STUDY GUIDE AND COMPUTER WORKBOOK

Catherine Renner

STATISTICS FOR THE BEHAVIORAL AND SOCIAL SCIENCES

SECOND EDITION

ARTHUR ARON

ELAINE N. ARON

PRENTICE HALL, UPPER SADDLE RIVER, NEW JERSEY 07458

©2002 by PEARSON EDUCATION, INC.
Upper Saddle River, New Jersey 07458

ISBN 0-13-041965-6

Printed in the United States of America

Table of Contents

Introduction
(How to Use this Study Guide and Computer Workbook)

This study guide is designed to help you master the material in your text. *First*, you should read the chapter in the text and work the practice problems. *Then*, you should work through the material in the corresponding chapter here.

The first part of each chapter in this *Guide* helps you solidify your knowledge. It includes a list of learning objectives, a thorough outline of the chapter, formulas (including their expression in words and numbers, as well as what all the symbols stand for), and step-by-step instructions for doing the various procedures covered in the chapter.

In most chapters, the next part of each chapter in this *Guide* is a detailed outline of one or more of those essays on explaining the material in the chapter "to a person who has never had a course in statistics." These sections will help you carry out these essay exercises in each chapter (and to prepare you for possible exam questions of this kind). Plus, being able to write a strong essay of this kind is the surest way to be confident you have really mastered the material.

Next in each chapter is a set of Self-Tests--multiple-choice, fill-in, and problem/essays--to help you evaluate how well you have learned the material and to give you practice for course exams. The answers are in the back of this *Guide*.

The last part of each chapter helps you use one of the standardly available statistical computer program -- SPSS -- to carry out the procedures and deepen your knowledge of the material covered in the text chapter. In addition to these sections in each chapter for the two programs, there is an appendix at the end of the book on how to get started using each of these program.

Finally, at the very end of this *Guide* there is a set of glossary flash-cards to be cut out. Many students find that in statistics conquering the terminology is half the battle. These flash cards are designed to help you in that process.

Acknowledgements from first edition: Arthur Aron and Christina Norman. Many people helped in the preparation of the first edition of this manual. Elijah Aron, Ken Galaka, Kip Obenauf, Paul Sanders, and Rosemary Torrano all prepared draft items for the Self-Tests; and Ken, Rosemary, and Miles Holland reviewed the finished items for accuracy. Sami Corn and Elijah helped with the typing, and Menko Johnson formatted the typing for the final typeset printing. Above all, I am grateful to Elaine Aron who read, checked for accuracy, and offered helpful advice on the entire manuscript.

Acknowledgements for the second edition: Catherine Hackett Renner. Revising this study guide was made easier due to the efforts of those individuals who laid the ground work in the first edition. I would like to thank Annarose Pandey for her help with concept checking. I would also like to thank Michael and Moriah Renner who provided patience and support during this revision process.

Chapter 1
Displaying the Order in a Group of Numbers

Learning Objectives

By the end of this chapter, you should be able to:

- Define descriptive versus inferential statistics.
- Define and describe the differences between variable, value, and score.
- Create ungrouped and grouped frequency tables using the four steps provided.
- Identify variables as either equal-interval, rank-order, or nominal.
- Create histograms and frequency polygons.
- Identify the shape of a frequency distribution with respect to modality, symmetry, skewness, and kurtosis.

Chapter Outline

I. **The Two Branches of Statistical Methods**
   A. *Descriptive statistics* are used to summarize and make understandable a group of numbers collected in a research study.
   B. *Inferential statistics* are used to draw conclusions and go beyond the numbers actually collected in the research study.

II. **Frequency Tables**
   A. They show how frequently each rating number or value was used.
   B. They make the pattern of numbers clear at a glance.
   C. To understand them, some basic statistics terminology is needed.
      1. *Variable*–a characteristic that can take on different values.
      2. *Value*–a number that represents a rating or measurement of a variable.
      3. *Score*–a particular person's value on a variable.
   D. There are four steps to creating a frequency table.
      1. Make a list down the page of each possible value, starting from the highest and ending with the lowest.
      2. Go one by one through the scores making a mark for each next to the corresponding value on your list.
      3. Make a table indicating how many times each value on your list of scores occurs.
      4. Figure the percent of scores for each value.

III. **Grouped Frequency Tables**
   A. They are used when there are so many different possible values that a frequency table is too cumbersome to give a simple account of the information.
   B. They combine individual values into intervals or groups of adjacent values.
   C. There are five steps to creating a grouped frequency table.
      1. Subtract the lowest from the highest value to find the range.
      2. Divide the range by a reasonable interval size.
         a. Use 2, 3, 5, 10, or a multiple of 10 if possible.
         b. The size, after rounding up, should represent a reasonable number of intervals (in general, no fewer than 5, no more than 15).

1

3. Make a table with the first column listing nonoverlapping intervals, ordered highest to lowest, with the lower end of each interval equal to a multiple of the interval size.
4. Make second column in the table indicating how many times a value on your list falls into each interval.
5. Make a third column in the table that figures the percent of scores for each interval.

IV. Kinds of Variables
A. There are numeric (or quantitative) variables and nominal (or categorical) variables.
B. There are two kinds of numeric variables:
   1. Equal-interval variables – numbers stand for approximately equal amounts of what is being measured.
   2. Rank-order variables – numbers stand only for relative ranking in a distribution.
C. Nominal variables refers to categories where the values are names for categories.

V. Histograms
A. They are one type of graphic display of the information in a frequency table.
B. They are a kind of bar chart (in which the bars are put right next to each other without divisions); the height of each bar corresponds to the frequency of each value or interval in the frequency table.
C. There are four steps to creating a histogram.
   1. Make a frequency table (or a grouped frequency table).
   2. Place the scale of values (or intervals) along the bottom of a page.
     a. The values (or intervals) should go from left to right, from lowest to highest.
     b. For a grouped frequency table it is conventional to mark only the midpoint of each interval, in the center of each bar. (The midpoint is figured as the point between the start of the interval and the start of the next interval.)
   3. Make a scale of frequencies along the left edge of the page.
   4. Make a bar for each value (or interval); the height corresponding to the frequency of the value (or interval) it represents.

VI. Frequency Polygons
A. They are a line graph in which the bottom of the graph shows the values or intervals (as in a histogram), and the line moves from point to point, with the height of each point showing the number of scores of that value or in that interval.
B. There are five steps to creating a frequency polygon.
   1. Make a frequency table (or a grouped frequency table).
   2. Place the values (or intervals) along the bottom.
     a. The values (or intervals) should go from left to right, from lowest to highest.
     b. Be sure to include one extra value (or interval) above and one extra value (or interval) below the values (or intervals) that actually have any scores in them.
     c. For a grouped frequency table, use the midpoint of each interval. (The midpoint is figured as the point between the start of the interval and the start of the next interval.)
   3. Along the left of the page make a scale of frequencies that runs from 0 at the bottom to the highest frequency in any value (or interval).
   4. Mark a point above the center of each value (or interval) corresponding to the frequency of that value (or interval).
   5. Connect the points with lines.

VII. Shapes of Frequency Distributions
  A. A frequency table, histogram, or frequency polygon describes a *frequency distribution*–how the number of scores or "frequencies" are spread out or "distributed."
  B. It is useful to describe in words the key aspects of the way numbers are distributed–which can be thought of as the shape of the histogram or frequency polygon that represents the frequency distribution.
  C. Unimodal and bimodal.
    1. A distribution with a single high peak is *unimodal*.
    2. A distribution with two major peaks is *bimodal*.
    3. Any distribution with two or more peaks is called *multimodal*.
    4. A distribution in which all the values have about the same frequency is called *rectangular*.
  D. Symmetrical and skewed.
    1. A distribution with approximately equal numbers of scores (and a similar shape) on both sides of the middle is *symmetrical*.
    2. A distribution that is clearly not symmetrical is *skewed*.
      a. The direction of skew refers to the side with the long tail; the side with the fewer scores describes the direction of the skew.
      b. A distribution with fewer scores to the right is called *positively skewed*.
      c. A distribution with fewer scores to the left is called *negatively skewed*.
    3. In practice, highly skewed distributions come up in psychology mainly when what is being measured has some upper or lower limit.
      a. The situation in which many scores pile up at the low end because it is not possible to have any lower score is called a *floor effect*.
      b. The situation in which many scores pile up at the high end because it is not possible to have any higher score is called a *ceiling effect*.
  E. Kurtosis.
    1. If a distribution is particularly flat or particularly peaked it has something called *kurtosis*.
    2. The standard of comparison is the *normal curve*, a bell–shaped curve that is widely approximated in frequency distributions in psychological research–and in nature generally (this will be important again in chapter 5).
    3. How peaked and pinched together versus flat and spread out a distribution is, compared to the normal curve, is called its degree of kurtosis.

VIII. Frequency Tables, Histograms, and Frequency Polygons in Research Articles
  A. They are mainly used by researchers as an intermediary step in the process of more elaborate statistical analyses.
  B. Frequency tables are used in two situations.
    1. Sometimes they are presented to compare frequencies on two or more variables or for two or more groups.
    2. Most often they are used when the values of the variable are categories rather than numbers.
  C. Histograms and frequency polygons almost never appear in research articles (except articles *about* statistics); but their shape is sometimes commented on in the text of the article, particularly if the distribution seems to be far from normal.

How to Make a Frequency Table

I. **Make a list down the page of each possible value, starting from the highest and ending with the lowest.**

II. **Go one by one through the group of scores you wish to describe, making a mark for each next to the corresponding value on your list.**

III. **Make a neat table showing how many times each value on your list occurs.**

How to Make a Grouped Frequency Table

I. **Subtract the lowest from the highest value to find the range.**

II. **Divide the range by a reasonable interval size.**
   A. Use 2, 3, 5, 10, or a multiple of 10 if possible.
   B. The size, after rounding up, should represent a reasonable number of intervals (in general, no fewer than 5, no more than 15).

III. **Make a list of the intervals, from highest to lowest–making the lower end of each interval equal to a multiple of the interval size. (Be sure that the intervals do not overlap.)**

IV. **Proceed as you would for an ordinary frequency table.**

How to Make a Histogram

I. **Make a frequency table (or a grouped frequency table).**

II. **Place the scale of values (or intervals) along the bottom of a page.**
   A. The values (or intervals) should go from left to right, from lowest to highest.
   B. For a grouped frequency table, it is conventional to mark only the midpoint of each interval, placed in the center of each bar. (The midpoint is figured as the point between the start of the interval and the start of the next interval.)

III. **Along the left of the page make a scale of frequencies that runs from 0 at the bottom to the highest frequency in any value (or interval).**

IV. **Make a bar for each value (or interval), the height corresponding to the frequency of the value (or interval) it represents.**

How to Make a Frequency Polygon

I. **Make a frequency table (or a grouped frequency table).**

II. **Place the scale of values (or intervals) along the bottom of a page.**
   A. Be sure to include one extra value (or interval) above and one extra value (or interval) below the values (or intervals) that actually have any scores in them.
   B. For a grouped frequency table, use the midpoint of each interval. (The midpoint is figured as the point between the start of the interval and the start of the next interval.)

III. **Along the left of the page make a scale of frequencies that runs from 0 at the bottom to the highest frequency in any value (or interval).**

IV. **Mark a point above the center of each value (or interval) corresponding to the frequency of that value (or interval).**

V. **Connect the points with lines.**

Chapter Self–Tests

1. Social Scientists use __*b*__ statistics like frequency tables to help make sense of the numbers they collect.
   a. inferential
   b. descriptive
   c. intuitive
   d. abstract

2. A researcher studies the amount of self–confidence people have after doing well on a test. Self–confidence in this study is a
   a. score.
   b. descriptive statistic.
   c. value.
   d. variable.

3. A psychologist administers a personality scale on which people can get a score of any number between 24 to 86. The results would be described using a grouped frequency table rather than an ordinary frequency table because an ordinary frequency table would
   a. have too many values.
   b. not be able to include all scores.
   c. create a skewed distribution.
   d. has to start at 0 (or 0%).

4. To determine the interval size to use in a grouped frequency table, you first find the range and then try different numbers to divide it by, trying to end up with an interval size that is
   a. twice the range.
   b. an odd number if possible.
   c. some common regular number (such as 2, 3, 5 or 10).
   d. some even number if possible.

5. What is generally the largest number of intervals you would want in a grouped frequency table?
   a. 5
   b. 15
   c. 45
   d. 60

6. A histogram
   a. is similar to a line graph.
   b. always approximates a normal curve.
   c. is a graphic description of frequency table.
   d. describes the relation between two variables.

7. In a frequency polygon, the vertical (up and down) dimension represents
   a. frequency.
   b. possible values the variable can take.

c. intensity of the variable.

d. mean score.

8. Suppose 50 people take a math exam–25 math experts, 25 people very poor at math. This distribution will probably be _____.

a. unimodal

b. bimodal

c. normal

d. skewed

9. Describe the distribution of the following scores (you will probably need to make a frequency table, histogram, or frequency polygon to do this).

1,10,6,8,7,5,5,4,9,2,9,8,6,7,8,3,4,3,5,5,7,6,4,6,6,7

a unimodal and approximately normal

b. bimodal and negatively skewed

c. normal and positively skewed

d. unimodal and positively skewed

10. A graphic display of a frequency distribution is misleading when

a. the proportions are close to 1–1/2 across to 1 up.

b. the frequencies are grouped or percentages are used.

c. some of the intervals are larger than others.

d. the intervals (or values) are put across the bottom.

Fill–In Questions

1. When making a frequency table, the _____Value_____ are listed in the first column and the frequencies corresponding to each of these are listed in the next column.

2. A researcher used a(n) __grouped__ because there were too many different values for an ordinary frequency table.

3. Because the range went from 10 to 99, the researcher used a(n) __interval__ of 10 for the grouped frequency table.

4. A graph describing a frequency table and looking like a city skyline is called a(n) __histogram__

5. A(n) __bimodal__ distribution shows up in a frequency polygon as two peaks that are much higher than all the others.

6. If the number of scores at each value is approximately the same, this creates a(n) __rectangular__ distribution, which is also symmetrical.

7. The distribution of incomes in a small community tends to be __negative__ skewed, because most people earn small to modest incomes, and a decreasing number earn large incomes (though a very small number earn a very great deal).

8. In a pilot test of a planned memory study, the majority received a perfect score. Seeking to avoid such a(n) _____ in the real study, the researcher made the task more difficult.

Ceiling

9. The _____ [*normal curve*] represents a particular unimodal, symmetrical distribution commonly found in social science research and nature generally.

10. _____ [*heavier tail or light tail?*] refers to a distribution being much more peaked or flat than is typical of distributions in social science research.

Essays and Problems   *Kurosis*

1. Under what conditions would you prefer to make a grouped frequency table over an ordinary frequency table? Why?

2. Twenty–four adolescent girls whose parents had just divorced completed a questionnaire about their attitudes toward their parents. Their scores were as follows (the scale goes from 0, very negative attitude, to 80, very positive attitude):

   17,73,8,19,68,11,41,24,61,44,53,18,0,21,75,3,18,11,72,12,11,79,71,4

   (a) Make a grouped frequency table.
   (b) Make a histogram based on the grouped frequency table.
   (c) Describe in words the shape of the histogram.

3. The average life spans in captivity for 43 different mammals (as reported in the *1989 World Almanac*, p. 258) are as follows:

   12 20 18 25 20 5 15 12 12 20 6 15 8 12 35 40 15 7 10 8 15

   20 4 25 20 7 12 15 15 12 3 3 1 10 12 5 15 20 12 12 10 16 5

   (a) Make a grouped frequency table.
   (b) Make a frequency polygon based on the grouped frequency table.
   (c) Describe in words the shape of the histogram.

4. Explain what it means to have a floor effect in a distribution of scores. Give an example.

Using SPSS 10.0 For Windows with this Chapter

If you are using SPSS for the first time, before proceeding with the material in this section, read the Appendix on Getting Started.

You can use SPSS to create frequency tables and histograms, including grouped frequency tables and histograms based on those grouped frequency tables. You should work through the example, following the procedures step by step. Then look over the description of the general principles involved and try to create frequency tables and histograms on your own for some of the problems listed in the Suggestions for Additional Practice. Finally, you may want to try the suggestions for using the computer to deepen your understanding.

I.   An Example
   A. Data: Fourteen students rated the quality of social life in their dormitory on a 1 to 10 scale. The ratings were 6, 9, 9, 4, 9, 7, 1, 7, 4, 10, 7, 1, 9, and 4.
   B. Follow the instructions in the SPSS Appendix for starting up SPSS.
   C. Enter the data as follows.
      1. Type **6**, the score for the first subject, and press Enter.
      2. Type **9**, the score for the second subject, and press Enter. At this point, the screen should look like Figure SG1-1.

3. Type the remaining scores, one per line. You can always move back
   to an earlier line by clicking the arrow in the space you wish to
   edit.

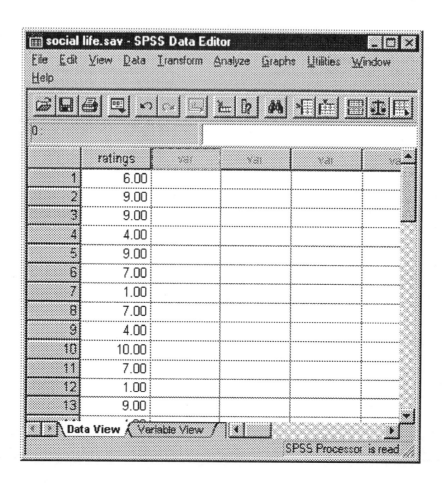

Figure SG1–1

D. Name your variable.
   1. To replace the default variable name with a more descriptive variable name, click on the "Variable
      View" tab. This will display another spreadsheet that allows you to define characteristics of your
      variables. In the Column marked "Name" type in the name of the first variable. This opens the
      Define Variable dialogue box. After you have typed in the variable name of ratings, you can click on
      the "Data View" tab to return you to the data window.
E. Make a frequency table and histogram, as follows.
   1. Analyze
      Descriptive Statistics >
      Frequencies
   At this point the screen should look like Figure SG1-2.
         [Select RATINGS by highlighting it with the mouse and then clicking on the
         arrow.]
            Charts
               [Select Histogram]

8

Continue
    OK

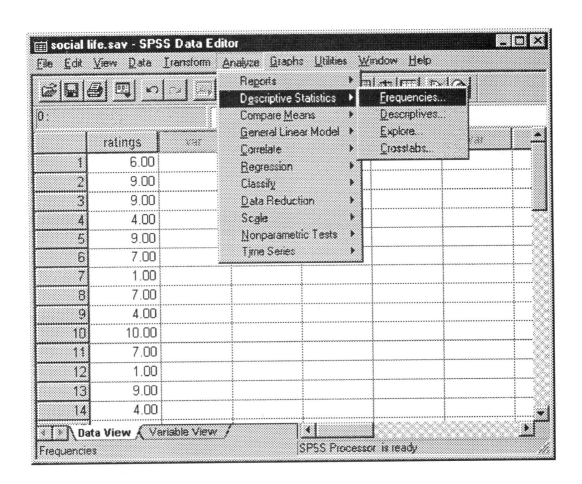

Figure SG1–2

2. A frequency table will appear in the output window.
3. Double click on the Chart Carousel icon for the histogram. The results should look like Figure SG1–3.
4. Inspect the results.
   a. At the top of the screen (on the left), SPSS reminds you of the name of the variable you are examining (in this case, Ratings).
   b. The two columns of numbers are the frequency table itself. The left column, labeled VALUE, gives the various values, from lowest to highest. The column to its right, labeled **FREQUENCY,** gives the frequency. (This is different from an ordinary frequency table, such as those shown in the text, and the values would be listed going down from highest to lowest.)
   c. The histogram is shown in the Chart Carousel. It is like the histograms in the text.
5. Print out the frequency table from the output window by going into File and selecting Print.
6. Print out the histogram from the Chart Carousel by going into File and selecting Print.

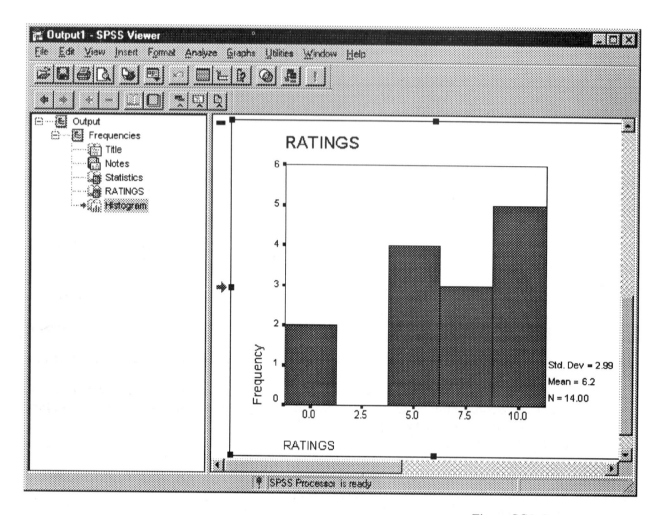

Figure SG1–3

F. Save your lines of data as follows:
      File
        Save Data
          [Type in file name using a '.sav' as the extension]
            [Indicate drive you would like it saved in]
              [Press OK]

II. Systematic Instructions for Making a Frequency Table and Histogram and Grouped Frequency Table and Histogram

A. Start up SPSS.

B. Enter the data as follows.
      1. Type in a data point and press Enter. Continue until all data has been entered.
      2. Name your variable by selecting the Variable View tab

C. Make a frequency table and histogram as follows.
      Analyze
        Descriptive Statistics >

10

Frequencies

         [Select variable by highlighting it with the mouse and then clicking on the arrow.]
         Charts
         [Select Histogram]
         Continue
         OK

D. Save your lines of data as follows.
    File
    Save Data
       [Type in file name using '.sav' extension]
        [Indicate drive you would like it saved in]
        OK

III. Additional Practice

(For each data set, enter the data, create a frequency table and histogram and compare your results to those in the text. Also, be sure to save your data sets so that you can use them again in Chapter 2.)

A. Text examples.
1. Use the data shown in the text for the stress levels of students in the first week of their statistics class (from Aron, Paris, & Aron, 1993).
2. Use the data shown in the text for children's attitudes toward achievement (from Moorehouse & Sanders, 1992).
3. Use the data shown in the text for milliseconds to read ambiguous and nonambiguous sentences (fictional data).
4. Note that these examples have a lot of data to enter, but they have the advantage of providing sufficient numbers of scores to give you a real sense of the value of a frequency table and histogram and of having a computer set it up for you.

B. Practice problems in the text.
1. Questions 1 and 2.

IV. Using the Computer to Deepen Your Knowledge

A. Getting a sense of a normal distribution.
1. Make up a data set of any 15 numbers and then make a histogram of it.
2. Print out the histogram and then go back to your data set and try to modify it to come out closer to a normal curve.
3. Repeat this process until your results are very close to a normal curve.
4. Try the process again starting with a whole new group of numbers.
5. Try to write down what you have learned about what goes into making a distribution come out normal.

B. Getting a sense of skew.
1. Take one of the data sets from your normal curve approximations from the previous exercise and modify it to make the curve come out slightly skewed to one side.
2. Now try to make it more skewed.
3. Repeat this process, creating several different degrees of skew.
4. Try to write down what you have learned about what goes into creating different degrees of skew.

Chapter 2
The Mean, Variance, Standard Deviation, and *Z* Scores

Learning Objectives

By the end of this chapter, you should be able to:

- Figure the mean from a group of scores.
- Understand the meaning behind statistical symbols and formulas.
- Determine the median and mode from a group of scores.
- Understand what the standard deviation and variance are.
- Figure the standard deviation and variance from a group of scores.
- Define Z scores and converting to and from raw scores.
- Understand the information the mean, variance, and standard deviation conveys as reported in research articles.

Chapter Outline

I. Measures of the Representative Value of a Score

  A. The Mean.
  1. It is usually the best single number for describing a group of scores.
  2. It is the ordinary average, the sum of all the scores divided by the number of scores.
  3. You can visualize the mean as a kind of balancing point for the distribution of scores: Imagine a board balanced over a log; on the board are piles of blocks distributed along the board, one for each score in the distribution; and the mean would be the point on the board where the weight of the blocks on each side would exactly balance.

  B. The Mode.
  1. It is the value with the largest frequency in a frequency table, the high point or peak of a distribution's frequency polygon or histogram.
  2. In a perfectly symmetrical unimodal distribution, the mode is the same as the mean.
  3. When the mode is not the same as the mean, it is not a very good representative value. In fact, it can be a poor representative value because it is not reflective of many aspects of the distribution.
  4. The mode is unaffected by changes in some scores.
  5. Researchers rarely use the mode.

  C. The Median.
  1. It is the middle score if you line up all the scores from highest to lowest.
  2. If there are two middle scores, it is their average.
  3. It is less distorted by a few extreme scores (outliers) than the mean.

II. The Variance and the Standard Deviation

  A. Variance.
  1. How spread out the scores in a distribution are.
  2. It is the average of each score's squared difference from the mean.
  3. You can visualize the variance as an average area, considering each squared deviation as a square whose sides are the amount of deviation.
  4. A more spread out distribution has a larger variance.
  5. The variance plays an important role in many other statistical procedures, but is used only occasionally by itself as a descriptive statistic since it is scaled in squared units, a metric that is not very intuitively direct for giving a sense of just how spread out the distribution is.
  6. The variance formula is $SD^2 = \Sigma(X-M)^2 / N$.

B. The standard deviation.
   1. The most widely used for describing the spread of a distribution.
   2. It is the square root of the variance.
   3. Roughly speaking, the standard deviation is the average amount that scores differ from the mean. (It is not exactly this because the squaring, summing, and taking the square root does not quite give the same result.)
   4. The standard deviation formula is $SD = \sqrt{SD^2}$.
C. The formulas used for the variance and standard deviation are "definitional"; in other books you may see them in a different "computational" form.
   1. Computational and definitional formulas are mathematically the same.
   2. Computational formulas are easier to use when computing by hand but are rarely used today in research practice because most statistical computations are done by computer.
   3. This textbook emphasizes the definitional formulas, thus, doing exercises reinforces understanding.
   4. The computational formulas are provided in a Chapter Appendix.
D. Variance and standard deviation are sometimes computed using the sum of squared deviations divided by N-1 when you want to estimate what these values would be for a larger group of people. Hand calculators and computer outputs sometimes give this figure instead of the formula emphasized in this chapter.

III. *Z* Scores
A. It is an ordinary score transformed so that it better describes that score's location in a distribution.
B. It is the number of standard deviations the score is above the mean (if it is a positive Z score) or below the mean (if it is a negative Z score). Thus, the standard deviation serves as a kind of standard yardstick through changing raw scores to Z scores.
C. Scores on different scales can be easily compared once they are converted to Z scores.
D. The formula for converting *from* a raw score is $Z = (X\text{-}M) / SD$.
E. The formula for converting *to* a raw score is $X = (Z)(SD) + M$.

IV. **The Mean, Variance, Standard Deviation, and *Z* Scores as Described in Research Articles**
A. The mean, variance and standard deviation are commonly reported, and in a variety of ways–either in the text, in tables, or in graphs.
B. *Z* scores rarely appear in research articles.

Understanding What Formulas Mean

I.   Mean (*M*)
Formula in words: Sum of all the scores divided by the number of scores.
Formula in symbols: $M = \Sigma X / N$ (2-1)
    Σ is an instruction to sum all the scores.
    X is each score in the distribution of the variable X.
    ΣX is the sum of all the scores in the distribution of the variable X.
    N is the number of scores in the distribution.

II. Variance (*SD²*)
Formula in words: Average of each score's squared difference from the mean.
Formula in symbols: $SD^2 = \Sigma(X\text{-}M)^2 / N$ (2-2)
    $\Sigma(X\text{-}M)^2$ is the sum of squared deviations from the mean.

III. Standard Deviation (*SD*)

Formula in words: Square root of the variance (square root of the average of each score's squared difference from the mean).

Formula in symbols: $SD = \sqrt{SD^2}$ (2-3)

IV. *Z* Scores from Raw Scores

Formula in words: The number of standard deviations above or below the mean–the deviation score (the score minus the mean) divided by the standard deviation.

Formula in symbols: $Z = (X - M) / SD$ (2-4)

V. Raw Scores from *Z* Scores

Formula in words: Multiply the *Z* score times the standard deviation (to get the raw deviation above or below the mean) and add the mean.

Formula in symbols: $X = (Z)(SD) + M$ (2-5)

How to Compute the Mean

I. Add up all the scores.
II. Divide by the number of scores.

How to Compute the Variance and the Standard Deviation

I.   Compute the mean (*M*): Add up all the scores and divide by the number of scores.
II. Compute the deviation scores: Subtract the mean from each score.
III. Compute the squared deviations scores: Multiply each deviation score times itself.
IV. Compute the sum of the squared deviation scores (*SS*): Add up all the squared deviation scores.
V.   Compute the variance (*SD²*), the average of the squared deviation scores: Divide the sum of the squared deviation scores by the number of scores.
VI. Compute the standard deviation (*SD*), the square root of the average of the squared deviation scores: Find the square root of the number computed above.

How to Convert a Raw Score to a *Z* Score

I. Compute the deviation score: Subtract the mean from the raw score.
II. Compute the *Z* score: Divide the deviation score by the standard deviation.

How to Convert a *Z* Score to a Raw Score

I. Compute the deviation score: Multiply the *Z* score by the standard deviation.
II. Compute the raw score: Add the mean to the deviation score.

Outline for Writing Essays on the Logic and Computations for the Mean, Variance, Standard Deviation, and Z Scores

The reason for your writing essay questions in the practice problems and tests is that this task develops and then demonstrates what matters so very much–your comprehension of the logic behind the computations. (It is also a place where those better at words than numbers can shine, and for those better at numbers to develop their skills at explaining in words.)

Thus, to do well, be sure to do the following in each essay: (a) give the reasoning behind each step; (b) relate each step to the specifics of the content of the particular study you are analyzing; (c) state the various formulas in nontechnical language, because as you define each term you show you understand it (although once you have defined it in nontechnical language, you can use it from then on in the essay); (d) look back and be absolutely certain that you made it clear just *why* that formula or procedure was applied and *why* it is the way it is.

The outlines below are *examples* of ways to structure your essays. There are other completely correct ways to go about it. And this is an *outline* for an answer–you are to write the answer out in paragraph form.

These essays are sometimes long for you to write (and for others to grade). But this is the very best way to be sure you understand everything thoroughly. You engrain it in your mind. The time is never wasted. It is an excellent way to study.

Essays on Finding the Mean, Variance, and Standard Deviation

I. Find mean.
  A. Procedure: $M = \Sigma X / N$.
  B. Explanation: This is the ordinary average, the sum of the scores divided by the number of scores.

II. Find the variance.
  A. Procedure: $SD^2 = \Sigma(X\text{-}M)^2 / N$.
  B. Explanation.
      1. Describes the spread of the scores.
      2. Finds the average of the squared amount each score differs from the mean.

III. Find the standard deviation.
  A. Procedure: $SD = \sqrt{SD^2}$.
  B. Explanation.
      1. The variance is an average of squared scores; by taking its square root, the measure of spread of the scores is returned to ordinary nonsquared scores.
      2. The result is approximately the average amount each score varies from the mean.
      3. To be exact it is the square root of the average squared deviation from the mean.
      4. Due to the squaring, averaging, and square root process, it is not quite the same as the average amount each score varies from the mean, but the use of squaring in the process avoids mathematical problems (for example, it eliminates the sign of the deviations–the fact that some are negative and some positive).

Essays Involving Z Scores

I. Find a Z score based on a raw score.
  A. Procedure: $Z = (X - M) / SD$.
  B. Explanation.
      1. Explain mean and standard deviation (as described in outline above).

2. Finding a Z score converts an ordinary score to its number of standard deviations above or below the mean.
3. This is done by subtracting the mean from the score and dividing the result by the standard deviation.
4. This puts the score on a scale that is highly standard–for example, high scores (those above the mean) are always positive Z scores, low scores (those below the mean) are always negative Z scores, and the amount a Z score is above or below the mean is in direct proportion to the standard deviation.
5. This procedure puts scores on different variables onto the same scale, permitting comparisons between them.

II. Find a raw score based on a Z score.
A. Procedure: $X = (Z)(SD) + M$.
B. Explanation.
1. Explain mean and standard deviation (as described in outline above).
2. This converts a Z score, a special score that indicates a score's number of standard deviations above or below the mean, back to an ordinary score.
3. This is done by multiplying the Z score times the standard deviation to get the number of ordinary score units above or below the mean, and then adding this to the mean to get the actual raw score.

Chapter Self-Tests

Multiple-Choice Questions

1. Six students record the amount of time studied on a particular evening (rounded off to the nearest hour). They report 0, 0, 1, 1, 4 and 6 hours. What is the mean time studied?
   a. 1
   b. 2
   c. 2.5
   d. 3.5

2. A score that is not representative of other scores in a distribution:
   a. should be deleted
   b. should be transformed
   c. is called a deviation score
   d. is called an outlier

3. The "balancing point" for a distribution of scores is:
   a. the average score
   b. the middle score
   c. the most frequently occurring score
   d. any score chosen randomly

4. What is the median of the following scores? 0,1,1,1,2,3,7,8,8,9,15
   a. 1
   b. 3
   c. 5
   d. 8

5. In the following set of scores, which would be the preferred measure of central tendency?
   5,41,42,42,44,46,47,47,47

   a. mean
   b. median
   c. mode
   d. standard error

6. The variance is

   a. the sum of the squared deviations from the mean
   b. the average of the deviations from the mean
   c. the sum of the square roots of the deviations from the mean
   d. the average of the squared deviations from the mean

7. A value that represents how far a raw score is from the mean in standard deviation units is a

   a. z-score
   b. variance score
   c. deviation score
   d. computational score

8. What is the variance of the four scores, 1, 5, 5, and 9?

   a. 4
   b. 5
   c. 8
   d. 16

9. N-1 is used when

   a. you don't know the value of a score in your distribution
   b. it has never been used
   c. the distribution is skewed
   d. you want to estimate the values to a larger group of people

   b

10. A person has a Z score of .5. If the mean of the distribution is 71 and the standard deviation is 20, what is this person's raw score?

    a. 70.5
    b. 71.5
    c. 76
    d. 81

Fill-In Questions

1. The sum of the scores divided by the number of scores is the ___mean___.

2. The ___variance___ is the average of each score's squared difference from the mean.

3. A study produces the scores 14, 15, 17, 18 and 18. What is N? ___5___.

4. The ___mode___ of the scores 6, 6, 6, 7, and 9 is 6.

5. If you line up all the scores from highest to lowest, the middle score is the ___median___.

17

6. If a group of scores are 14, 17, 17, 18, 18, and 91, the score of 91 is called a(n) _outlier_

7. The _____ is less distorted by extreme scores than the mean.

8. A deviation score is the score minus _mean_ .

9. The ~~mode~~ _standard deviation_ is the value that represents the peak of a distribution in a frequency polygon.

10. When a distribution of scores is _normal_ _____ the mean, median, and mode are the same.

Problems and Essays

1. A psychologist administers a test of hand-eye coordination to eight severely depressed adult men and finds scores of 3.1, 3.8, 4.0, 4.5, 4.5, 5.4, 6.0 and 8.7.

   (a) Compute the mean, variance, and standard deviation.
   (b) Explain what you have done and what the results mean to a person who has never had a course in statistics.

2. A person visits a vocational counselor and is administered various tests. The person scores 50 on a test that measures aptitude for a career in sales (for people in general on this test, $M = 40$, $SD = 4$) and 95 on a test of aptitude for a career in education (for people in general on this test, $M = 80$, $SD = 20$). (On both tests high scores mean greater aptitude.)

   (a) In relation to other people, what is this person's greater aptitude? (Be sure to show the calculations that are the basis of your answer.)
   (b) Explain what you have done and the basis of your conclusion to a person who has never had a course in statistics.

3. Two children completed a standard test of vocabulary, which was sent off to a special service for scoring. The school counselor received the results in terms of Z scores. One child, Mary, received a Z score of 1.23 and the other child, Susan, received a Z score of -.62. The school counselor is interested also in the raw number correct each student received. Looking up the information in the test's manual, the school counselor found out that the mean raw score for this test is 42 questions correct, with a standard deviation of 6.5.

   (a) What are the raw numbers correct for each child?
   (b) Explain what you have done to a person who has never had a course in statistics.

4. A researcher administered a questionnaire to a group of healthy adults all over 80 years old. The questionnaire included one item that asked about happiness with life, using a 10-point scale from 1 = very unhappy to 10 = very happy. The researcher reported the result on this scale as follows: "For the 65 subjects who completed this item, $M = 6.83$, $SD = 2.41$." Explain what this result means to a person who has never had a course in statistics.

Using SPSS 10.0 with this Chapter

You can use SPSS to compute the mean and variance and to convert a series of raw scores to Z scores. However, as you will see, the variance that SPSS gives you is computed using a slightly different formula than what you have been using in Chapter 2–instead of dividing the sum of squared deviations by N, it divides by N-1. (This other way of computing the variance is also correct, but is used for a different purpose.) Thus, when computing the variance using SPSS, you have to make an adjustment to what SPSS gives you, using your hand calculator. Once you have made the adjustment, you can take the square root of your result (again with your hand calculator) to get the standard deviation.

You should work through the example, following the procedures step by step. Then look over the description of the general principles involved and try the procedures on your own for some of the problems listed in the Suggestions for Additional Practice. Finally, you may want to try the suggestions for using the computer to deepen your understanding, and you can explore the additional, advanced SPSS procedure at the end, involving skew and kurtosis.

I. Example
    A. Data: The number of therapy sessions for each of 10 clients of a psychotherapist
       (fictional data), from the example in the text. The numbers of sessions are 7, 8, 8, 7, 3,
       1, 6, 9, 3, and 8.
    B. Repeat the process in Chapter 1 starting up SPSS and entering this new data until your
       data looks like Figure SG2-1.

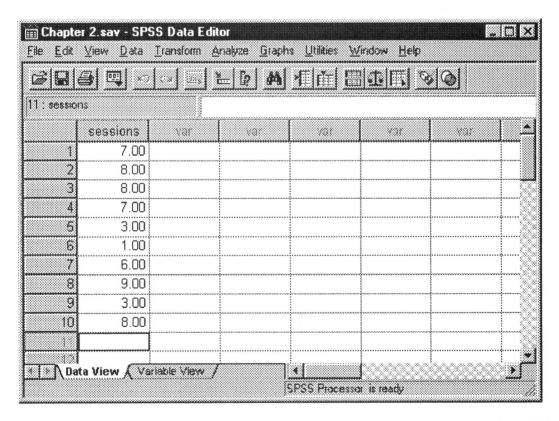

Figure SG2-1

C. Compute the mean and variance for the number of sessions as follows.
    1. Analyze
       Descriptive Statistics>
         Descriptives
         [At this point your screen should look like Figure SG2-2]
             [Highlight Sessions and then click on the arrow to move the
             Sessions over to the Variable(s) box.]
                Options
                    [Check Mean and Variance, and Uncheck the boxes that are checked]
                        Continue
                            OK

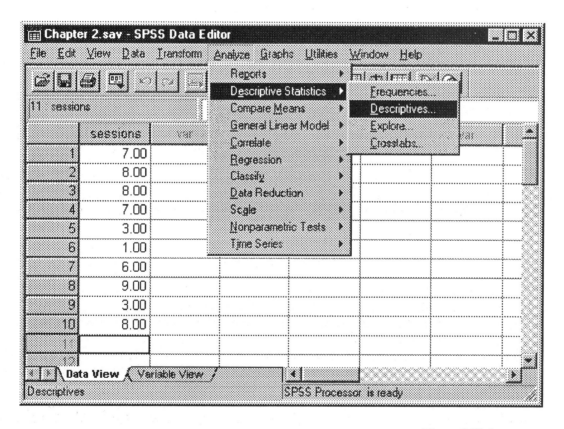

Figure SG2-2

2. The results should appear on the screen in the Output window and should look like Figure SG2-3.

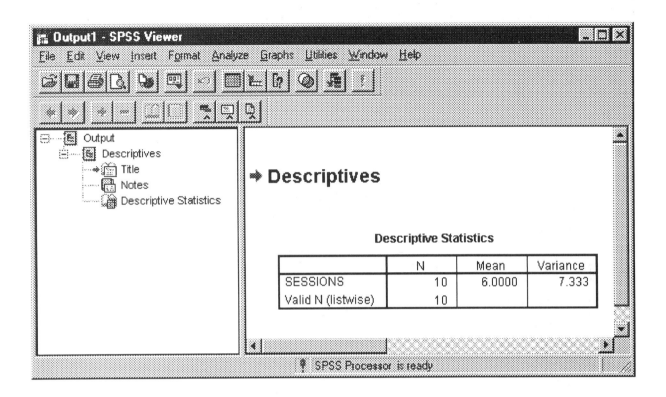

Figure SG2-3

D. Inspect and adjust the result.
   1. At the left is **SESSIONS**, the name of the variable being analyzed.
   2. The second column gives the **Mean,** which SPSS computed to be **6.00**, the same as was computed in the text for this example.
   3. The second line continues with the **Variance**. However this "variance" is based on the formula of $SS/(N\text{-}1)$ instead of the formula we are using in this chapter of SS/N. To adjust the result SPSS gives, you must multiply it by $N\text{-}1$ and then divide by N. In this example, SPSS displays **7.33**. There are 10 scores, so the adjustment is 9 times 7.333, divided by 10–which comes out to 6.6, the same as what was computed in the text. The square root of 6.6, the standard deviation, 2.57, is also the same as was computed in the text.
   4. The next row indicates the number of **Valid Scores**–the number of subjects who did not have missing values on the variable being measured. In your work in this course, you are not likely to have any missing values. However, in actual research situations it is quite common that some subjects will not have answered a particular question or participated in a particular condition of an experiment.
E. Print out a copy of the result by going to File and clicking on Print.
F. Find the Z scores corresponding to the raw scores, using the following steps:
   1. Transform
      Compute
         [Under target variable tell SPSS to create a new variable that consists of Z scores, labeled ZSESS]

21

[Highlight SESSIONS and click on the arrow to move it over into the
Numeric Expression box]
[Type (SESSIONS-6)/2.57 in the Numeric Expressions box--your screen should now
appear as Figure SG2-4]
OK

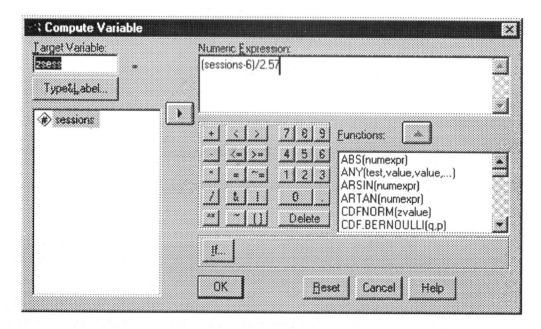

Figure SG2-4

2. The results should appear as shown below in Figure SG2-5.

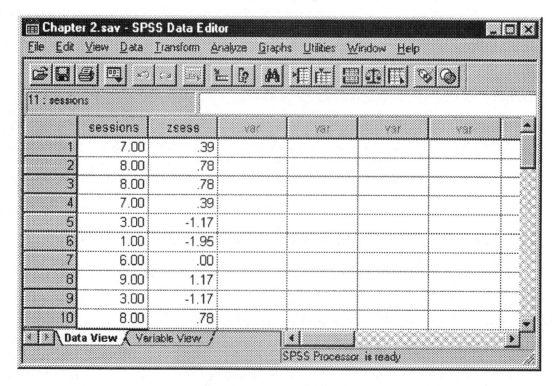

Figure SG2-5

3. Print out a copy of the result by going into File and clicking on Print.
4. Save your lines of data as follows:
   File
     Save Data
       [Name your data file followed by .sav and designate the drive you would like your data saved on]
         OK

II. Additional Practice

(For each data set, enter the data and compute the mean and variance–adjusting the latter and determining the standard deviation. Then make *Z* scores. Finally, compare your results to those in the text.)

A. Text examples–use same data sets as for Chapter 1 computer problems.

B. Practice problems in the text.
   1. All problems listed for use with the computer in the last chapter.
   2. Problems 1-3 from Chapter 2 in the text.

III. Using the Computer to Deepen Your Knowledge

A. The effect of outliers (extreme scores) on the mean.
   1. Use SPSS to compute the mean and variance for the example several times, each time changing one of the numbers of sessions to a more extreme number–such as changing the 9 to a 10, then to a 15, then a 20, then a 100 (someone getting long-term depth therapy perhaps).
   2. For each run record the mean and variance.
   3. Make a chart of the results and notice how sensitive both statistics are to the changes in a single score. (For purposes of this exercise, the unadjusted variance will be adequate to make the point clear.)

B. Mean and variance of *Z* scores.
   1. Use SPSS to compute the mean and variance of the *Z* scores created in the example and also in one of the other additional problems.
   2. Note that whatever the original mean and variance, the mean and variance of *Z* scores are always 0 and 1, respectively (within rounding error). (The variance is 1 only after you have made the adjustment to have a variance that was computed with N, not N-1.)

C. The effects of adding or subtracting a constant.
   1. Using the example, create a new variable that is the same as the number of sessions, but in which 8 is added to each score. (You can do this by going into Transform and clicking on Compute. Then enter a new Target Variable name and type in SESSIONS + 8 in the Numeric Expression box.) Then run the mean and variance and compare to the original.
   2. Do the same thing, but this time subtracting 3 from each score. (This will create some negative numbers of sessions!)
   3. Notice that the mean is affected; it is the original mean but with the number you added or subtracted to each score added or subtracted to it.
   4. But also notice that the variance (whether you adjust it or not) is not affected by adding or subtracting a constant.
   5. If you think in terms of a histogram of the distribution of scores, adding or subtracting a number to each score moves the whole distribution over to one side or the other, thus changing the mean. But the variation among the scores stays the same.

D. The effects of multiplying or dividing by a constant.
   1. Using the example, create a new variable that is the same as the number of sessions, but in which each is multiplied by 8. Then have SPSS compute the mean and variance; make the adjustment of the variance and take its square root to get the standard deviation.
   2. Do the same thing, but this time, dividing each score by 3.

3. Compare your results to the original.
   a. Notice that the mean is affected; it is the original mean, but multiplied or divided by the number by which you multiplied or divided each score.
   b. Also notice that in this case the variance and standard deviation are also affected.

Chapter 3
Correlation and Prediction

Learning Objectives

By the end of this chapter, you should be able to:

- Understand the nature of correlation.
- Describe the different types of relationships represented in linear, curvilinear, positive, and negative correlations.
- Describe the relationship between correlation and causality.
- Create a scattergram.
- Figure a bivariate prediction model with Z scores and associated formulas, terminology, and symbols.
- Explain why prediction is sometimes called regression.
- Figure bivariate prediction with raw scores and associated terminology, formulas, and symbols.
- Explain the nature and use of multiple regression.
- Explain what information the multiple regression coefficient provides.
- Be able to appropriately use r^2 to compare correlations.
- Explain the impact of restriction in range and unreliability of measurement on the correlation coefficients.

Chapter Outline

I. **Correlation and Causality**
   A. Correlation is when scores on one variable systematically vary with scores on another variable.
   B. When two variables are correlated it is not clear what their casual relationship is.
      1. This is a common situation in research involving correlations. Given this we often speak of predicting one variable from the other.
      2. The variable being predicted from is called the *predictor variable*.
      3. The variable being predicted about is still usually called the dependent or criterion variable
   C. In order to determine causality, the direction of causality needs to be determined.
   D. Strategies to rule out one direction of causality involve measuring variables at different time points (longitudinal studies) or in different groups (true experiment).

II. **Graphing Correlations: The Scatter Diagram**
   A. A *scatter diagram* displays the degree and pattern of relation of the two variables.
   B. Making a scatter diagram involves three steps.
      1. Draw the axes and determine which variable should go on which axis.
      2. Determine the range of values to use for each variable and mark them on the axes.
      3. Mark a dot for the pair of scores for each score.

III. **Patterns of Correlation**
   A. These can be identified by the general pattern of dots on the scatter diagram.
   B. Linear correlation is where the pattern of dots follows a straight line.
      1. Positive correlation (or positive linear correlation) is one pattern.
         a. It refers to low scores on one variable going with low scores on the other variable, mediums with mediums, and highs with highs.
         b. On the scatter diagram, the dots follow a line that slopes up and to the right. (That is, the line has a positive slope.)

2. Negative correlation (or negative linear correlation) is the other pattern.
   a. It refers to low scores on one variable going with high scores on the other variable, mediums with mediums, and highs with lows.
   b. On the scatter diagram, the dots follow a line that slopes up and to the left. (That is, the line has a negative slope.)

C. Curvilinear correlation is where the pattern of dots does not follow a straight line.
   1. Sometimes the relationship between two variables does not follow any kind of straight line, but instead follows a curving or more complex pattern.
   2. If the true pattern is curvilinear, figuring the correlation should show a small or zero correlation coefficient.
D. No correlation means no pattern–the two variables are completely unrelated to each other.
   1. On the scatter diagram the dots are spread everywhere, and there is no line, straight or otherwise, that is any reasonable representation of a simple trend.
   2. Note that in actual research situations sometimes the relationship between two variables does exist (that is, it is not really a no–correlation situation), but it is not very strong and thus hard to see visually in a scatter diagram.

IV. Figuring the Degree of Linear Correlation: The Pearson Correlation Coefficient (*r*)
   A. The degree of linear correlation is the extent to which there is a clear pattern, some particular relationship, between the distributions of scores on two variables.
   B. Figuring the degree of linear correlation is best solved using z-scores because:
      1. Scores on different variables must be compared in a consistent way puts both variables on the same scale.
      2. Z scores allow you to combine this information to get a number that reflects the *degree* to which highs go with highs, etc.–this is accomplished by computing the sum of cross–products of Z scores.
         a. A cross–product of Z scores is the Z score of the subject on one variable times the Z score of that subject on the other variable.
         b. If highs go with highs (positive Z times positive Z) or lows with lows (negative Z times negative Z), the result is positive in either case–thus a high positive sum (of these cross–products, over all subjects) results when there is a strong positive linear correlation.
         c. If highs go with lows (positive Z times negative Z) or lows with highs (positive Z times negative Z), the result is negative in either case–thus a high negative sum results when there is a strong negative linear correlation.
         d. If highs sometimes go with highs (positive Z times positive Z) but sometimes highs go with lows (positive Z times negative Z), and so forth, the result is that positives and negatives cancel out–thus the sum is near zero when there is no correlation.
      3. The degree of correlation will have a standard scale by finding the average of the cross–products of Z scores (dividing the sum by the number of scores).
         a. When there is a perfect positive linear correlation, $r = 1$.
         b. When there is a perfect negative linear correlation, $r = -1$.
         c. When there is no linear correlation, $r = 0$.
         d. In between degrees of correlation have values between 0 and 1 (for positive correlations) and between 0 and –1 (for negative correlations).
   C. The formula for figuring the correlation coefficient is: $r = \Sigma(Z_X Z_Y) / N$.

V. Testing the Statistical Significance of the Correlation Coefficient
   A. The correlation coefficient, by itself, is a descriptive statistic–it describes the degree and direction of linear correlation in the particular group measured.

26

C. A correlation is said to be "significant" if:
    1. It is very unlikely that we could have obtained a correlation this big if in fact the overall group had no correlation.
    2. We determine this likelihood using probability.
    3. We say that a correlation is "statistically significant" if $p < .05$.
D. The logic and procedures of statistical significance are the major focus of the text starting with Chapter 4, but are not considered in any more detail in this chapter on correlation.

VI. Prediction
A. In prediction (same as regression), we use a person's score on one variable to make predictions about a person's score on another variable.
B. The predictor variable is the variable being predicted from and is labeled X.
C. The criterion variable is variable being predicted to and is labeled Y.

VII. The Prediction Model using Z Scores
A. A person's predicted Z score on the dependent variable is found by multiplying a particular number, called a *regression coefficient*, times that person's Z score on the predictor variable.
B. Because we are working with Z scores (which are also called standard scores), the regression coefficient in this case is called a *standardized regression coefficient*.
    1. It is symbolized by the Greek letter beta (ß).
    2. Because it is a kind of measure of how much weight or importance to give the predictor variable, it is called a "beta weight."
C. Formula and symbols: Predicted $Z_Y = (\beta)(Z_X)$.
D. Why prediction is sometimes called regression.
    1. When there is less than a perfect correlation between two variables, the dependent variable Z score is some fraction (the value of r) of the predictor variable Z score.
    2. As a result, the dependent variable Z score is closer to its mean (that is, it regresses or returns to a Z of zero).

VIII. Prediction Using Raw Scores
A. Convert the raw score on the predictor variable to a Z score.
B. Multiply beta times this Z score to get the predicted Z score on the dependent variable.
C. Convert the predicted Z score on the dependent variable to a raw score.

IX. Extension to Multiple Regression and Correlation
A. The association between a dependent/criterion variable and two or more predictor variables is called *multiple correlation*; making predictions in this situation is called *multiple regression*.
B. Z score prediction model in multiple regression: Predicted $Z_Y = (\beta_1)(Z_{X1}) + (\beta_2)(Z_{X2}) + (\beta_3)(Z_{X3})$ ......
C. In multiple regression, ß for a predictor variable is *not* the same as r for that predictor variable with the dependent variable.
    1. ß is usually lower (closer to 0) than r because part of what any one predictor variable measures will overlap with what the other predictor variables measure.
    2. In multiple regression, ß is based on the unique, distinctive contribution of the variable, excluding any overlap with other predictor variables.

D. Raw-score prediction model in multiple regression: $\hat{Y} = a + (b_1)(X_1) + (b_2)(X_2) + (b_3)(X_3)$
...... (each b gives the raw-score rates of exchange for its predictor variable at any given levels of the other predictor variables).
E. The multiple correlation coefficient (R) describes the overall correlation between the predictor variables, taken together, and the dependent variable.
   1. Due to overlap in predicting the dependent variable, R is usually less than (and can not be more than) the sum of each predictor variable's r with the dependent variable.
   2. R ranges from 0 to 1.0 (unlike r, it can not be negative).

X. Correlation and Prediction as Described in Research Articles
A. Correlation coefficients are often described in the text of a research article.
   1. They are usually reported with the letter r, an equal sign, and the correlation coefficient (e.g., $r = .31$).
   2. Sometimes the significance level, such as "$p < .05$," will also be reported.
B. A table of correlations, called a *correlation matrix*, is common when correlations have been computed among many variables.
C. When multiple regression models are used (either in the text or a table), the following information is usually reported:
   1. The regression coefficients.
   2. R^2.
   3. R.
   4. Statistical significance of R^2, regression coefficients, or both.
   5. The standardized and unstandardized β
   6. The standardized error or SE β which gives an indication of the accuracy of the estimation.

XI. The Proportion of Variance Explained
A. The size of the correlation coefficient indicates the strength of the linear relationship.
B. To compare two or more correlations with each other you have to square each correlation (r^2).
   1. r^2 is called the proportion of variance accounted for.
   2. It reflects the amount of variability in the criterion variable that is due to the predictor variable.

Understanding What Formulas Mean

I. Correlation coefficient (r)

Formula in words: Average of the cross–product of Z scores.

Formulas in symbols: $r = \Sigma(Z_X Z_Y) / N$ (3–1)

Z_X is the Z score for each person on the X variable.

Z_Y is the Z score for each person on the Y variable.

$Z_X Z_Y$ is the cross–product of Z scores (for each person, Z_X times Z_Y).

N is the number of people.

II. Predicted Z score for a particular subject on the dependent variable (predicted Z_Y) in bivariate prediction.

Formula in words: Standardized regression coefficient times the subject's Z score on the predictor variable.

Formula in symbols: Predicted $Z_Y = (\beta)(Z_X)$ (3-2)

β is the standardized regression coefficient.

Z_X is the known subject's known Z score on the predictor variable.

III. Standardized regression coefficient (ß) in bivariate prediction.

Formula in words: It is the same as the correlation coefficient.

Formula in symbols: $\beta = r$ (3-3)

r is the ordinary correlation coefficient between the predictor variable and the dependent variable.

IV. Predicted Z score for a particular subject on the dependent variable (predicted Z_Y) in multiple prediction.

Formula in words: Sum, over all predictor variables, of the product of each predictor variable's standardized regression coefficient times the subject's Z score on that predictor variable.

Formula in symbols: Predicted $Z_Y = (\beta_1)(Z_{X1}) + (\beta_2)(Z_{X2}) + (\beta_3)(Z_{X3})$. . (3-4)

How to Graph and Compute a Correlation

I. How to construct a scatter diagram.

A. Draw the axes and determine which variable should go on which axis.

B. Determine the range of values to use for each variable and mark them on the axes.

C. Mark a dot for the pair of scores for each individual.

D. Determine if clearly curvilinear–if so, do not compute the correlation coefficient (or do so with the understanding that you are only describing the degree of linear relationship).

II. How to figure the correlation coefficient.

A. Convert all scores to Z scores.

 1. This requires figuring the mean and standard deviation for each variable.

 2. Once you have the mean and standard deviation figured you need to figure the z-score for each raw score.

B. Compute the cross–product of the Z scores.

 1. For each person, multiply the z-score for one variable times the z-score for the other variable.

C. Sum the cross–products of the Z scores.

D. Divide by the number of people in the study (N).

How to Construct a Z-Score Prediction Model in Bivariate Regression

I. **Compute the correlation coefficient.**
II. **Set ß equal to *r*.**
III. **The prediction model: Predicted $Z_Y = (\beta)(Z_X)$.**

How to Make a Z-Score Prediction for a Particular Subject in Bivariate Regression

I. **Determine the Z-score prediction model.**
II. **Find the Z score for that subject's score on the predictor variable: $Z_X = (X - M_X)/SD_X)$.**
III. **Substitute the above Z score into the prediction model and solve.**

Outline for Writing Essays on the Logic and Computations
for a Correlation Problem

The reason for your writing essay questions in the practice problems and tests is that this task develops and then demonstrates what matters so very much–your comprehension of the logic behind the computations. (It is also a place where those better at words than numbers can shine, and for those better at numbers to develop their skills at explaining in words.)

Thus, to do well, be sure to do the following in each essay: (a) give the reasoning behind each step; (b) relate each step to the specifics of the content of the particular study you are analyzing; (c) state the various formulas in nontechnical language, because as you define each term you show you understand it (although once you have defined it in nontechnical language, you can use it from then on in the essay); (d) look back and be absolutely certain that you made it clear just *why* that formula or procedure was applied and *why* it is the way it is.

The outlines below are *examples* of ways to structure your essays. There are other completely correct ways to go about it. And this is an *outline* for an answer–you are to write the answer out in paragraph form.

These essays are necessarily very long for you to write (and for others to grade). But this is the very best way to be sure you understand everything thoroughly. One short cut you may see on a test is that you'll be asked to write your answer for someone who understands statistics up to the point of the new material you are studying. You can choose to take the same short cut in these practice problems (maybe writing for someone who understands right up to whatever point you yourself start being just a little unclear). But every time you write for a person who has never had statistics at all, you review the logic behind the entire course. You engrain it in your mind. Over and over. The time is never wasted. It is an excellent way to study.

I. Construct a scatter diagram.

A. Procedure: A two–dimensional graph with each variable on one axis and a dot for each score representing its score on the two variables.

B. Explanation: This graph shows the pattern of relationship among the two variables.

II. Estimate the direction and degree of linear correlation.

A. Procedure: Inspect the pattern of dots.

B. Explanation: The general pattern of dots shows whether highs go with highs, lows with lows (or the reverse), indicating the degree of association. (Note the pattern for your particular data.)

III. Compute the correlation coefficient.

A. Procedure: $r = \Sigma(Z_X Z_Y) / N$.

B. Explanation.

1. The correlation represents the degree high scores go with high scores and low scores with low scores (or if describing a negative correlation, the reverse).

2. One can identify the extent to which a score is high or low by converting to Z scores (explain meaning of a Z score, and mean and standard deviation in lay terms, as per the explanation in the outline for writing essays in Chapter 2 of this *Study Guide*).

   a. With Z scores, a high score is always positive.

   b. A low score is always negative.

   c. The degree to which a score is high or low is in proportion to the standard deviation.

3. After converting all scores to Z scores, one multiplies each individual's Z score on one variable times that individual's Z score on the other variable.

a. If describing a positive correlation, note that if highs go with highs then positives will always be multiplied by positives (giving a positive product) and if lows go with lows then negatives will always be multiplied by negatives (also giving a positive product)–the sum over all scores will thus be high and positive.

b. If describing a negative correlation, note that if highs go with lows then positives will always be multiplied by negatives (giving a negative product)–the sum over all scores will thus be a large negative number.

4. One then sums the cross–products and divides by the number of scores to get an average cross–product (called r).

a. If describing a positive correlation, note that the more highs go with highs and lows with lows (or the dots fall near a straight line that slopes up), the closer r is to 1, with no association being an r of 0. (Discuss the degree of correlation of your particular result.)

b. If describing a negative correlation, note that the more highs go with lows and lows with highs (or the dots fall near a straight line that slopes down), the closer r is to –1, with no association being an r of 0. (Discuss the degree of correlation of your particular result.)

IV. Check the sign and size of your computed correlation coefficient against your estimate from the scatter diagram (Step II above).

Chapter Self–Tests

Multiple Choice Questions

1. A relationship between two variables that does not follow a straight line is a _____ relationship.

   a. curvilinear
   b. positive
   c. negative
   d. inverse

2. A correlation coefficient is simply:

   a. a ratio of mean variability.
   b. the distance from the mean in standard deviation units.
   c. the sum of the squared deviations from the mean.
   d. the average of the cross-products of the z-scores.

3. A study finds that the more exercise people do, the less money they spend on medical treatment, but only up to a point. Beyond that point, the more exercise they do, the more money they spend on medical treatment. The relation between amount of exercise and money spent on medical treatment represents

   a. a positive linear correlation.
   b. a negative linear correlation.
   c. a curvilinear correlation.
   d. no correlation (that is, neither linear nor curvilinear).

4. Which choice best describes the data on this scatter diagram?

a. no correlation
b. curvilinear correlation
c. positive linear correlation
d. negative linear correlation

5. The degree of linear correlation is measured by the:

    a. regression coefficient.
    b. correlation coefficient.
    c. standardized regression coefficient.
    d. predictor variable.

6. An employer conducts a survey of how much coffee workers drink each day and how much work they get done. The result is a positive correlation that is statistically significant at the .05 level. What should she conclude?

    a. Coffee increases the rate at which people work.
    b. Working quickly causes people to drink more coffee.
    c. Having a faster metabolism causes people to work faster and to crave coffee.
    d. She cannot make any definite conclusions about the direction of causality just from knowing that the correlation is positive and significant.

7. When using SAT scores to determine ones future college GPA, the SAT score is the _____ variable and college GPA is the _____ variable.

    a. predictor; criterion
    b. dependent; predictor
    c. dependent; criterion
    d. criterion; predictor

8. In a research article, the correlations among several variables are often presented in a table called a

    a. contingency table.
    b. scatter diagram.
    c. correlation matrix.
    d. C table.

9. In the equation, predicted $Z_Y = (\beta)(Z_X)$, the symbol Z_X stands for the

    a. known Z score of the predictor variable.
    b. standardized regression coefficient.
    c. predicted value of the Z score for the dependent variable.
    d. regression constant.

10. Suppose that there is a .52 correlation between performance on the midterm exam and performance on the final exam. If a person's midterm exam score is 3 standard deviations above the mean (Z score = +3), then what is the person's predicted Z score on the final?

    a. $3/.52 = 5.8$
    b. $.52 + 3 = 3.52$
    c. $.52/3 = .17$
    d. $(.52)(3) = 1.56$

Fill–In Questions

1. An association between a criterion variable and two or more predictor variables is called _____.

2. Making a prediction using a criterion variable and two or more predictor variables is called _____.

3. A scatter diagram shows a pattern of dots that follow a line that starts going up and to the right and then about half–way along stops going up and just stays flat as it continues to the right. This pattern is an example of _____ correlation.

4. A study finds that the more self–confidence people have, the less fear they have of meeting new people. The relation between self–confidence and fear of meeting new people is an example of a(n) _____ correlation.

5. The overall correlation between the criterion variables and all predictor variables is called the _____.

6. The more accurate the prediction, the _____ the variance of the actual scores will be to the predicted scores.

7. If pairs of scores for a group of people are highly correlated, a researcher will often conclude that it is likely that for people in general these scores are highly correlated. The researcher would say that this result is statistically _____.

8. _____ is the symbol for the standardized regression coefficient.

9. In a multiple prediction situation with two predictor variables, it has been found that $ß_1 = .3$, $ß_2 = -.4$. A particular subject's Z score on the first predictor variable is -1.5, and this subject's Z score on the second predictor variable is .8. This subject's predicted Z score on the dependent variable is _____.

10. In the bivariate prediction model for your data, $a=15$ and $b=3$. For an individual whose score on X is 8, the predicted score for Y is _____.

Problems and Essays

1. Four individuals kept records for a month on how many eggs they ate per day and then were measured on their cholesterol level. Here are the (fictional) results:

Average Eggs Eaten Per Day	Cholesterol Level
2	210
0	100
1	180
5	270

(a) Make a scatter diagram of the raw data.
(b) Describe the general pattern of the data in words.
(c) Compute the correlation coefficient.
(d) Compute the proportionate reduction in error.
(e) Indicate plausible directions of causality in terms of the variables involved.
(f) Explain your result to a person who has never had a course in statistics.

2. The following (fictional) data are from six LA gang leaders. Here are raw scores and Z scores of the size of each leader's gang and of each leader's willingness to help in a campaign to stop gang violence:

Gang Leader	Size of Gang Raw	Z	Rated Willingness to Help Campaign Raw	Z
Gang A	24	–1.2	10	1.6
Gang B	106	.4	4	–.5
Gang C	42	–.9	7	.5
Gang D	70	–.3	6	.2
Gang E	90	.1	5	–.2
Gang F	178	1.9	1	–1.6

(a) Make a scatter diagram of the raw data.
(b) Describe the general pattern of the data in words.
(c) Compute the correlation coefficient.
(d) Compute the proportion of variance accounted for.
(e) Indicate plausible directions of causality in terms of the variables involved.
(f) Explain your answer to a person who has never had a course in statistics.

3. A Canadian sociologist conducted a (fictional) survey of attitudes towards a particular immigrant nationality among members of that nationality. The survey also included questions about how much the respondents identified with their group of national origin and about how many generations the person's parents had been in Canada (which ranged from 1–first–generation immigrants–through 6). The researcher reported the following results: "There appears to be a strong association between positive attitudes and degree of identification, with a correlation between the two measures of $r = .51$, $p < .01$. However, there was little association between positive attitudes and number of generations, $r = .16$, not significant." Explain this result to a person who has never had a course in statistics. (Discuss the statistical–significance aspect only in a very general way.)

4. An educational psychologist analyzed the relation between high school students' performance in various classes as measured by their grades and reported the (fictional) results in the following table.

	English	Math	Science	History
English		.12	.19	.53**
Math			.68**	.09
Science				.28*
History				

$*p < .05$; $**p < .01$

Explain these results to a person who has never had a course in statistics. (Discuss the statistical–significance aspect only in a very general way.)

5. A researcher is interested in predicting how well people will do who participate in an outdoor training program (ratings by instructor at end of program on a 100-point scale from 0 to 10) on the number of hours they exercise each week. In a pilot study of five people, these results were obtained.

Person Tested	Hours Exercised Per Week		Performance in Training Program	
	X	Z_X	Y	Z_Y
1	3	-.59	45	-.54
2	11	1.76	90	1.47
3	6	.29	53	-.18
4	1	-1.17	25	-1.43
5	4	-.29	72	.67
	$M=5$		$M=57$	
	$SD=3.41$		$SD=22.35$	

The correlation was found to be .87. Based on the above information, (a) give the Z-score prediction formula for predicting performance in the training program based on number of hours of exercise per week; (b) using the bivariate prediction rule, predict the performance in the training program for a person who has exercised 8 hours per week; and (c) explain what you have done to a person who has never taken a course in statistics.

Using SPSS 10.0 with this Chapter

You can use SPSS to create a scatter diagram and to compute a correlation coefficient. You should work through the example, following the procedures step by step. Then look over the description of the general principles involved and try the procedures on your own for some of the problems listed in the Suggestions for Additional Practice. Finally, you may want to try the suggestions for using the computer to deepen your understanding, and you can explore the advanced SPSS procedure, a correlation matrix, at the end.

I. Example

A. Data: The number supervised and stress level for five managers (fictional data), from the example in the text. The scores for the managers for the two variables are number supervised 6, stress 7; 8, 8; 3, 1; 10, 8; and 8, 6.

B. Follow the instructions in the SPSS Appendix for starting up SPSS.

C. Enter the data as follows.

1. Type 6 and press enter. Then click on the next box on the same line and type 7 and enter. This will put the subjects two scores on the same line next to each other.

2. Click on the first box on the next line and type 8 and then enter. Then click on the second box on the second line and type 8 and enter.

3. Type the scores for the remaining subjects, on each line one subject's number supervised and stress level, in that order.

4. To name the two variables, click on the variable view tab at the bottom of the screen. This will bring up a spreadsheet that allows you to define characteristics about your variables. In the first column of the first row, type in NUMSUPD under the Name column. In the first column of the second row type in STRESS under the name column. The screen that allows you to name your variables should now appear as shown in Figure SG3–1. The screen that allows you to enter your data should now appear as shown in Figure SG3-2.

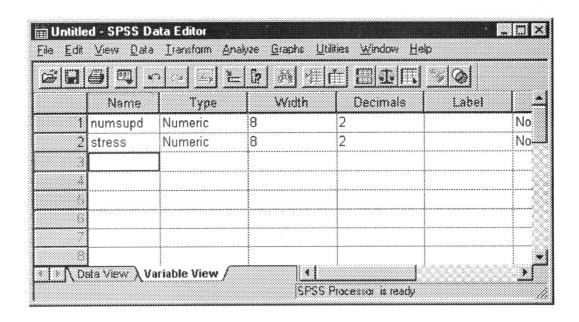

Figure SG3–1

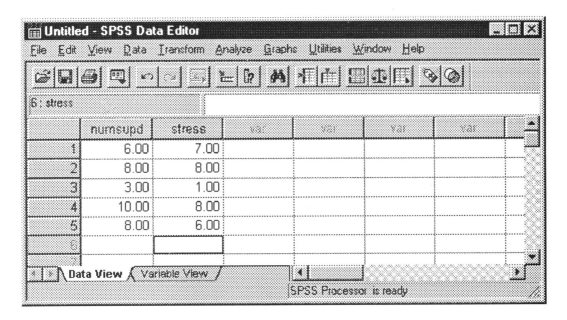

Figure SG3–2

D. Create a scatter diagram for the two variables as follows:
　　　　Graphs
　　　　　Scatter
　　　　　　Simple
　　　　　　　Define
　　　　　　　　[Highlight STRESS and move it into the Y-axis box.
　　　　　　　　Then highlight NUMSUPD and move it into the X-axis box and click OK.

37

Your screen should now look like Figure SG3-3.]

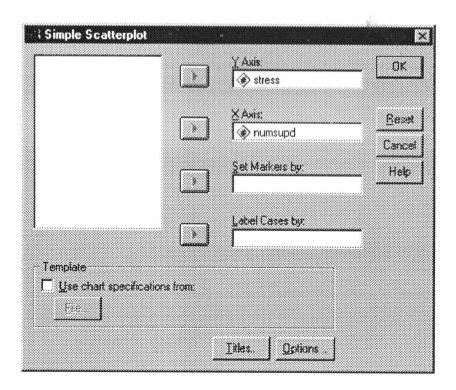

Figure SG3-3

The scatter diagram should look like Figure SG3–4.

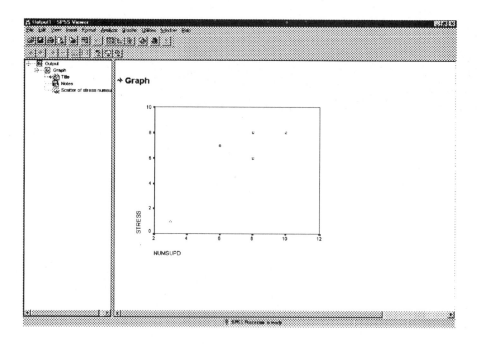

Figure SG3-4

E. Inspect the result.
    1. The label for the vertical axis, **STRESS**, is shown along the left side, and the label for the horizontal axis, **NUMSUPD**, is shown along the bottom of the screen.
    2. The **dots** represent the data points.
    3. Notice that this scatter diagram corresponds closely to the one in the text for these data.
F. Print out a copy of the result by going to File and clicking on Print.
    1. Click on the Chart Carousel icon and go to Close. This will return you to the Data window.
G. Compute the correlation coefficient as follows:
    Statistics
      Correlate >
        Bivariate
          [Move Stress and Numsupd under Variables by highlighting them and clicking on the arrow. Your should appear as Figure SG3-5]
            OK

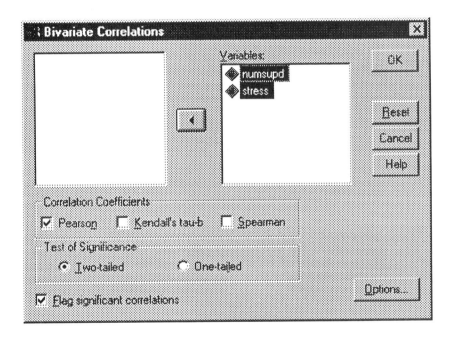

Figure SG3-5

The results should appear as shown in Figure SG3-6.

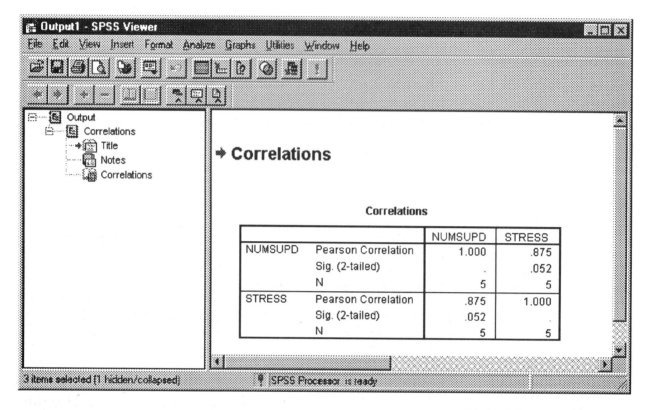

Figure SG3–6

1. Inspect the result: The screen shows the combination of variables with **1.000** for each variable's correlation with itself, and **.875** for the correlation between the two variables (the correlation in the chapter, in which everything was rounded off to two decimal places, was .88).
2. Print out a copy of the result by going to File and then Print.
3. Save your lines of data as follows:
   File
      Save Data
         [Name your data file followed by the extension ".sav" and designate the drive you would like your data saved in.]

II. Additional Practice

(For each data set, create a scatter diagram, compute the correlation coefficient, and compare your results to those in the text.)

A. Text examples.
   1. Fictional study of class size and achievement test scores of five elementary schools (from Table 3–3).
B. Practice problems in the text.
   1. Questions 1 and 2.

III. Using the Computer to Deepen Your Knowledge

A. The effect of outliers (extreme scores) on the correlation coefficient.
   1. Use SPSS to compute correlations for the example several times, each time changing one of the numbers supervised to a more extreme number–such as changing the 10 to a 11, then to a 15, then a 20, then a 100. For each run record the correlation.
   2. Do the same with the original numbers, but changing one of the stress ratings, perhaps one of the 8s. For each run record the correlation.
   3. Do the same thing with the original numbers, but this time creating a joint outlier–perhaps making the 10,8 pair into a 20,16 pair, then a 40,32 pair, etc. For each run record the correlation.

40

4. Do the same thing, but this time creating a joint outlier that is not an outlier on either variable by itself. Try 2,8 and 10,0.
5. Make a chart of the results and notice how sensitive the correlation coefficient is to outliers involving one variable and outliers involving two variables.

B. The effect of adding, subtracting, multiplying, or dividing by a constant on the correlation coefficient.
   1. Use SPSS to compute the correlation coefficient using the example data–except this time add five to every stress score. Then add 10. Then try adding 5 to every number–supervised score. Note that the correlations in each case are the same.
   2. Do the same, this time multiplying one of the scores by 5. Then try dividing one of the scores by 8. Again, there is no effect.
   3. Do the same, this time using Z scores. Again there is no effect.

C. Estimating correlations.
   1. Begin with the example and modify the scores for two of the subjects until you have reduced the correlation to as close to .50 as you can.
   2. Modify as many scores as necessary to create a correlation near to zero.
   3. Modify as many scores as necessary to create a correlation near to –.50.
   4. Create a scatter diagram on paper that you think represents a correlation of about .25. Then enter the numbers and try it on the computer to see how close you get. Modify the scatter diagram until you have achieved a correlation of about .25.
   5. Do the same for correlations of –.50, –.25, 0, .50, and .75.

IV. **Advanced Procedure: Correlation Matrix**
   A. Add a third variable to your data representing job difficulty. The scores for the managers (in the same order) are 35, 30, 25, 40, and 35. (To do this, you must add a variable name for this variable, such as **JOBDIFF**, and add each subject's scores to his or her line of scores.)
   B. Have SPSS compute the correlations among all three variables.

Chapter 4
Some Key Ingredients for Inferential Statistics:
The Normal Curve, Probability, and Population Versus Sample

Learning Objectives

By the end of this chapter you should be able to:
- Describe the characteristics of the normal distribution.
- Choose values from the normal curve table.
- Convert raw scores to Z scores.
- Determine the percentage of the population between any two raw scores.
- Determine the raw score from a Z score.
- Understand the information conveyed in a probability statement.
- Calculating probabilities.
- Interpret the normal curve as a probability distribution.
- Explain the difference between a sample and population.
- Explain how random and nonrandom methods of sampling differ.

Chapter Outline

I. **The Normal Distribution**
   A. The distributions of many variables that psychologists measure follow a unimodal, symmetrical, bell-shaped distribution.
   B. These bell-shaped histograms or frequency polygons approximate a precise and important mathematical distribution called the *normal distribution*, or more simply, the *normal curve*.
   C. Because this shape is standard, there is a known percentage of scores below or above any particular point such that:
      1. Exactly 50% of the scores fall below the mean and exactly 50% above the mean.
      2. Approximately 34% of the scores fall between the mean and one standard deviation from the mean in each direction.
      3. Approximately 14% of the scores fall between one and two standard deviations from the mean in each direction.
   D. Because the normal curve is mathematically exact you can determine the percentage of people that:
      1. Fall between any two Z scores.
      2. Fall above or below any Z scores.
   E. The normal curve table and Z scores.
      1. Instead of having to perform the calculations involved, statisticians have created helpful tables of the normal curve that give the percentage of scores between the mean (a Z score of 0) and any other Z score. (Table B-1 in the text is a normal curve table.)
      2. This table can be used to compute the percentage of scores from Z scores or from raw scores (by converting them to Z scores).
      3. This table can be used to compute a Z score or raw score (by converting from a Z score) from percentage of scores.

II. Probability

A. Inferential statistics can be applied to results of research to permit probabilistic conclusions about theories or applied procedures.

B. There are only a few key ideas within probability you need to know to understand basic inferential statistical procedures.

C. Probability is the long-run, expected relative frequency of a particular outcome in which:

    1. An *outcome* is the result of an experiment (or virtually any event, such as a coin coming up heads or it raining tomorrow).

    2. *Frequency* means how many times something occurs.

    3. *Relative frequency* means the number of times something occurs relative to the number of times it could have occurred.

    4. Hence, *Long run relative frequency* is what you would expect to get, in the long run, if you were to repeat the experiment many times.

D. Probabilities are figured as the number of possible successful outcomes divided by the number of all possible outcomes.

E. Probabilities can take the range of 0-1 in which:

    1. Something that has no chance of happening has a probability of 0.

    2. Something that is certain to happen has a probability of 1.

F. Probability is usually symbolized by the letter p and expressed as equaling, greater than, or less than some fraction or percentage.

G. The normal distribution can also be thought of as a probability distribution: The proportion of scores between any two Z scores is the same as the probability of selecting a score between those two Z scores.

III. Sample and Population

A. A *population* is the entire set of things of interest.

B. A *sample* is the subset of the population about which you actually have information.

C. Why samples are studied (instead of populations).

    1. Usually it is not practical to study entire populations.

    2. The goal of science is to make generalizations or predictions about events beyond our reach, such as the behavior of entire populations.

D. The general strategy of psychology research is to study a sample of individuals who are believed to be representative of the general population (or of some particular population of interest).

E. At the minimum, researchers try to study people who at least do not differ from the general population in any systematic way that would be expected to matter for that topic of research.

F. There are several methods of sampling.

    1. The ideal method of sampling is *random selection*: The researcher obtains a complete list of all the members of a population and randomly selects some number of them to study.

    2. *Haphazard selection* is quite different from true random selection and is likely to produce a sample that is a biased subset of the population as a whole.

    3. In psychology research it is rarely possible to employ true random sampling, but researchers try to study a sample that is not systematically *un*representative of the population in any known way.

G. Statistical terminology for samples and populations.

    1. The mean, variance, and standard deviation of a population are called population parameters.

        a. A population parameter is usually an unknown that is, at best, estimated from sample information.

    2. The mean, variance, and standard deviation you calculate to describe a sample are *sample statistics*.

      a. A sample statistic is computed from known information.

      b. Generally, the symbols for sample statistics (which is what we have used so far) are ordinary letters.

        i. Sample mean = M.

        ii. Sample standard deviation = SD.

IV. Normal Curves, Probabilities, Samples, and Populations as Described in Research Articles

    A. These topics, which are important fundamentals, are rarely found discussed explicitly in research articles (except articles *about* methods or statistics).

    B. The normal curve is sometimes mentioned when describing the distribution of scores on a particular variable.

    C. Probability is rarely discussed directly, except in the context of statistical significance (see Chapter 5 and beyond).

    D. The method of selecting the sample from the population is sometimes described, particularly if the study is a survey.

How to Determine the Percentage of Scores Above or Below a Particular Score Using a Normal Curve Table

I. **If it is a raw score, convert it to a Z score: $Z = (X-M)/SD$.**

II. **Draw a picture of the normal curve and indicate where the Z score falls on it. Shade in the area you for which you wish to find the percentage.**

III. **Look up the Z score in the Z column and find the percentage in the adjacent *% Mean to Z* column.**

IV. **For a percentage of scores above a particular Z score.**

    A. If the Z score is positive, subtract this percentage from 50% (that is, 50% minus this percentage).

    B. If the Z score is negative, add 50% to it.

V. **For a percentage of scores below a particular Z score.**

    A. If the Z score is positive, add 50% to this percentage.

    B. If the Z score is negative, subtract this percentage from 50% (that is, 50% minus this percentage).

How to Determine a Score from Knowing the Percentages of Scores Above or Below that Score Using a Normal Curve Table

I. **For a situation in which there is a particular percentage of scores higher than the score.**

    A. If the percentage is less than 50%.

      1. Subtract the percentage from 50% (that is, 50% minus the percentage).

      2. Look up the closest percentage to this difference in the *% Mean to Z* column and find the Z score in the adjacent Z column.

B. If the percentage is greater than 50%.
  1. Subtract 50% from the percentage (that is, the percentage minus 50%).
  2. Look up the closest percentage to this difference in the *% Mean to Z* column and find the *Z* score in the adjacent *Z* column.
  3. Make this *Z* score negative (put a minus sign in front of it).

II. **For a situation in which there is a particular percentage of scores lower than the score.**
  A. If the percentage is less than 50%.
    1. Subtract the percentage from 50% (that is, 50% minus the percentage).
    2. Look up the closest percentage to this difference in the *% Mean to Z* column and find the *Z* score in the adjacent *Z* column.
    3. Make this *Z* score negative (put a minus sign in front of it).
  B. If the percentage is more than 50%.
    1. Subtract 50% from the percentage (that is, the percentage minus 50%).
    2. Look up the closest percentage to this difference in the *% Mean to Z* column and find the *Z* score in the adjacent *Z* column.

III. **Convert the *Z* score to a raw score:** $X = (Z)(SD) + M.$

Outline for Writing Essays on the Logic and Computations for Determining a Percentage of Scores in a Normal Distribution
(from a Score or Vice Versa)

The reason for your writing essay questions in the practice problems and tests is that this task develops and then demonstrates what matters so very much--your comprehension of the logic behind the computations. (It is also a place where those better at words than numbers can shine, and for those better at numbers to develop their skills at explaining in words.)

Thus, to do well, be sure to do the following in each essay: (a) give the reasoning behind each step; (b) relate each step to the specifics of the content of the particular study you are analyzing; (c) state the various formulas in nontechnical language, because as you define each term you show you understand it (although once you have defined it in nontechnical language, you can use it from then on in the essay); (d) look back and be absolutely certain that you made it clear just *why* that formula or procedure was applied and *why* it is the way it is.

The outlines below are *examples* of ways to structure your essays. There are other completely correct ways to go about it. And this is an *outline* for an answer--you are to write the answer out in paragraph form.

These essays are necessarily very long for you to write (and for others to grade). But this is the very best way to be sure you understand everything thoroughly. One short cut you may see on a test is that you may be asked to write your answer for someone who understands statistics up to the point of the new material you are studying. You can choose to take the same short cut in these practice problems (maybe writing for someone who understands right up to whatever point you yourself start being just a little unclear). But every time you write for a person who has never had statistics at all, you review the logic behind the entire course. You engrain it in your mind. Over and over. The time is never wasted. It is an excellent way to study.

How to Figure the Percentage of Scores from Raw Scores and from Z Scores Using the Normal Curve Table.

I. If a raw score, convert it to a Z score.

II. Draw a picture of the normal curve, where the Z score falls on it, and shade in the area for which you are finding the percentage.

III. Using the Normal Curve Table, find the exact percentage of scores between this Z score and the mean.
    A. Procedure: Look up the Z score in the Z column and find the percentage in the adjacent *% Mean to Z* column.

IV. To determine the percentage above your score.
    A. If the Z score is positive.
        1. Procedure: Subtract this percentage from 50%.
        2. Explanation.
            a. Since the Z score is positive (that is, it is above the mean), the amount above this score is the 50% above the mean less what is between this score and the mean (the percentage from the table).
            b. Give your actual difference.
            c. Illustrate with a picture of a normal curve showing your situation.
    B. If the Z score is negative.
        1. Procedure: Add 50% to this percentage.
        2. Explanation.
            a. Since the Z score is negative (that is, it is below the mean), the total above this score is what is between it and the mean (the percentage from the table) plus the 50% above the mean.
            b. Give your actual sum.
            c. Illustrate with a picture of a normal curve showing your situation.

V. To determine the percentage below your score.
    A. If the Z score is positive.
        1. Procedure: Add 50% to this percentage.
        2. Explanation.
            a. Since the Z score is positive (that is, it is above the mean), the total below this score is the amount between it and the mean (the percentage from the table) plus the 50% below the mean.
            b. Give your actual total.
            c. Illustrate with a picture of a normal curve showing your situation.
    B. If the Z score is negative.
        1. Procedure: Subtract this percentage from 50%.
        2. Explanation.
            a. Since the Z score is negative (that is, it is below the mean), the amount below this score is the 50% below the mean less the percentage between the mean and this score (the amount computed earlier).
            b. Give your actual difference.
            c. Illustrate with a picture of a normal curve showing your situation.

VI. If the percentage is less than 50%.
    A. Procedure.
        1. Subtract the percentage from 50% (that is, 50% minus the percentage).
        2. Look up the closest percentage to this difference in the *% Mean to Z* column and find the Z score in the adjacent Z column.
    B. Explanation.

1. The percentage between the mean and the score (the percentage that can be looked up on the table to find the corresponding Z score) is what remains between the percentage above the score and 50% (the total above the mean).
2. Give your figures.
3. Illustrate with a picture of a normal curve showing your situation.

VII. If the percentage is greater than 50%.
A. Procedure.
1. Subtract 50% from the percentage (that is, the percentage minus 50%).
2. Look up the closest percentage to this difference in the *% Mean to Z* column and find the Z score in the adjacent Z column.
3. Make this Z score negative (put a minus sign in front of it).

B. Explanation.
1. The percentage between the mean and the score (the percentage that can be looked up on the table to find the corresponding Z score) is what remains after subtracting out the 50% above the mean.
2. Since there are more than 50% above this score, the score must be below the mean, and hence a negative Z score.
3. Give your figures.
4. Illustrate with a picture of a normal curve showing your situation.

VIII. For a situation in which there is a particular percentage of scores lower than the score.
A. If the percentage is less than 50%.
1. Procedure.
   a. Subtract the percentage from 50%.
   b. Look up the closest percentage to this difference in the *% Mean to Z* column and find the Z score in the adjacent Z column.
   c. Make this Z score negative (put a minus sign in front of it).
2. Explanation.
   a. The percentage between the mean and the score (the percentage that can be looked up on the table to find the corresponding Z score) is what remains after subtracting it from the total of 50% below the mean.
   b. Since there are less than 50% below this score, the score must be below the mean and hence a negative Z score.
   c. Give your figures.
   d. Illustrate with a picture of a normal curve showing your situation.
B. If the percentage is more than 50%.
1. Procedure.
   a. Subtract 50% from the percentage (that is, the percentage minus 50%).
   b. Look up the closest percentage to this difference in the *% Mean to Z* column and find the Z score in the adjacent Z column.
2. Explanation.
   a. The percentage between the mean and the score (the percentage that can be looked up on the table to find the corresponding Z score) is what remains above the mean after subtracting out the 50% below the mean.
   b. Give your figures.
   c. Illustrate with a picture of a normal curve showing your situation.

Chapter Self-Tests

Multiple-Choice Questions

1. A normal curve is
   a. bimodal and slightly skewed to the right.
   b. unimodal and symmetrical.
   c. unimodal and slightly skewed to the left.
   d. bimodal and roughly symmetrical.

2. The mean score on a depression scale is 10 and the standard deviation is 3. The distribution is normal. Using the approximation rules for normal curves, how many people would get a score between 10 and 16?
   a. 50%
   b. 34%
   c. 34% + 14% = 48%
   d. 34% + 34% = 68%

3. A person received a test score that was in the top 30% of all the scores. Using the normal curve table, what was this person's *Z* score?
   a. .52
   b. .84
   c. 5.03
   d. 5.34

4. What is the *Z* score a person would have to receive to be in the top 2% of their class?
   a. -2.05
   b. 0.05
   c. .48
   d. 2.05

5. *Approximately* what *Z* score would a person have to have to be in the bottom 16% of their group?
   a. -2
   b. 1
   c. 0
   d. +1

6. How do you calculate probability?
   a. The number of all possible outcomes divided by the number of possible successful outcomes.
   b. The number of all possible outcomes multiplied by the number of possible successful outcomes.
   c. The number of possible successful outcomes divided by the number of possible outcomes.
   d. The number of all possible outcomes minus the number of possible successful outcomes.

7. A(n) _____ is the number of times something happens relative to the number of times it could have happened.
   a. percentile rank
   b. expected relative frequency
   c. relative frequency
   d. outcome

8. The result of an experiment is a(n) _____.

a. outcome
b. statistic
c. probability
d. parameter

9. In the behavioral and social sciences it is important to select a sample that is _____ the population.
   a. exactly like
   b. representative of
   c. contains the majority of
   d. dissimilar from

10. A(n) _____ sample is choosing a sample from those who are available.
   a. random
   b. representative
   c. haphazard
   d. estimated

Fill-In Questions

1. In a normal curve approximately _____ percent of the scores fall between the mean and one standard deviation above the mean.

2. A distribution in which most scores are in the middle and fewer are at the extremes is a _____ distribution but not necessarily a _____ distribution.

3. The shape of the normal curve is considered _____, thus there is a known percentage at any point.

4. A probability is also a _____.

5. A Z score is a raw score converted into the number of _____ the raw score is from the mean.

6. To pick 15 people for a study of faculty opinion at a particular college, a student gives a questionnaire to each faculty member who arrives at the faculty club on a particular evening. This is an example of _____ selection.

7. A characteristic of a population, such as its mean, is called a(n) _____.

8. A characteristic of a sample, such as its standard deviation, is called a(n) _____.

9. _____ is the expected relative frequency of a particular outcome.

10. A _____ is usually unknown and can only be estimated from what you know about a sample from that population.

50

Problems and Essays

1. Suppose a test of musical ability has a normal distribution with a mean of 50 and a standard deviation of 5. Approximately what percentage of people are (a) above 55, (b) below 40, and (c) above 45. (Use the normal curve approximation rules.) (d) Explain your answers to a person who has never had a course in statistics.

2. Suppose the number of clients seen in any given week by full time psychotherapists in a particular city is normally distributed with a mean of 15.3 and a standard deviation of 2.8. (a) A therapist who is in the top 5% of number of clients seen would be seeing at least how many? (b) What is the most a therapist could be seeing and still be in the bottom 10%. (c) Explain your answers to a person who has never had a course in statistics.

3. Thirty students in a particular elementary school classroom include 8 girls who are of an ethnic minority, 4 boys of an ethnic minority, 7 girls who are not of an ethnic minority, and 11 boys not of an ethnic minority. A student is selected at random to represent the class. (a) What is the probability that student will be a girl? (b) What is the probability the student will be of an ethnic minority?

4. A health researcher plans to conduct a mail survey of a sample of doctors in a particular U.S. state to ask about their attitudes toward drug advertisements. What would be the best way to go about selecting the sample of doctors to study? Explain what you would do and why to a person who is unfamiliar with research methods or statistics.

Note. There is no section on using SPSS 10.0 with this chapter because none of the procedures covered are easily implemented using standard computerized statistical packages.

Chapter 5
Introduction to Hypothesis Testing

Learning Objectives

By the end of this chapter you should be able to:

■ Describe the core logic behind hypothesis testing.
■ Apply the 5-step hypothesis testing process.
■ Describe the populations involved in hypothesis testing.
■ Construct appropriate null and research (alternative) hypotheses.
■ Figure the cutoff score on the comparison distribution.
■ Appropriately use significance and conventional levels of significance.
■ Decide when to, and not to, reject the null hypothesis and explain the implications of this decision.
■ Explain the difference between one-tailed and two-tailed tests as well as the difference between directional and nondirectional hypotheses.
■ Recognize how results of studies using hypothesis–testing procedures are reported in research articles.

Chapter Outline

I. **The Core Logic of Hypothesis Testing**
   A. Hypothesis testing is a systematic procedure for deciding whether the results of a research study supports a particular theory which applies to a population.
   B. The key idea is that we test the notion that the experimental manipulation made no difference. If the notion of no difference can be rejected, this supports the idea it does make a difference.
   C. Put another way; we draw conclusions by evaluating the probability of getting our research results if the opposite of what we are predicting were true.
   D. This double–negative is awkward at the heart of inferential statistics.

II. **The Steps of Hypothesis Testing (as applied to the situation in which a single individual is exposed to the experimental manipulation and compared to a known population distribution of people not so exposed)**
   A. Step 1: Reframe the question into a research hypothesis and a null hypothesis about populations.
      1. Research is conducted using samples to test hypotheses about populations.
      2. One population (Population 1) is the people who are exposed to the experimental manipulation.
      3. The other population (Population 2) is the people who have not been exposed to the experimental manipulation.
      4. The research (or alternative) hypothesis is a statement about a predicted difference between populations.
         a. Typically the difference predicted is that the mean of one population is different (or more specifically, higher or lower) than the mean of the other.
         b. The prediction is usually based on theory or practical experience.
      5. The null hypothesis is a statement about a relation between populations that represents the crucial opposite of the research hypothesis.

a. It usually is a prediction of no difference (or that if there is a difference it is in the direction opposite tc what is predicted).

b. It has this name because it predicts a "null" or nondifference.

6. The research hypothesis and the null hypothesis are opposites and mutually exclusive.

a. It is this oppositeness that is at the heart of the hypothesis–testing process.

B. Step 2: Determine the characteristics of the comparison distribution.

1. In terms of hypothesis–testing language, the crucial question is as follows: Given a particular sample value, what is the probability of obtaining the result if the null hypothesis is true?

2. To answer this, we need to know the characteristics of the population from which the sample would be coming from if the null hypothesis were true.

3. If the null hypothesis is true, both populations are the same and the score in Population 1 comes from a distribution with the same characteristics as that of Population 2.

4. This crucial distribution is called the *comparison distribution.*

C. Step 3: Determine the cutoff sample score on the comparison distribution at which the null hypothesis should be rejected.

1. Before making an observation, researchers consider what kind of observation would be sufficiently extreme to reject the null hypothesis.

2. Researchers do not usually use an actual number of units on the direct scale of measurement of the comparison distribution; instead they state how extreme a score should be in terms of a Z score on this distribution (and the associated probability of getting a Z score that extreme on this distribution).

3. Since the comparison distribution is ordinarily a normal curve, the cutoff is found in a normal curve table.

4. The cutoff percentage is called the "level of significance."

5. Conventional levels of significance used by psychology researchers are 5% (the .05 significance level) or 1% (the .01 significance level).

6. When a sample value is so extreme that the null hypothesis is rejected, the result is said to be *statistically significant.*

D. Step 4: Determine the sample's score on the comparison distribution.

1. This is the result of the actual experiment or observation.

2. The raw–score result is converted to a Z score on the scale of the comparison distribution to make it comparable to the cutoff Z score.

E. Step 5: Compare the scores obtained in Steps 3 and 4 to determine whether or not to reject the null hypothesis.

1. If the actual sample's Z score (from Step 4) is more extreme than the cutoff Z score (from Step 3), the null hypothesis is rejected.

a. Thus, the research hypothesis is supported.

b. However, the research hypothesis is not "proven" or shown to be "true"–no pattern of results can prove a hypothesis based on research data; it can only support or fail to support a particular hypothesis.

2. If the actual sample's Z score (from Step 4) is not more extreme than the cutoff Z score (from Step 3), the null hypothesis is not rejected.

a. Thus, the experiment is inconclusive.

b. However, because hypothesis testing is based on probability, we do not say the null hypothesis is proven or true.

c. The null hypothesis could be false, even though the study does not succeed in rejecting it–for example, we could fail to reject it because the effect was too weak to show up significantly in the study.

III. One–Tailed and Two–Tailed Hypothesis Tests

A. A *directional hypotheses* is used when there is a specific predicted direction of effect, such as predicting an increase or predicting a decrease.

    1. The research hypothesis is that Population 1's mean is higher (or lower, if that is the prediction) than Population 2's mean.

    2. Significance testing is carried out as follows (for simplicity, points a and b below assume a higher score was predicted and the 5% significance level used).

        a. To reject the null hypothesis, the obtained score has to be in a region of the comparison distribution that is in its upper 5%.

        b. That is, it has to be in the area on one tail only, and thus this is called a *one–tailed test*.

B. A *nondirectional hypothesis* is used when the researcher predicts one population will be different from the other, without specifying how they will be different.

    1. The research hypothesis is that Population 1's mean is different from Population 2's mean.

    2. Significance testing is carried out as follows (for simplicity, points a through c below assumes the 5% significance level is used).

        a. To reject the null hypothesis, the obtained score has to be in a region of the comparison distribution that is in either the upper 2.5% or the lower 2.5%, making a total of 5% of the area in which the null hypothesis could be rejected.

        b. That is, it can be in either tail of the distribution, and thus this is called a *two–tailed test*.

        c. Using a two–tailed test requires a more extreme cutoff than a one–tailed test for the same situation.

C. When to use one–tailed versus two–tailed tests.

    1. In principle you plan to use a one–tailed test when you have a clearly directional hypothesis and a two–tailed test when you have a clearly nondirectional hypothesis.

    2. In practice, the situation is not so simple.

        a. Even when a theory clearly predicts a particular result, we sometimes find that the result is just the opposite of what we expected and that this reverse of what we expected may actually be more interesting.

        b. For this reason, by using one–tailed tests we run the risk of having to ignore possibly important results.

    3. There is debate as to whether one–tailed tests should be used, even when there is a clearly directional hypothesis.

    4. In most cases the final conclusion is not really affected by whether a one– or two–tailed test is used (the result is either extreme enough to reject the null hypothesis either way, or not extreme enough to reject the null hypothesis either way).

    5. If a result is so close that it matters which method is used, results should be interpreted cautiously pending further research.

IV. Hypothesis Tests as Reported in Research Articles

A. Hypothesis tests are usually reported in the context of one of the specific statistical procedures covered in later chapters.

B. For each result of interest, the article usually gives the following information.

    1. Whether the result was statistically significant.

    2. The name of the specific technique used in determining the probabilities (these are what are covered in later chapters).

    3. An indication of the significance level, such as "$p < .05$," or "$p < .01$."

        a. "$p < .05$" means that the probability of these results if the null hypothesis were true is less than .05 (5%).

        b. If a result is close but did not reach the significance level chosen, it may be reported anyway as a "near significant trend," with "$p < .10$," for example.

c. If the result is not significant, sometimes the actual *p* level will be given (for example, "*p* = .27"), or the abbreviation "ns," for "not significant," will be used.

   4. If a one–tailed test was used, that will usually also be noted. (Otherwise assume a two–tailed test was used.)

C. Sometimes the results of hypothesis testing are shown simply as starred results in a table; a result with a star has attained significance (at a level given in a footnote) and one without has not.

D. The steps of hypothesis testing, or which is the null and which is the research hypothesis, are rarely made explicit.

How to Test an Hypothesis

(When the sample consists of one individual and the distribution of the
population not exposed to the experimental manipulation is known.)

I. Reframe the question into a research hypothesis and a null hypothesis about populations. (Step 1.)

A. Identify the two populations.

   1. Population 1 is people like those studied who have been exposed to the experimental manipulation.
   2. Population 2 is people like those studied but who have not been exposed to the experimental manipulation (this is usually people of the category studied from the general public).

B. State the research hypothesis.

   1. Decide whether this will be directional or nondirectional.
   2. State in terms of the two populations (that the mean of one will be higher, lower, or the same as the other).

C. State the null hypothesis: Populations 1 and 2 are the same; the manipulation lacks impact.

D. Check that the research and null hypothesis are consistent (in terms of both being in relation to a directional or nondirectional prediction).

II. Determine the characteristics of the comparison distribution. (Step 2.)

A. This will be the distribution of Population 2.

B. Note its Population M, Population SD^2 and shape (which will usually be normal).

III. Determine the cutoff sample score on the comparison distribution at which the null hypothesis should be rejected. (Step 3.)

A. Decide on the significance level (1% or 5%).

B. Determine the percentage of individuals between the mean and where the appropriate percentage begins on the normal curve.

   1. If a one–tailed test, this is 50% minus the significance level.
   2. If a two–tailed test, this is 50% minus 1/2 the significance level.

C. Look up the *Z* corresponding to this percentage in the *% Mean to Z* column in the normal table–this is the cutoff *Z*.

IV. Determine the sample's score on the comparison distribution. (Step 4.)

A. Conduct the study and note the score of the individual (or note the result as given to you in the problem).

B. Convert the raw-score result to a *Z* score on the comparison distribution: *Z*= (M-Population M)/Population SD.

V. **Compare the scores obtained in Steps 3 and 4 to determine whether or not to reject the null hypothesis. (Step 5.)**

  A. If the actual sample's Z score (from Step 4) is more extreme than the cutoff Z score (from step 3).

    1. The null hypothesis is rejected.
    2. Thus, the research hypothesis is supported.

VI. **Convert the raw–score result to a Z score on the comparison distribution: $Z =$ the scores obtained in Steps 3 and 4 to determine whether or not to reject the null hypothesis. (Step 5.)**

  A. If the actual sample's Z score (from Step 4) is more extreme than the cutoff Z score (from Step 3).

    1. The null hypothesis is rejected.
    2. Thus, the research hypothesis is accepted.

  B. If the actual sample's Z score (from Step 4) is not more extreme than the cutoff Z score (from Step 3).

    1. The null hypothesis is not rejected.
    2. Thus, the experiment is inconclusive.

Outline for Writing Essays for Hypothesis–Testing Problems Involving a Single Sample of One Subject and a Known Population

The reason for your writing essay questions in the practice problems and tests is that this task develops and then demonstrates what matters so very much–your comprehension of the logic behind the computations. (It is also a place where those better at words than numbers can shine, and for those better at numbers to develop their skills at explaining in words.)

Thus, to do well, be sure to do the following in each essay: (a) give the reasoning behind each step; (b) relate each step to the specifics of the content of the particular study you are analyzing; (c) state the various formulas in nontechnical language, because as you define each term you show you understand it (although once you have defined it in nontechnical language, you can use it from then on in the essay); (d) look back and be absolutely certain that you made it clear just *why* that formula or procedure was applied and *why* it is the way it is.

The outlines below are *examples* of ways to structure your essays. There are other completely correct ways to go about it. And this is an *outline* for an answer–you are to write the answer out in paragraph form.

These essays are necessarily very long for you to write (and for others to grade). But this is the very best way to be sure you understand everything thoroughly. One short cut you may see on a test is that you may be asked to write your answer for someone who understands statistics up to the point of the new material you are studying. You can choose to take the same short cut in these practice problems (maybe writing for someone who understands right up to whatever point you yourself start being just a little unclear). But every time you write for a person who has never had statistics at all, you review the logic behind the entire course. You engrain it in your mind. Over and over. The time is never wasted. It is an excellent way to study.

I. **Reframe the question into a research hypothesis and a null hypothesis about populations. (Step 1 of hypothesis testing.)**

  A. State in ordinary language the hypothesis–testing issue: Does the score of the person studied represent a higher (or lower or different) score than would be expected if this person had just been a randomly selected example of people in general–that is, does this person represent a different group of people from people in general?

B. Explain language (to make the rest of the essay easier to write by not having to repeat long explanations), focusing on the meaning of each term in the concrete example of the study at hand.
   1. Populations.
   2. Research hypothesis.
   3. Null hypothesis.
   4. Rejecting the null hypothesis to provide support for the research hypothesis.

II. Determine the characteristics of the comparison distribution. (Step 2 of hypothesis testing.)

A. Explain the principle that the comparison distribution is the distribution (pattern of spread of the scores) of the population which did not undergo the experimental manipulation–this is the distribution from which we would expect our sample to be a random sample if the null hypothesis were true.

B. Explicitly identify the characteristics of your comparison distribution, explaining what each characteristic means.
   1. Its mean (explain that this is the arithmetic average).
   2. Its standard deviation.
      a. This is a standard measure of how spread out it is.
      b. It is roughly the average amount scores vary from the mean.
      c. Exactly speaking, the square root of the average of the squares of the amount that each score differs from the mean.
   3. Its shape.
      a. Usually it is a normal curve.
      b. Describe the shape (or draw it).
      c. Note that this is a highly common shape for distributions; the percentage of scores above any given point (as measured in standard deviations from the mean) is available in tables.

III. Determine the cutoff score on the comparison distribution at which the null hypothesis should be rejected. (Step 3 of hypothesis testing.)

A. Before you figure out how extreme your particular score is on this distribution, you want to know how extreme it would have to be to decide it was too unlikely that it could be just a randomly drawn score from this comparison distribution.

B. Since this is a normal curve, you can use a table to tell you how many standard deviations from the mean your score would have to be to be in the top so many percent.

C. Note that the number of standard deviations from the mean is called a Z score. (By explaining this term, you make writing simpler later on.)

D. To use these tables, you have to decide the kind of situation you have; there are two considerations.
   1. Are you interested in the chances of getting this extreme a score that is extreme in only one direction (such as only higher than for people in general) or in both? (Explain which is appropriate for your study.)
   2. Just how unlikely would the extremeness of a particular group's average have to be? The standard figure used in psychology is less likely than 5% (though 1% is sometimes used to be especially safe). (Say which you are using in your study–if no figure is stated in the problem and no special reason given for using one or the other, the general rule is to use 5%.)

E. With a little manipulation of numbers you can then look up the percentage in the table and find the Z score corresponding to that percentage.

IV. **Determine the score of your sample on the comparison distribution. (Step 4 of hypothesis testing.)**
   A. At this point the study would be conducted and the score of the individual obtained.
   B. The next step is to find where your actual score would fall on the comparison distribution, in terms of a Z score–that is, how many standard deviations it is above or below the mean on this distribution.
   C. State this Z score.

V. **Compare the scores obtained in Steps 3 and 4 to decide whether to reject the null hypothesis. (Step 5 of hypothesis testing.)**
   A. State whether your score (from Step 4) does or does not exceed the cutoff (from Step 3).
   B. If your score exceeds the cutoff.
      1. State that you can reject the null hypothesis.
      2. State that by elimination, the research hypothesis is thus accepted.
      3. State in words what it means that the research hypothesis is accepted (that is, the study shows that the particular experimental manipulation appears to make a difference in the particular thing being measured).
   C. If your score does not exceed the cutoff.
      1. State that you can not reject the null hypothesis.
      2. State that the experiment is inconclusive.
      3. State in words what it means that the study is inconclusive (that is, the study did not yield results which give a clear indication of whether or not the particular experimental manipulation appears to make a difference in the particular thing being measured).
      4. Explicitly note that even though the research hypothesis was not supported in this study, this is not evidence that it is false–it is quite possible that it is true but it has only a small effect which was not sufficient to produce a score extreme enough to yield a significant result in this study.

Chapter Self–Tests

Multiple–Choice Questions

1. If we reject the null hypothesis we are consequently:
   a. Proving the research hypothesis is true.
   b. Accepting the research hypothesis.
   c. Proving the independent variable had an impact on the dependent variable.
   d. Proving the difference between the two populations is a statistically significant difference.

2. Suppose that a researcher wants to know if college students drink more coffee than people in general of college–student age. What would the research hypothesis be in this case?
   a. People over college–student age will drink less coffee than the students will.
   b. There will be no difference between the two populations.
   c. College students do not drink more coffee than people in general of college–student age.
   d. College students drink more coffee than people in general of college–student age.

3. The crucial element in the null hypothesis is:

   a. It is the real interest in the research study.
   b. It determines the direction of the significance tests.
   c. It states the situation in which there is no difference between the populations.
   d. It defines the comparison distributions.

4. What does it mean when a researcher chooses the cutoff on the comparison distribution to be .01?

   a. It means that to reject the null hypothesis the result must be higher than a Z score of .01.
   b. It means that to reject the null hypothesis there must be less than a 1% chance that the result would have happened by chance if the null hypothesis were true.
   c. It means that if the result is larger than .01 (such as .02 or .03), it is "statistically significant."
   d. It means that the research hypothesis is definitely true if the sample's score on the comparison distribution is less extreme than the cutoff that corresponds to the most extreme .1% of that comparison distribution.

5. The cutoff sample score is also know as:

   a. The critical value.
   b. The p-value.
   c. The significance level.
   d. The t score.

6. A comparison distribution is

   a. Another sample not used in the study.
   b. The same as an experimental group.
   c. The same as a control group.
   d. The normal distribution.

7. What should you do if you want to use a 5% significance level on a two–tailed test?

   a. Reject the null hypothesis if the sample is so extreme that it is in either the top 5% or the bottom 5% of the comparison distribution.
   b. Reject the null hypothesis if the sample is so extreme that it is in either the top 2.5% or the bottom 2.5% of the comparison distribution.
   c. Use a comparison distribution that is not a normal curve, such as a Poisson distribution.
   d. Use a comparison distribution that is a normal curve, but which has a standard deviation twice as large as you would use for a one–tailed test.

8. What does it mean if the research hypothesis is clearly directional?

   a. You use a one–tailed test.
   b. You use a two–tailed test.
   c. It is fairly clear that the null hypothesis will be supported so long as the comparison distribution follows a normal curve.
   d. It is fairly clear that the research hypothesis will be supported so long as the comparison distribution follows a normal curve.

9. Researchers are reluctant to use one–tailed tests because

   a. Using a one–tailed test dramatically reduces the chance of getting a significant result, even if your research hypothesis is true (that is, even if the null hypothesis is false).
   b. Research in psychology rarely involves studies which have a basis for predicting a particular direction of result.
   c. When using a one–tailed test, if a result comes out opposite to that which is predicted, it can not be considered significant no matter how extreme it is.
   d. All of the above.

10. If a research report describes a result and notes "$p < .05$," this means
   a. The result is not statistically significant at the .05 level.
   b. The sample score falls in either the upper 5% or the lower 5% of the comparison distribution (making in reality a 10% chance of getting this result by chance).
   c. There is a 95% chance that the research hypothesis is true.
   d. The chances of getting this result if the null hypothesis is true are less than 5%.

   d

Fill–In Questions

1. ___hypothesis test___ is a systematic procedure for deciding whether the results of a research study supports a particular theory's application to a population.

2–5 A study is conducted to test whether people who have taken a growth hormone are taller (that is, whether their height is greater) than people in general.

2. Population 1 is people who have taken the growth hormone. Population 2 is ___people in general___

3. What is the research hypothesis? ___$P1$ would grew higher than $P2$___
   (State in terms of Populations 1 and 2.)

4. What is the null hypothesis? ___$P1$ is the same to $P2$___
   (State in terms of Population 1 and 2.)

5. The comparison distribution is the distribution of ___$P2$ (general P)___

6. If we have rejected the null hypothesis, we have ___support___ the research hypothesis.

7. Conventional levels of significance are __0.5__ and __0.1__.

8. If the cutoff Z score is -1.96 and the score of your sample is -2.13, what should you conclude? ___statistic significant___

9. The ___comparison___ distribution is similar to a control group.

10. When a sample score is so extreme we can reject the null hypothesis, the result is said to be ___statistically significant___.

Problems and Essays

1. A researcher was interested in whether "mom's old cure," a glass of warm milk before bedtime, actually facilitates falling asleep. His previous research indicated that an unassisted subject falls asleep in a laboratory situation after an average of 27 minutes with a standard deviation of 7 minutes. He had a test subject drink a glass of warm milk and then measured the amount of time it took for the subject to fall asleep. It took the subject 14 minutes. (These are all fictional data.)

   (a) Based on these data, did the subject fall asleep significantly faster? (Use the .05 significance level.)
   (b) Explain your conclusion and procedure to a person who has never had a course in statistics.

60

2. The government reports that the average plane arrives 10 minutes late, with a standard deviation of 1.5 minutes. Your experience, however, is that a particular airline typically arrives later than other airlines. To test this, you go to the airport and check the arrival on a randomly selected flight from this company. The flight arrives 13.25 minutes late. (These are all fictional data.)

(a) Based on these data, what should you conclude about this company's timeliness compared to airlines in general? (Use the .05 significance level.)

(b) Explain your conclusion and procedure to a person who has never had a course in statistics.

3. Can drugs affect memory? A neurologist interested in this question administered a new drug to a group of students in order to see if their ability to immediately recall information was affected in any way. The neurologist had been using nonsense syllables in her studies and found that the average subject was able to immediately recall 7 items with a standard deviation of 2. The first data available from the drug study indicated that the subject had been able to recall only 4 items.

(a) Was this finding significant at the .05 level?

(b) Explain your conclusion and procedure to a person who has never had a course in statistics.

4. A social psychologist was interested in whether teenagers who had played a lot of video games as a child were able to learn to drive more quickly than the average. He obtained previous data regarding the amount of time (in hours) that it took the average teenager to learn to drive. Then he selected one high school student who reported having spent many hours playing video games and measured the amount of time it took for her to learn how to drive. Her Z score ($Z = 1.23$) was not significant at the .05 level.

Explain these results and the steps of hypothesis testing to someone unfamiliar with statistics.

Note. There is no section on using SPSS 10.0 with this chapter because none of the procedures covered are easily implemented using standard computerized statistical packages. The material in this chapter is mainly preparation for carrying out procedures that are widely used, however, and for which the computer can be very helpful.

Chapter 6
Hypothesis Tests With Means of Samples

Learning Objectives

By the end of this chapter you should be able to:

- Explain why the distribution of means is the appropriate comparison distribution when using a sample of more than one person.
- State the characteristics of the distribution of means and its relation to the Central Limit Theorem.
- Figure the variance and standard deviation of the distribution of means.
- Explain why the variance of the distribution of means is less than the variance of the population.
- Explain why the larger the sample size, the smaller the variance of the distribution of means.
- Explain the difference between point estimates and interval estimates.
- Discuss the conditions under which the distribution of means is or closely approximates a normal curve.
- Conduct a hypothesis test with a sample of more than one person and a known population distribution.
- Figure a confidence interval.
- Understand the use of the standard error in reporting research results.

Chapter Outline

I. The Distribution of Means as a Comparison Distribution
   A. When testing hypotheses with a sample of more than one person, the comparison distribution is not simply the distribution of Population 2 (the general population, people not exposed to the experimental manipulation).
      1. The score of interest in your sample in this case is the mean of the group of scores.
      2. But the distribution of Population 2 is a distribution of individual persons.
      3. Thus using Population 2's distribution as the comparison distribution would be a mismatch. *Why?*
   B. The appropriate comparison distribution in this case is a *distribution of means*, the distribution of all possible means of samples of the same size of your sample.
   C. It helps to have an intuitive understanding of how one would construct such a distribution.
      1. Note that this procedure is only to explain the idea, and would be too much work and unnecessary in practice.
      2. Select a random sample of individuals from the population and compute its mean.
      3. Select another random sample of this size from the population and compute its mean.
      4. Repeat this process until the population is depleted.
      5. Make a distribution of these means.

II. Characteristics of a Distribution of Means
   A. There is an exact mathematical relation of a distribution of means to the population of individuals the samples are drawn from. This means that the characteristics of the distribution of means can be determined directly from knowledge of the characteristics of the population and the size of the samples involved.
   B. The mean of a distribution of means (M_M).

1. Rule: The mean of the distribution of means is the same as the mean of the population of individuals from which the samples are taken.
2. Formula: M_M = Population M
3. Explanation.
   a. Each sample is based on randomly selected values from the population.
   b. Thus, sometimes the mean of a sample will be higher and sometimes lower than the mean of the whole population of individuals.
   c. There is no reason for these to average out higher or lower than the original population mean.
   d. Thus the average of these means (the mean of the distribution of means) should in the long run equal the population mean.

C. The Variance of a distribution of means (Population SD_M^2).
   1. Principle: The distribution of means will be less spread out than the population of individual scores from which the samples are taken.
   2. Explanation.
      a. Any one score, even an extreme score, has some chance of being selected in a random sample.
      b. However, the chance is less of two extreme scores being selected in the same random sample, particularly since in order to create an extreme sample mean they would have to be two scores which were extreme in the same direction.
      c. Thus, there is a moderating effect of numbers: In any one sample, the deviants tend to be balanced out by middle scores or by deviants in the opposite direction, making each sample tend towards the middle and away from extreme values.
      d. With fewer extreme values for the means, the variance of the means is less.
   3. Principle: The more individuals in each sample, the less spread out is the distribution of means of that sample size. With a larger number of individuals in each sample, it is even harder for extreme scores in that sample not to be balanced out by middle scores or extremes in the other direction in the same sample.
   4. Rule: The variance of a distribution of means is the variance of the distribution of the population of individual scores divided by the number of scores in the samples being selected.
   5. Formula: Population SD_M^2 = Population SD^2/N. (N is the number of scores in each sample.)

D. The standard deviation of a distribution of means (Population SD_M).
   1. Rule: The standard deviation of the distribution of means is the square root of the variance of the distribution of means.
   2. Formula: Population $SD_M = \sqrt{\text{Population } SD_M^2}$
   3. Explanation: Represents the degree to which particular means of samples are typically "in error" as estimates of the mean of the entire population.
   4. Special name: The standard error of the mean or the standard error, for short.

E. The shape of a distribution of means.
   1. It tends to be unimodal and symmetrical.
   2. As the number of subjects in each sample gets larger, the distribution of means of all possible samples of that number of subjects is a better and better approximation to the normal curve.
   3. With samples of 30 or more each, even with a quite nonnormal population of individual scores, the approximation of the distribution of means to a normal curve is so close that the percentages in the normal curve table will be extremely accurate.
   4. Whenever the population distribution of individual scores is normal, a distribution of means, of whatever sample size, will always be normal.

III. Hypothesis Testing Involving a Distribution of Means

A. The distribution of means is the comparison distribution to which the sample mean can be compared in order to see how likely it is that such a sample mean could have been selected if the null hypothesis is true.

B. It is the characteristics of the distribution of means that must be determined in Step 2 of the hypothesis testing process.

C. It is the location of your sample on the comparison distribution that must be determined in Step 4 of hypothesis testing.
1. You are now finding a Z score of a sample mean on a distribution of means (instead of the Z score of a single subject on a distribution of a population of single subjects).
2. Thus, the formula is $Z = (M\text{-Population } M)/\text{Population } SD_M$.

D. Other than using the distribution of means as the comparison distribution and locating the mean of your sample on this distribution, the process of hypothesis testing is exactly the same as in Chapter 5 (which focused on hypothesis testing involving a sample of just one subject).

IV. Estimation and Confidence Intervals

A. Sometimes it is necessary to estimate an unknown population mean based on the scores in a sample.
1. The best estimate of a population mean is the sample mean.
2. Whenever we estimate a specific value of a population parameter, it is called a point estimate.
3. Whenever we estimate a range of possible means that are likely to include the population mean, it is called an interval estimate.

B. A confidence interval is an interval which is wide enough to be quite sure it includes the population mean.
1. A 95% confidence interval means that you can be 95% sure that the true population mean falls within this interval.

C. Confidence limits are the upper and lower boundaries of a confidence interval.
1. To find a 95% confidence interval, you need to find the cutoff points for the top and bottom 2.5% (this leaves a total of 95% in the middle).
2. Here are three steps for computing confidence intervals:
   a. Determine the characteristics of the distribution of means.
   b. Use the normal curve table to find the Z scores that go with the upper and lower percentages that you want.
   c. Convert these Z scores to a raw score on your distribution of means. These are the upper and lower confidence limits.
3. You can use confidence intervals as a way to do hypothesis testing. If the confidence interval does not include the mean of the null hypothesis distribution, then the result is significant.

V. Topics of this Chapter as Reported in Research Articles

A. Research situations in which there is a known population mean and standard deviation are quite rare in psychology, so they seldom appear in research articles; the main reason we have asked you to learn about this situation is because it is a necessary building block to understanding hypothesis testing in the more common research situations.

B. When such hypothesis tests are reported, the procedure may be described as a "Z test."

C. Researchers will sometimes report the standard deviation of the distribution of means.
1. This is done as an indication of the amount of variation that might be expected among means of samples of a given size from this population.
2. In this context it is usually identified as the "standard error" or abbreviated as SE.
3. Often the lines that go above and below the tops of the bars in a bar graph refer to standard error (instead of standard deviation).

D. Confidence intervals are also sometimes reported in research articles, particularly when describing results of surveys.

Formulas

I. Variance of a distribution of means (Population SD_M^2)

        Formula in words: The variance of the distribution of the population of individual scores divided by the number of individual scores in each sample.

        Formula in symbols: Population SD_M^2 = Population SD^2/N (6-1)

        Population SD^2 is the variance of the population of individual scores.

            N is the number of individual scores in each sample.

II. Standard deviation of a distribution of means, standard error (Population SD_M)

        Formula in words: The square root of the variance of the distribution of means.

        Formula in symbols: Population $SD_M = \sqrt{\text{Population } SD_M^2}$ (6-2)

III. Location of the sample mean on the distribution of means (Z)

        Formula in words: Deviation of the mean of the sample from the mean of the known population (same as mean of the distribution of means), divided by the standard deviation of the distribution of means.

        Formula in symbols: $Z = M - M_M / \text{Population } SD_M$ (6-3)

          M is the mean of the sample.

         M_M is the mean of the known population (same as the mean of the distribution of means).

        Population SD_M is the standard deviation of the distribution of means.

How to Figure Confidence Limits

I. Determine the characteristics of the distribution of means.

II. Use the normal curve to find the Z scores that go with the upper and lower percentage you want.

    A. For a 95% confidence interval, this is the Z score that goes with the top and bottom 2.5%.

    B. For a 99% confidence interval, this is the Z score that goes with the top and bottom .5%.

III. Convert these Z scores to raw scores on your distribution of means to create the upper and lower limits.

How to Test an Hypothesis Involving a Single Sample of More than One Subject and a Known Population

I. Reframe the question into a research hypothesis and a null hypothesis about populations. (Step 1.)

    A. Identify the two populations.

        1. Population 1 is people like those studied who have been exposed to the experimental manipulation.

        2. Population 2 is people like those studied but who have not been exposed to the experimental manipulation. (This is usually people from the general public, of the category studied.)

    B. State the research hypothesis.

1. Decide whether this will be directional or nondirectional.
2. State in terms of the two populations (that the mean of one will be higher, lower, or the same as the other).

C. State the null hypothesis–Populations 1 and 2 are the same; the manipulation had no impact.

D. Check that the research and null hypothesis are consistent (in terms of both being in relation to a directional or nondirectional prediction.)

II. **Determine the characteristics of the comparison distribution. (Step 2.)**

A. This will be a distribution of means of samples of the number of subjects in the sample being studied.

B. Its mean is the same as the mean of the population of individual scores from which the samples are taken: $M_M = M$.

C. Its standard deviation is the square root of the result of dividing the variance of the distribution of the population of individual scores by the number of individuals in the samples being selected: Population $SD_M = \sqrt{(\text{Population } SD^2_M / N)}$. (N is the number of individuals in each sample.)

D. Its shape.
1. Normal if the population is normal.
2. Very close to normal if N is greater than 30, regardless of population shape.
4. Otherwise, unimodal and symmetrical, but not normal.

III. **Determine the cutoff sample score on the comparison distribution at which the null hypothesis should be rejected. (Step 3.)**

A. Decide on the significance level (1% or 5%).

B. Determine the percentage of individuals between the mean and where the appropriate percentage begins on the normal curve.
1. If a one-tailed test, this is 50% minus the significance level.
2. If a two-tailed test, this is 50% minus 1/2 the significance level.

C. Look up the Z corresponding to this percentage in the *% Mean to Z* column in the normal table–this is the cutoff Z.

IV. **Determine the sample's score on the comparison distribution. (Step 4.)**

A. Conduct the study and compute the mean of the scores in the sample studied (or note the result as given to you in the problem).

B. Convert the raw score result to a Z score on the comparison distribution (the distribution of means): $Z = (M - M_M)/\text{Population } SD_M$.

V. **Compare the scores obtained in Steps 3 and 4 to determine whether or not to reject the null hypothesis. (Step 5.)**

A. If the actual sample's Z score (from Step 4) is more extreme than the cutoff Z score (from Step 3).
1. The null hypothesis is rejected.
2. Thus, the research hypothesis is supported.

B. If the actual sample's Z score (from Step 4) is not more extreme than the cutoff Z score (from Step 3).
1. The null hypothesis is not rejected.
2. Thus, the experiment is inconclusive.

Outline for Writing Essays for Hypothesis-Testing Problems Involving a Single Sample of More than One Subject and a Known Population

The reason for your writing essay questions in the practice problems and tests is that this task develops and then demonstrates what matters so very much–your comprehension of the logic behind the computations. (It is also a place for those of you who are better at words than numbers to shine. And for those better at numbers to develop their skills at explaining in words.)

Thus, to do well you need to be sure to do the following in each essay: (a) give the reasoning behind each step; (b) relate each step to the specifics of the content of the particular study you are analyzing; (c) state the various formulas in nontechnical language, because as you define each term you show you understand it (although once you have defined it in nontechnical language, you can use it from then on in the essay); (d) look back and be absolutely certain that you made it clear just why that formula or procedure was applied and why it is the way it is.

The outlines below are *examples* of ways to structure your essays. There are other completely correct ways to go about it. And this is an *outline* for an answer–you must write the answer out in paragraph form. Examples of full essays are in the answers to Set I Practice Problems in the back of the text.

These essays are necessarily very long for you to write (and for others to grade). But this is the very best way to be sure you understand everything thoroughly. One short cut you may see on a test is to write your answer for someone who understands statistics up to the point of the new material you are studying. You can choose to take the same short cut in these practice problems (maybe writing for someone who understands right up to whatever point you yourself start being just a little unclear). But every time you write for a person who has never had statistics at all, you review the logic behind the entire course. You engrain it in your mind. Over and over. The time is never wasted. It is an excellent way to study.

I. **Reframe the question into a research hypothesis and a null hypothesis about populations. (Step 1 of hypothesis testing.)**
   A. State in ordinary language the hypothesis-testing issue: Does the average of the scores of the group of persons studied represent a higher (or lower or different) mean than would be expected if this group of persons had just been a randomly selected example of people in general–that is does this set of people studied represent a different group of people from people in general?
   B. Explain language (to make rest of essay easier to write by not having to repeat long explanations each time), focusing on the meaning of each term in the concrete example of the study at hand.
      1. Populations.
      2. Sample.
      3. Mean.
      4. Research hypothesis.
      5. Null hypothesis.
      6. Rejecting the null hypothesis to provide support for the research hypothesis.

II. **Determine the characteristics of the comparison distribution. (Step 2 of hypothesis testing.)**
   A. Explain principle that the comparison distribution is the distribution (pattern of spread of the means of scores) that represents what we would expect if the null hypothesis were true and our particular mean were just randomly sampled from this population of means.

B. Note that because we are interested in the mean of a sample of more than one individual, we have to compare our actual mean to a distribution not of individual scores but of means.

C. Give an intuitive understanding of how one might construct a distribution of means for samples of a given size from a particular population.
    1. Select a random sample of the given size (number of subjects) from the population and compute its mean.
    2. Select another random sample of this size from the population and compute its mean.
    3. Repeat this process a very large number of times.
    4. Make a distribution of these means.
    5. Note that this procedure is only to explain the idea, and would be too much work and unnecessary in practice.

D. There is an exact mathematical relation of a distribution of means to the population the means are drawn from, so that in practice the characteristics of the distribution of means can be determined directly from knowledge of the characteristics of the population and the size of the samples involved.

E. The mean of a distribution of means.
    1. It is the same as the mean (average) of the scores in the known population of individual scores.
    2. State what it is in the particular problem you are working on.
    3. Explanation.
        a. Each sample is based on randomly selected values from the population.
        b. Thus, sometimes the mean of a sample will be higher and sometimes lower than the mean of the whole population of individuals.
        c. There is no reason for these to average out higher or lower than the original population mean.
        d. Thus the average of these means (the mean of the distribution of means) should in the long run equal the population mean.

F. The standard deviation of a distribution of means.
    1. The distribution of means will be less spread out than the population of individual scores from that the samples are taken.
        a. Any one score, even an extreme score, has some chance of being selected in a random sample.
        b. However, the chance is less of several extreme scores being selected in the same random sample, particularly since in order to create an extreme sample mean they would all have to be scores which were extreme in the same direction.
        c. Thus, there is a moderating effect of numbers. In any one sample, the deviants tend to be balanced out by many more middle scores or by deviants in the opposite direction, making each sample tend towards the middle and away from extreme values.
        d. With fewer extreme values for the means, the variation among the means is less.
    2. The more individuals in each sample, the less spread out is the distribution of means of that sample size. With a larger number of individuals in each sample, it is even harder for extreme scores in that sample not to be balanced out by middle scores or extremes in the other direction in the same sample.
    3. Explain the idea of standard deviation.
        a. It is a standard measure of how spread out it is.
        b. It is roughly the average amount scores that vary from the mean.
        c. Exactly speaking, it is the square root of the average of the squares of the amount that each score differs from the mean.
    4. The standard deviation of the distribution of means is found by a formula that divides the average of squared deviations from the mean of the population by the number of subjects in the sample (thus making it smaller in proportion to the number of subjects in the sample), and taking the square root of this result.
    5. State what it is in the particular problem you are working on, describing the steps of computation.

G. The shape of a distribution of means.
   1. If your N is greater than 30.
      a. The distribution of means will be approximately normal.
      b. Explain that a normal curve is a bell-shaped distribution that is very common in psychology.
      c. The distribution tends to be normal due to the same basic process of extremes balancing each other out that we noted in the discussion of the standard deviation–middle values are more likely and extreme values less likely.
   2. If the population of individual scores in your situation is normal.
      a. The distribution of means will be approximately normal.
      b. This is because the distribution of means will have nothing to distort it from looking like the distribution of individual scores.

III. Determine the cutoff score on the comparison distribution at which the null hypothesis should be rejected. (Step 3 of hypothesis testing.)
   A. Before you figure out how extreme your particular sample's mean is on this distribution of means, you want to know how extreme it would have to be to decide it was too unlikely that it could have been a randomly drawn mean from this comparison distribution of means.
   B. Since in this problem the comparison distribution is a normal curve, you can use a table to tell you how many standard deviations from the mean your score would have to be to be in the top so many percent.
   C. Note that the number of standard deviations from the mean is called a Z score. (By explaining this term, you make the writing simpler later on.)
   D. To use these tables you have to decide the kind of situation you have; there are two considerations.
      1. Are you interested in the chances of getting this extreme of a mean that is extreme in only one direction (such as only higher than for people in general) or in both? (Explain which is appropriate for your study.)
      2. Just how unlikely would the extremeness of a particular mean have to be? The standard figure used in psychology is less likely than 5% (though 1% is sometimes used to be especially safe). (Say which you are using in your study–if no figure is stated in the problem and no special reason given for using one or the other, the general rule is to use 5%.)
   E. With a little manipulation of numbers you can then look up the percentage in the table and find the Z score corresponding to that percentage.
   F. State the cutoff for your particular problem.

IV. Determine the score of your sample on the comparison distribution. (Step 4 of hypothesis testing.)
   A. At this point the study would be conducted and the mean score of the sample studied obtained. (State what it is.)
   B. The next step is to find where your actual sample's mean would fall on the comparison distribution, in terms of a Z score.
   C. State this Z score.

V. Compare the scores obtained in Steps 3 and 4 to decide whether to reject the null hypothesis. (Step 5 of hypothesis testing.)
   A. State whether your mean (from Step 4) does or does not exceed the cutoff (from Step 3).
   B. If your mean exceeds the cutoff.
      1. State that you can reject the null hypothesis.
      2. State that by elimination, the research hypothesis is thus supported.

3. State in words what it means that the research hypothesis is supported (that is, the study shows that the particular experimental manipulation appears to make a difference in the particular thing being measured).

C. If your score does not exceed the cutoff.
   1. State that you can not reject the null hypothesis.
   2. State that the experiment is inconclusive.
   3. State in words what it means that the study is inconclusive (that is, the study did not yield results that give a clear indication of whether or not the particular experimental manipulation appears to make a difference in the particular thing being measured).
   4. Explicitly note that even though the research hypothesis was not supported in this study, this is not evidence that it is false–it is quite possible that it is true but it has only a small effect, which was not sufficient to produce a mean extreme enough to yield a significant result in this study.

Chapter Self-Tests

Multiple-Choice Questions

1. When testing an hypothesis in which the group studied is a mean of a sample of scores, the proper comparison distribution is
   a. the original population from which the sample was taken.
   b. the population that would exist if the null hypothesis were true.
   c. the distribution of all possible means of the sample size (N) from the known population.
   d. the distribution of the individual scores from which the sample mean was calculated.

2. The mean of the distribution of means is the same as:
   a. The mean of any sample drawn from the population.
   b. The mean of several, but not all, of the samples drawn from the population.
   c. The mean of the population of individuals.
   d. The mean of any sample drawn from the population minus the standard error of the means.

3. The shape of the distribution of means is
   a. rectangular.
   b. unimodal and symmetrical.
   c. unimodal and modest asymmetry.
   d. dependent upon the number of people in the sample.

4. An estimate of the specific value of a population parameter is called a(n)
   a. interval estimate.
   b. cutoff score.
   c. predicted score.
   d. point estimate.

5. A _____ is a range of values that includes the population mean.
   a. population interval
   b. confidence interval
   c. point estimate interval
   d. sample interval

6-9 An experimenter was interested in the relation of social class to motivation, using a standard test of motivation (for the general population, the mean is 90 and the standard deviation is 10). Based on a theory she had constructed, she expected that those in the upper class would score lower. She administered the test to 20 members of an upper-class community. Her obtained sample mean on the test was 87.

6. In this example, the null hypothesis would be

    a. upper-class communities have higher motivation than the population in general.
    b. the mean of the population the sample represents is no lower than the mean of the general population.
    c. the sample variance will equal the population variance.
    d. there will be no difference between the population and the distribution of means.

7. The characteristics of the comparison distribution are

    a. mean=90, variance=5.
    b. mean=90, variance=.5.
    c. mean=90, variance=9.
    d. mean=90, variance=20.

8. The cutoff Z score (using the .05 level) is

    a. ±1.64.
    b. +1.96.
    c. -1.64.
    d. -2.33.

9. If the sample mean's score on the comparison distribution is more extreme than the cutoff, what should the researcher conclude?

    a. upper class people are more motivated.
    b. upper class people are less motivated.
    c. upper class people are neither more nor less motivated, but have approximately the same level of motivation.
    d. the results are inconclusive.

10. If a researcher uses a 99% confidence interval instead of a 95% confidence interval

    a. it is more difficult to reject the null hypothesis.
    b. their results will be significant 99% of the time.
    c. they will reject the null more often.
    d. they will find their results to be significant more easily.

Fill-In Questions

1. When a study is being conducted in which a group of people are studied to see if they represent a group that is different from the general population, the comparison distribution is a(n) _____ distribution. of mean

2. The best estimate of the population mean is the _____ Sample mean

3. _____ Point estimate is an estimate of a specific value of a population parameter.

4. The characteristics of the distribution of the means are based upon the _____ Central limit theorem

5. In a study where, $M_M = 107$, $SD_M = 3$. If a group of 40 people studied has a mean of 101, what is their Z score on the comparison distribution? -2

6. _____ standard error of the distribution mean _____ is the degree to which particular means in the distribution deviate from the population mean.

7. The standard error of the mean is the same as ___ SD_M ___.

8. An ___ interval estimate ___ is an estimate of the range of possible means that are likely to include the population mean.

9. If the mean of Population 1 falls outside of the 95% confidence interval, we ___ reject ___ the null.

10. It is rare that psychologists actually carry out hypothesis-testing procedures involving a single sample and a population whose mean and variance are known (the kind of hypothesis tests we are considering in this chapter). But when they do carry out such a procedure and report the result in a research article, it is called a(n) ___ Z test ___

Problems and Essays

1. A researcher who is interested in the effects of music administers a measure of logical reasoning ability to 5 subjects (randomly selected from the general population of adults) while they are listening to soothing music. Their scores on the test were 68, 39, 55, 73, and 80. Previous research using this test indicates that in the general population the distribution is normal, with Population M = 48 and Population SD = 12.

   (a) Do people do better when listening to soothing music (use the .01 level).
   (b) Explain what you have done and your conclusions to a person who has never had a coursein statistics.

2. A learning psychologist was interested in whether providing a stationary pattern of small lights on the ceiling and walls of a darkened laboratory would decrease the time it took for rats to learn a maze. (She was wondering if the rats would be able to use the stationary cues to aid in their navigation.) From her previous research she knew that on the average it took a rat 38 trials, with a standard deviation of 6, to learn a particular maze, and that the distribution is normal. She then tested a group of 10 rats in the changed laboratory and found their average number of trials to learn the maze was 36.

   (a) Was this difference significant at the .05 level?
   (b) Explain what you have done and your conclusions to a person who has never had a course in statistics.

3. A school psychologist was wondering how the preschoolers at the school where he worked compared to other preschoolers who have taken a standardized problem-solving test. He therefore administered the test to all the preschool children and found that their average was significantly higher than the mean for the general population (the Z score +1.97) at the .05 level. How would the psychologist interpret these findings and report them to a group of people unfamiliar with statistics?

Note: There is no section on using SPSS 10.0 with this chapter because none of the procedures covered are easily implemented using standard computerized statistical packages. The material in this chapter is mainly preparation for carrying out procedures that are widely used, however, and for which the computer can be very helpful.

Chapter 7
Making Sense of Statistical Significance:
Decision Error, Statistical Power, and Effect Size

Learning Objectives

By the end of this chapter you should be able to:

- Describe and identify the types of decision errors in hypothesis testing.
- Explain the role of statistical power in an experiment.
- Describe how sample size and effect size affect power.
- Figure the effect size of a study.
- Discuss how variance affects power.
- Figure the power of a study.
- Evaluate the outcome of a study with respect to its statistical significance, power, and practical importance.
- Identify how the power of a particular study can be increased.

Chapter Outline

I. Decision Errors
   A. A situation in which the right procedures lead to the wrong decisions.
      1. Not about making mistakes in calculations.
      2. These errors are possible because the whole hypothesis testing process is based on probability.
   B. Two types of decision errors.
      1. Type I error.
         a. Mistakenly rejecting the null hypothesis is called a Type I error.
         b. Type I errors are of serious concern to scientists, who could construct entire theories and research programs–let alone practical applications–based on a result that in fact is fallacious.
         c. The conservative approach is to set a very stringent significance level so that the results have to be quite extreme to reject the null hypothesis.
         d. The likelihood of making a Type I error is equal to the significance level.
      2. Type II error.
         a. Mistakenly failing to reject the null hypothesis is called a Type II error.
         b. Type II errors concern scientists, and especially those interested in applications of psychological knowledge, because a Type II error could mean that a good theory or useful practical procedure is not used.
         c. If you set a very stringent significance level, you may fail to reject the null hypothesis–that is, you may fail to decide the research hypothesis is demonstrated by the evidence of the sample–when in fact the research hypothesis is true.
   C. Minimizing the chance of making one kind of error increases the chance of making the other.
   D. Summary of possible outcomes in hypothesis testing.
      1. There are two kinds of possible correct decisions and two kinds of possible erroneous decisions you can make in hypothesis testing.
         a. The research hypothesis is actually true and the hypothesis-testing procedure results in rejecting the null hypothesis (a correct decision).

b. The research hypothesis is actually false and the hypothesis-testing procedure results in rejecting the null hypothesis (a Type I error).
c. The research hypothesis is actually true and the hypothesis-testing procedure results in failing to reject the null hypothesis (a Type II error).
d. The research hypothesis is actually false and the hypothesis-testing procedure results in failing to reject the null hypothesis (a correct decision).

2. These are hypothetical possibilities useful for understanding the logic of setting significance levels, but we never actually know whether the research hypothesis is true or false.

II. Statistical Power

A. The probability that a study will yield significant results if the research hypothesis is true.

B. Even if the research hypothesis is true, the study may not necessarily give significant results–the particular sample that happens to be selected from the population studied may not turn out to be extreme enough to provide a clear case for rejecting the null hypothesis.

C. Power tables.
1. Calculations are labor intensive and complex.
2. Statisticians have prepared power tables that simplify the process of figuring power.

III. Influences on Power

A. Primary influences.
1. Effect size, which has two elements:
   a. One element is the magnitude of the difference between the comparison and the predicted means.
   b. The other element is the standard deviation of the populations of individual scores.
2. Sample size. In general increasing sample size increases power.

B. Secondary influences.
1. Level of statistical significance (α).
2. Two-tailed versus one-tailed tests.
3. Type of hypothesis-testing procedure used.

IV. Effect Size

A. The amount the two population distributions do not overlap.

B. The larger the difference between the two means (and thus the more offset the two distributions are from each other, minimizing their overlap), the greater the effect size.

C. The larger the effect size, the greater the power.

D. The smaller the population standard deviation (and thus the less overlap because each distribution is narrower), the greater the effect size.

E. One measure of effect size is the difference between the two means divided by the population standard deviation: Effect size = (Population 1 $\underline{M}$ - Population 2 $\underline{M}$)/ Population SD.

F. The general importance of effect size.
1. Dividing the mean difference by the standard deviation of the population of individual scores standardizes the difference in the same way that a Z score gives us a standard metric for comparison to other scores, even other scores on different scales.
2. Because it provides a standard metric for comparison, especially by using the standard deviation of the population of individual scores, we bypass the dissimilarity from study to study of different sample sizes, making comparison even easier and effect size even more of a standard metric.
3. Thus, knowing the effect size of a study permits us to compare results with effect sizes found in other studies, even other studies using different sample sizes.
4. Equally important, knowing effect size can permit us to compare studies using different measures, which may have scales with quite different means and variances.
5. Even within a particular study, we can apply our general knowledge of what is a small or large effect size.

G. Effect size conventions: Developed by Cohen, based on what is typically found in psychology research.
    1. Small effect size.
      a. About 85% overlap of the two populations.
      b. Effect size= .2: That is, the predicted mean is about two-tenths of a standard deviation higher than the mean of the known population.
    2. Medium effect size.
      a. About 67% overlap of the two populations.
      b. Effect size = .5: That is, the predicted mean is about half a standard deviation higher than the mean of the known population.
    3. Large effect size.
      a. About 53% overlap of the two populations.
      b. Effect size = .8: That is, the predicted mean is about eight-tenths of a standard deviation higher than the mean of the known population.
H. If you know the effect size (for example, based on Cohen's conventions) and the population standard deviation, it is possible to compute the expected mean difference by solving the effect size formula for (Population 1 $\underline{M}$ - Population 2 $\underline{M}$).

V. Sample Size
A. The larger the sample size, the greater the power.
B. This is because the variance of the distribution of means is based on the population variance divided by the sample size–the larger the sample size, the smaller the variance, and the smaller the variance, the less overlap of the distributions of means.
C. Figuring the needed sample size to attain a given level of power.
    1. One reason the influence of sample size on power is so very important is that the number of subjects is something the researcher can often control prior to the experiment.
    2. The number of subjects needed for a given level of power can be found by turning the steps of computing power on their head.
      a. Begin with a desired level of power (often 80% is used).
      b. Then calculate how many subjects are needed to get that level of power for a particular effect size.
    3. In practice researchers use special tables for this purpose (subsequent chapters of the text provide such tables for each new hypothesis testing procedure).

VI. Other Influences on Power
A. Significance level (α).
    1. The less stringent the significance level (for example, .05 versus .01), the more power.
    2. This is because the cutoff for a less stringent significance level will not be as extreme.
B. Two-tailed versus one-tailed tests.
    1. One-tailed tests have more power (for results in the predicted direction).
    2. This is because the cutoff in the predicted direction is less extreme (since all the α percentage is at that end, instead of being divided in half).

VII. Role of Power When Designing a Study
A. If a researcher checks and finds that the power of a planned experiment is low, it is clear that even if the research hypothesis is true that this study is not likely to yield significant results in support of that research hypothesis. Thus the researcher must seek practical ways to modify the study to increase the power to an acceptable level.
B. What is an acceptable level of power?
    1. 80% is a widely used convention.
    2. The acceptable level of power also depends on how difficult and costly it is to increase power
      a. If a study is very difficult or costly to conduct, a researcher might want even higher levels (such as 90% or even 95%) before undertaking the project.

b. If a study is very easy and inexpensive to conduct, a researcher might be willing to take a chance with a somewhat lower level of power (such as 60% or 70%).

VIII. How to Increase the Power of a Planned Study

    A. Increasing expected difference between population means.

        1. If the original prediction is the most accurate available, arbitrarily changing it would undermine the accuracy of the power calculation.

        2. However, it is sometimes possible to change the way the experiment is being conducted (for example, by increasing the intensity of the experimental manipulation) so that the researcher would have reason to expect a larger mean difference.

        3. Disadvantages of this approach.

          a. Can be difficult or costly to implement.

          b. Can create circumstances implementing the experimental treatment that are unrepresentative of those to which the results are intended to be generalized.

    B. Decreasing the population standard deviation.

        1. Conduct the study using a population that is less diverse than the one originally planned–however, this limits the scope of the population to which the results can be generalized.

        2. Use conditions of testing that are more constant (such as controlled laboratory conditions) and measures that are more precise–this is a highly recommended approach.

    C. Increasing sample size.

        1. The most commonly used, straightforward way to increase power.

        2. In some cases, however, there may be limits to the number of subjects available or great costs in recruiting or testing additional numbers.

    D. Using a less stringent significance level–however, this increases the risk of a Type I error, and thus should be used cautiously.

    E. Using a one-tailed test–however, one runs the various risks discussed in Chapter 5 with one-tailed tests, most notably the possibility of having to deal with opposite-to-predicted results.

    F. Using a more sensitive hypothesis-testing procedure–when choices are available (and there are no offsetting disadvantages), one should always use the procedure that gives greatest power.

IX. Role of Power in Evaluating Results of a Study

    A. When a result is significant.

        1. Statistical significance is a necessary prerequisite to considering a result as either theoretically or practically important. For a result to be practically important, however, in addition to statistical significance, it should be of a reasonable effect size.

        2. It is easy for a study with a very small effect size, having little practical importance, to still come out significant–if the study has reasonable power due to other factors, especially a large sample size.

        3. When comparing two studies the effect sizes and not the significance levels obtained should be compared (since the significance levels could be due to different sample sizes and not to different underlying effects in the populations).

    B. When a result is not significant.

        1. If the power of the study was low, the non-significant outcome could be because the research hypothesis was false, or it could be because the research hypothesis was true but the study had too little power to come out significant.

        2. If the power of the study was high, failing to get a significant result suggests more strongly that the research hypothesis (as specified with a specific mean difference) is false.

X. Power and Effect Size as Discussed in Research Articles
   A. Power is not often mentioned directly in research articles (its greater role is in the planning of research and in interpreting research results).
   B. Power is occasionally mentioned in the context of justifying the number of subjects used in a study.
   C. Authors are also likely to mention effect size when comparing results of studies or parts of studies (or in meta-analysis articles).

Formula

Effect size

Formula in words: The difference between the hypothesized and known population means, divided by the population standard deviation.

Formula in symbols: Effect size = (Population 1 $\underline{M}$ - Population 2 $\underline{M}$)/ Population SD   (7-1)

Population 1 M   is the mean of Population 1 (the hypothesized mean for the population that is exposed to the experimental manipulation).

Population 2 M   is the mean of Population 2 (which is also the mean of the comparison distribution).

Population SD   is the standard deviation of Population 2 (and assumed to be the standard deviation of both populations).

Outline for Writing Essays on Power and Effect Size for Studies Involving a Single Sample of More than One Subject and a Known Population

The reason for your writing essay questions in the practice problems and tests is that this task develops and then demonstrates what matters so very much–your comprehension of the logic behind the computations. (It is also a place where those better at words than numbers can shine, and for those better at numbers to develop their skills at explaining in words.)

Thus, to do well, be sure to do the following in each essay: (a) give the reasoning behind each step; (b) relate each step to the specifics of the content of the particular study you are analyzing; (c) state the various formulas in nontechnical language, because as you define each term you show you understand it (although once you have defined it in nontechnical language, you can use it from then on in the essay); (d) look back and be absolutely certain that you made it clear just *why* that formula or procedure was applied and *why* it is the way it is. The outlines below are *examples* of ways to structure your essays. There are other completely correct ways to go about it. And this is an *outline* for an answer–you are to write the answer out in paragraph form.

These essays are necessarily very long for you to write (and for others to grade). But this is the very best way to be sure you understand everything thoroughly. One short cut you may see on a test is that you may be asked to write your answer for someone who understands statistics up to the point of the new material you are studying. You can choose to take the same short cut in these practice problems (maybe writing for someone who understands right up to whatever point you yourself start being just a little unclear). But every time you write for a person who has never had statistics at all, you review the logic behind the entire course. You engrain it in your mind. Over and over. The time is never wasted. It is an excellent way to study.

I. Explain the logic of hypothesis testing and associated terminology (as per the outline for essays in Chapter 6 of this *Study Guide*).

II. Explain the concept of power–the probability of getting significant results if the research hypothesis is true.

III. Explain the concept of effect size and how it is calculated, and it's relationship to power.

IV. Explain the relationship between effect size and power.

Chapter Self-Tests

Multiple-Choice Questions

1. If you use the .01 significance level instead of the .05 significance level, you increase the chance
    a. incorrectly supporting the research hypothesis.
    b. incorrectly rejecting the null hypothesis.
    c. a Type II error.
    d. a Type I error.

2. Statistical power can be defined as
    a. the effect that the result of the study will have on the area of applied psychology.
    b. the probability of rejecting the null hypothesis if in fact the null hypothesis is true.
    c. having a large enough effect size in order to always get a significant result.
    d. the probability that the study will yield a significant result if the research hypothesis is true.

3. Researchers interested in making practical applications are most likely to want to minimize

    a. significance levels.
    b. effect sizes.
    c. Type I errors.
    d. Type II errors.

4. If in a planned experiment the population distribution expected under the research hypothesis and the known population have almost no overlap at all, the planned experiment has

    a. a large effect size.
    b. a moderate effect size.
    c. a small effect size.
    d. no statistical importance.

5. How does the number of subjects affect power?

    a. by allowing the experimenter to remove results that are not extreme and so to significantly decrease variance.
    b. by reducing the amount of variance in each of the distributions of means, and thereby further separating these two distributions.
    c. by adding the effect of extreme scores to the population variance.
    d. by limiting the difference between the sample and population means.

6. When the standard deviation of the population of individual scores are low, this makes power

    a. low.
    b. high.
    c. irrelevant–the chances of getting a significant result are almost nil.
    d. none of the above–the standard deviation of the population of individual scores has nothing to do with power.

7. Two similar studies each investigated the effectiveness of a different job training program. If you wanted to compare the effectiveness of the two programs based on the results of these studies, it would be best to compare

    a. power.
    b. effect size.
    c. significance levels.
    d. Z scores on the comparison distribution.

8. Trying to avoid a Type I error results in

    a. increasing the significance level.
    b. increasing the likelihood of a Type II error.
    c. decreasing effect size.
    d. increasing variability.

9. Power is affected by

    a. sample size.
    b. variability.
    c. effect size.
    d. all of the above.

10. Increasing your sample size

    a. decreases your power.
    b. decreases effect size.
    c. decreases variability.
    d. none of the above.

Fill-In Questions

1. _____ errors occur when one rejects the null hypothesis when in fact it is true.

2. _____ errors are due to probability rather than errors in calculations.

3. Using a .001 significance level helps insure against making a _____ error.

4. An effect size of _____ is considered a large effect size.

5. The probability of getting a significant result if the research hypothesis is in fact true is called _____.

6. The extent to which two populations do not overlap is called the _____.

7. _____ does not affect effect size.

8. Using more accurate measurement in a study increases power by its direct effect in reducing _____.

9. Increasing the number of subjects in a study increases power by reducing _____.

10. A study with a _____ effect size is likely to be statistically significant.

Problems and Essays

1. For each of the following hypothetical studies, explain what a Type I and Type II error would be, and what each would mean.

   (a) A study comparing the mean test score for a class using a new learning technique (expected to improve test scores) with the average score on the same test.

   (b) A study testing whether chimpanzees injected with a new drug learn to use symbolic communication faster than the normal chimp.

2. A marketing researcher is planning a study of children's buying habits of candy. At a particular summer camp where this psychologist has previously done research, it is known that the amount spent on candy at the camp store by the children during a one-week period is roughly normally distributed with a mean of $3.80 and a standard deviation of $1.50. (The camp store is the only source of candy anywhere near the camp and records of all purchases are automatically kept because children have an account at the store that they use rather than actually carrying money.) In this study 25 randomly selected children at the camp will be given a special lecture on the effects of candy on teeth and general health. Then how much candy they buy at the camp store during the following week will be analyzed from the store records. The researchers are realistic and expect that such a lecture will have, at best, only a modest effect. But unless the effect is at least an average reduction of $.25, such lectures would be considered ineffective.

   (a) What is the predicted effect size?

   (b) Explain what power is.

   (c) Describe four things the researchers could do to try to increase the power of the study and say why each might work.

3. A study is reported in which baseball players are compared to the general public on how much they like chewing gum. The result was that the null hypothesis was not rejected; no significant difference was found. In this study 500 baseball players were tested, and in general the power was very high. What should you conclude from all this about whether baseball players like chewing gum more than people in general? Why?

4. A study reports that a particular kind of training workshop reduces burnout among school counselors. This was a large study, involving thousands of school counselors, and the study employed very accurate measures and generally had very high power. The result was that the null hypothesis was rejected at the .05 level of significance (one-tailed). What should you conclude from all this about the impact of the workshop? Why?

Note. There is no section on using SPSS 10.0 with this chapter because in general computers are not used in the computation of power.

Chapter 8
Introduction to the *t* Test

Learning Objectives

By the end of this chapter you should be able to:

- Explain the purpose of the *t* distribution and how it is different from a normal curve.
- Explain the difference between a biased and an unbiased estimate of the population variance.
- Determine the appropriate cut-off value using the *t* table.
- Figure the *t* test for a single sample and a known population mean.
- Figure the *t* test for dependent means.
- Determine if the normal-population-distribution assumption for the *t* test for dependent have been met.
- Figure the effect size for a study using a *t* test for dependent means, including whether it is a small, medium, or large effect, based on Cohen's conventions.
- Use a power table for the *t* test for dependent means to determine the number of subjects needed for the *t* test for dependent means.
- Interpret the results from *t* tests for dependent means as reported in psychology research articles.
- Explain the limitations of a pretest-posttest design.

Chapter Outline

I. **The *t* Test for a Single Sample**
   A. Hypothesis testing with a single sample and a population for which the mean is known but not the variance works the same way as you learned in Chapter 6, except that you estimate the population variance (for Step 2) and you use a different table to determine the cutoff point (Step 3).
   B. Estimating population variance from the sample information.
      1. Since a sample represents its population, its variance is representative of the population's variance.
      2. However, the variance of a random sample, on the average, will be slightly smaller than the variance of the population from which that sample is taken. (That is, the sample's variance is a *biased* estimator of the population's variance.)
      3. To figure an *unbiased* estimate of the population variance, divide the sum of squared deviations in the sample by the number of scores in the sample minus one or, $S^2 = \Sigma(X-M)^2/(N-1)$.
      4. The number you divide by in figuring the estimated population variance (N-1) is the degrees of freedom. Thus $S^2 = SS/df$.
      5. Once you know S^2, you compute the standard deviation of the comparison distribution in the usual way, except for using S^2 instead of *Population SD^2*. That is $S_M^2 = S^2/N$; $S_M = \sqrt{S_M^2}$.
   C. Shape of the comparison distribution when using an estimated population variance: The *t* distribution.
      1. When carrying out the hypothesis testing process using an estimated population variance, there is less true information and more room for error.
      2. Thus, extreme scores are more likely to occur in the distribution of means than would be found in a normal curve.
      3. The appropriate comparison distribution follows instead a mathematically defined curve called a *t* distribution.
      4. *t* distributions differ according to the degrees of freedom when figuring S^2.
      5. The more degrees of freedom on which the *t* distribution is based, the closer it is to a normal curve.

D. Determining the cutoff sample score for rejecting the null hypothesis: Using the *t* table.
  1. Appendix A of this book (and most statistics books) gives a simplified table of *t* distributions which includes only the crucial cutoff scores.
  2. To use the *t* table you need to know the degrees of freedom, the significance level, and whether it is a one- or two-tailed test.

E. Determining the score of your sample mean on the comparison distribution: The *t* score.
  1. Step 4 of the hypothesis testing process, determining the score of your sample's mean on the comparison distribution, is done exactly the same way with a *t* test.
  2. However, the resulting score is called a *t* score instead of a *Z* score.
  3. Thus, $t = (Sample\ M - Population\ M)/S_M$.

F. Deciding whether to reject the null hypothesis.
  1. This step is exactly the same as discussed previously.
  2. Compare the cutoff score with the sample's score on the comparison distribution.
  3. If the sample's score on the comparison distribution is equal to or higher than the cutoff score, you reject the null hypothesis.
  4. If the sample's score on the comparison distribution is lower than the cutoff score, you accept the null hypothesis.

II. The *t* Test for Dependent Means

A. A more common situation for a *t* test involves studies in which there are two scores for each of several subjects--often a before and after score or when each subject is tested under two different circumstances.
  1. These are called repeated-measures or within-subjects designs.
  2. The hypothesis testing procedure is called a *t* test for dependent means.
  3. SPSS calls this procedure t-test for related means.

B. A *t* test for dependent means is conducted in exactly the same way as the *t* test for a single sample (above), except you use difference scores and you assume the population mean (of difference scores) is zero.

C. Difference scores:
  1. A difference score is computed by subtracting, for each subject, one score from the other (for example, the before score from the after score).
  2. Using difference score converts two sets of scores into one.
  3. Once the difference score has been computed for each subject, the entire hypothesis testing procedure is carried out using difference scores.

D. The population of difference scores (*Population 2*, the one to which the population represented by your sample will be compared) is ordinarily assumed to have a mean of zero. (This makes sense because we are comparing our sample's population to one in which there is, on the average, no difference.)

III. Assumptions of the *t* Test

A. The comparison distribution will be a *t* distribution only if the population of individual scores (or difference scores, if conducting a *t* test for dependent means) from which we drew our sample follows a normal curve.
  1. Otherwise the appropriate comparison distribution will follow some unknown, other shape.
  2. Unfortunately, it is rarely possible to tell whether the population is normal based on the information in your sample.
  3. Fortunately, results are reasonably accurate when the population distribution is fairly far from normal.

B. Thus, psychologists use the *t* test so long as neither of the following is the case:
  1. There is reason to expect a very large discrepancy from normal.
  2. The population is highly skewed and a one-tailed test is being used.

IV. Effect Size and Power for the *t* Test for Dependent Means

A. Effect size:
1. Effect size for the *t* test for dependent means is computed in the same way as we did in Chapter 7: *t* = (*Population 1 Mean - Population 2 Mean*)/*S*.
2. Since the mean of Population 2 is ordinarily assumed to be zero and the standard deviation is of the populations of difference scores, the formula reduces to *t* = Population 1 Mean / S with both terms relating to difference scores.
3. Note: To compute effect size you divide by *Population SD* (or its estimate *S*), and not by SD_M.

B. Power:
1. The text provides a table (Table 8.7) that gives the approximate power for the .05 significance level for small, medium, and large effect sizes and one- or two-tailed tests.
2. This power table is especially useful when interpreting the practical importance of a nonsignificant result in a published study.

C. Planning sample size: The text provides a table (Table 8.8) that gives the approximate number of subjects needed to achieve 80% power for estimated small, medium, and large effect sizes using one- and two-tailed tests for the .05 significance levels. (Eighty percent is a common figure used by researchers for the minimum power needed to make it worth conducting a study.)

D. Studies using difference scores often have considerably larger effect sizes for a given amount of expected difference than other kinds of research designs.

V. How *t* Tests for Dependent Means Are Described in Research Articles

A. Research articles describe *t* tests in the text a standard format that includes the degrees of freedom, the *t*-score, and the significance level. For example: $t(24) = 2.8, p < .05$.

B. In addition, researchers may also present the means of the different groups on a table, often using stars to indicate the level of significance for each comparison.

Formulas

I. Unbiased estimate of the population variance (S^2) for a *t* test for a single sample or a *t* test for dependent means

Formula in words: Estimated population variance is the sum of deviations of the scores in the sample from the sample's mean, divided by the degrees of freedom (the number of scores in the sample minus one).

Formula in symbols: $S^2 = \Sigma(X-M)^2/(N-1) = SS/df$ (8-1)

$\Sigma(X-M)^2$ is the sum of squared deviations from the mean of the sample.

N is the number of scores in the sample (or number of pairs of scores).

df is the degrees of freedom.

II. Degrees of freedom (*df*) for a *t* test for a single sample or a *t* test for dependent means

Formula in words: Degrees of freedom are the number of difference scores minus one.
Formula in symbols: $df=N-1$ (8-2)

III. Estimated population standard deviation (*S*)

Formula in words: Estimated population standard deviation is the square root of the estimated population variance.
Formula in symbols: $S = \sqrt{S^2}$ (8-3)

IV. Variance of the distribution of means based on an estimated population variance (S_M^2)

Formula in words: Variance of the distribution of means based on an estimated population variance is the estimated population variance divided by the number of scores (or difference scores) in the sample.

Formula in symbols: $S_M^2 = S^2/N$ (8-4)

S^2 is the variance of the population of individual scores (or of difference scores in a *t* test for dependent means).

N is the number of scores (or difference scores) in the sample.

V. Standard deviation of the distribution of means based on an estimated population variance (S_M)

Formula in words: Standard deviation of the distribution of means based on an estimated population variance is the square root of the variance of the distribution of means based on an estimated population variance.

Formula in symbols: $S_M = \sqrt{S_M^2}$ (8-5)

VI. *t* score for a *t* test for a single sample or a *t* test for dependent means

Formula in words: *t* score is the difference between the mean of the sample and the known population mean, divided by the standard deviation of the distribution of means based on an estimated population variance.

Formula in symbols: $t = (Sample\ M - Population\ M)/S_M$ (8-6)

Sample M   is the mean of the sample of scores (or the mean of the sample of difference scores).

Population M is the mean of the population to which the sample's population is being compared (Population 2). In the case of a *t* test for dependent means, Population M is usually assumed to be 0.

S_M standard deviation of distribution of means based on an estimated population variance

VII. Effect size for *t* test for a single sample or for a *t* test for dependent means

Formula in words: A standard measure of effect size (*t*) is the difference between the hypothesized and known population means, divided by the population standard deviation.

Formula in symbols: *effect size = (Population 1 M - Population 2 M) /Population SD*

Population 1 M   is the hypothesized (or, if the study is completed, actual) mean of the population which the sample represents. (In a *t* test for dependent means, μ_1 is a mean of difference scores.)

Population 2 M   is the known mean of the population of scores (or difference scores) to which the sample's population is to be compared. (In a *t* test for dependent means, μ_2 is usually considered to be 0.)

Population SD   is the standard deviation of the scores (or difference scores) in the population. It may be estimated as *S*.

VIII. Alternative, simplified formula for effect size for a *t* test for dependent means when *Population 2 M* is considered to be 0

Formula in words: A standard measure of effect size (*t*) for the *t* test for dependent means can be computed by taking the hypothesized population mean difference score, divided by the standard deviation of the population of difference scores.

Formula in symbols: *effect size = Population 1 M / Population SD*

How to Conduct a *t* Test for a Single Sample
(Based on Table 8.3 in the Text)

I.   Reframe the question into a null and a research hypothesis about populations.

II. Determine the characteristics of the comparison distribution:
   A. The mean is the same as the known population mean.
   B. The standard deviation is computed as follows:
      1. Compute estimated population variance: $S^2 = \Sigma (X-M)2/(N-1)$.
      2. Compute variance of the distribution of means: $S_M^2 = S^2/N$.
      3. Compute standard deviation: $S_M = \sqrt{S_M^2}$.
   C. Shape will be a *t* distribution with *N*-1 degrees of freedom.

III. Determine the cutoff sample score on the comparison distribution at which the null hypothesis should be rejected.
   A. Determine the degrees of freedom, desired significance level, and whether to use a one-tailed or two-tailed test.
   B. Look up the appropriate cutoff on a *t* table.

IV. Determine the score of your sample's mean on the comparison distribution: *t = (Sample Mean- Population M)/S_M*

V. Compare the scores in 3 and 4 to decide whether or not to reject the null hypothesis.

How to Conduct a *t* Test for Dependent Means
(Based on Table 8.6 in the Text)

I.   Reframe the question into a null and a research hypothesis about populations.

II. Determine the characteristics of the comparison distribution:
   A. Convert each subject's two scores into difference scores. Carry out the remaining steps using these difference scores.
   B. Compute the mean of the difference scores.
   C. Assume the population mean is zero.
   D. Compute the estimated population variance of difference scores:
   $S^2 = \Sigma (X-M)^2/N-1$.
   E. Compute the variance of the distribution of means of difference scores: $S_M^2 = S^2/N$.
   F. Compute the standard deviation of the distribution of means of difference scores:
   $S_M = \sqrt{S_M^2}$.
   G. Note that it will be a *t* distribution with $df = N-1$.

III. Determine the cutoff sample score on the comparison distribution at which the null hypothesis should be rejected.
  A. Determine desired significance level and whether to use a one-tailed or two-tailed test.
  B. Look up the appropriate cutoff on a t table.
IV. Determine the score of your sample on the comparison distribution:
  $t = ($ *Sample M-Population M* $)/S_M.$
V. Compare the scores in 3 and 4 to decide whether or not to reject the null hypothesis.

Outlines for Writing Essays

The reason for your writing essay questions in the practice problems and tests is that this task develops and then demonstrates what matters so very much--your comprehension of the logic behind the computations. (It is also a place where those better at words than numbers can shine, and for those better at numbers to develop their skills at explaining in words.)

Thus, to do well, be sure to do the following in each essay: (a) give the reasoning behind each step; (b) relate each step to the specifics of the content of the particular study you are analyzing; (c) state the various formulas in nontechnical language, because as you define each term you show you understand it (although once you have defined it in nontechnical language, you can use it from then on in the essay); (d) look back and be absolutely certain that you made it clear just *why* that formula or procedure was applied and *why* it is the way it is.

The outlines below are *examples* of ways to structure your essays. There are other completely correct ways to go about it. And this is an *outline* for an answer--you are to write the answer out in paragraph form.

These essays are necessarily very long for you to write (and for others to grade). But this is the very best way to be sure you understand everything thoroughly. One short cut you may see on a test is that you may be asked to write your answer for someone who understands statistics up to the point of the new material you are studying. You can choose to take the same short cut in these practice problems (maybe writing for someone who understands right up to whatever point you yourself start being just a little unclear). But every time you write for a person who has never had statistics at all, you review the logic behind the entire course. You engrain it in your mind. Over and over. The time is never wasted. It is an excellent way to study.

I. Reframe the question into a research hypothesis and a null hypothesis about populations. (Step 1 of hypothesis testing.)
  A. State in ordinary language the hypothesis testing issue: Does the average of the scores of the group of persons studied represent a higher (or lower or different) mean than would be expected if this group of persons had just been a randomly selected example of people in general--that is, does this set of people studied represent a different group of people from people in general?
  B. Explain language (to make the rest of essay easier to write by not having to repeat long explanations), focusing on the meaning of each term in the concrete example of the study at hand.
      1. Populations.
      2. Sample.
      3. Mean.
      4. Research hypothesis.
      5. Null hypothesis.
      6. Rejecting the null hypothesis to provide support for the research hypothesis.

II. Determine the characteristics of the comparison distribution. (Step 2 of hypothesis testing.)

    A. Explain the principle that the comparison distribution is the distribution (pattern of spread of the means of scores) that represents what we would expect if the null hypothesis were true and our particular mean were just randomly sampled from this population of means.

    B. Note that because we are interested in the mean of a sample of more than one score, we have to compare our actual mean to a distribution not of individual scores but of means.

    C. Give an intuitive understanding of how one might construct a distribution of means for samples of a given size from a particular population.

        1. Select a random sample of the given size (number of subjects) from the population and compute its mean.

        2. Select another random sample of this size from the population and compute its mean.

        3. Repeat this process a very large number of times.

        4. Make a distribution of these means.

        5. Note that this procedure is only to explain the idea and would be too much work and unnecessary in practice.

    D. There is an exact mathematical relation of a distribution of means to the population the means are drawn from, so that in practice the characteristics of the distribution of means can be determined directly from knowledge of the characteristics of the population and the size of the samples involved.

    E. The mean of a distribution of means.

        1. It is the same as the mean (average) of the scores in the known population of individual scores.

        2. State what it is in the particular problem you are working on.

        3. Explanation.

           a. Each sample is based on randomly selected values from the population.

           b. Thus, sometimes the mean of a sample will be higher and sometimes lower than the mean of the whole population of individuals.

           c. There is no reason for these to average out higher or lower than the original population mean.

           d. Thus the average of these means (the mean of the distribution of means) should in the long run equal the population mean.

    F. The standard deviation of a distribution of means.

        1. The spread of a distribution of means will be less spread out than the population of individual scores from which the samples are taken.

           a. Any one score, even an extreme score, has some chance of being selected in a random sample.

           b. However, the chance is less of several extreme scores being selected in the same random sample, particularly since in order to create an extreme sample mean they would have to be scores which were extreme in the same direction.

           c. Thus, there is a moderating effect of numbers. In any one sample, the deviants tend to be balanced out by middle scores or by deviants in the opposite direction, making each sample tend towards the middle and away from extreme values.

           d. With fewer extreme values for the means, the variation among the means is less.

        2. The more scores in each sample, the less spread out is the distribution of means of that sample size: With a larger number of scores in each sample, it is even harder for extreme scores in that sample not to be balanced out by middle scores or extremes in the other direction in the same sample.

        3. Explain the idea of standard deviation.

           a. It is a standard measure of how spread out a distribution is.

           b. Roughly, it is the average amount scores vary from the mean.

           c. Exactly speaking, it is the square root of the average of the squares of the amount that each score differs from the mean.

4. The standard deviation of the distribution of means is found by a formula that divides the average of squared deviations from the mean of the population by the number of subjects in the sample (thus making it smaller in proportion to the number of subjects in the sample), and taking the square root of this result.

5. Computing this standard deviation requires knowing the variation in the population, and this is not known. But it can be estimated.

    a. Whatever the distribution your particular scores come from, it is reasonable to assume that the variation among your particular group is representative of the variation in that larger distribution of scores.

    b. A sample's variation is on the average slightly less than the population it comes from because it is less likely to include scores that are far from its mean.

    c. Thus, a special adjustment is made that exactly corrects for this: Instead of taking the average of the squared deviations--the sum of squared deviations divided by the number of subjects--one instead divides the sum of squared deviations by one less than the number of subjects in the sample.

6. Describe the steps of computing the estimated population variance and the standard deviation of the distribution of means for your example, stating the final result.

G. The shape of the distribution of means.

1. The distribution tends to be bell shaped, with most scores falling near the middle and fewer at the extremes, due to the same basic process of extremes balancing each other out that we noted in the discussion of the standard deviation--middle values are more likely and extreme values less likely.

2. Specifically, it can be shown that it will follow a precise shape called a *t* distribution.

3. Actually there are different *t* distributions according to the amount of information that goes into estimating the variation in the distribution from the sample, the number you divide by in making the estimate (the number of subjects minus one).

4. Also, the shape of the comparison distribution is only a precise *t* distribution if the population of individual scores follows a precise shape called a normal curve (also bell shaped) that is widely found in nature. Note that in the problem you are told that the distribution of the population is a normal curve so that this condition is met in your case.

III. **Determine the cutoff sample score on the comparison distribution at which the null hypothesis should be rejected. (Step 3 of hypothesis testing.)**

A. Before you figure out how extreme your particular sample's mean is on this distribution of means, you want to know how extreme it would have to be to decide it was too unlikely that it could have been a randomly drawn mean from this comparison distribution of means.

B. Since the shape of the comparison distribution follows a mathematically defined formula, you can use a table to tell you how many standard deviations from the mean your score would have to be to be in the top so many percent.

C. Note that the number of standard deviations from the mean on this *t* distribution is called a *t* score. (Explaining this term makes writing simpler later on.)

D. To use these tables, you have to decide the kind of situation you have; there are two considerations.

1. Are you interested in the chances of getting this extreme of a mean, one that is extreme in only one direction (such as only higher than for people in general) or in both? (Explain which is appropriate for your study.)

2. Just how unlikely would the extremeness of a particular mean have to be? The standard figure used in psychology is less likely than 5% (though 1% is sometimes used to be especially safe). (Say which you are using in your study--if no figure is stated in the problem and no special reason given for using one or the other, the general rule is to use 5%.)

E. State the cutoff for your particular problem.

IV. Determine the score of your sample on the comparison distribution. (Step 4 of hypothesis testing.)

    A. The next step is to find where your actual sample's mean would fall on the comparison distribution, in terms of a t score.

    B. State this t score.

V. Compare the scores in 3 and 4 to decide whether or not to reject the null hypothesis. (Step 5 of hypothesis testing.)

    A. State whether your mean (from Step 4) does or does not exceed the cutoff (from Step 3).

    B. If your mean exceeds the cutoff.

        1. State that you can reject the null hypothesis.

        2. State that by elimination, the research hypothesis is thus supported.

        3. State in words what it means that the research hypothesis is supported (that is, the study shows that the particular experimental manipulation appears to make a difference in the particular thing being measured).

    C. If your score does not exceed the cutoff.

        1. State that you can not reject the null hypothesis.

        2. State that the experiment is inconclusive.

        3. State in words what it means that the study is inconclusive (that is, the study did not yield results which give a clear indication of whether or not the particular experimental manipulation appears to make a difference in the particular variable being measured).

        4. Explicitly note that even though the research hypothesis was not supported in this study, this is not evidence that it is false--it is quite possible that it is true but it has only a small effect which was not sufficient to produce a mean extreme enough to yield a significant result in this study.

Chapter Self-Tests

Multiple-Choice Questions

1. The reason we use N-1 in the variance formula when using samples is

    a. to determine the degrees of freedom.
    b. because we randomly delete one score.
    c. to create an unbiased estimate of the population variance.
    d. none of the above.

2. When estimating the variance of a population from the sample, you divide by the sample size minus one, because using the sample size directly

    a. does not correct for squaring the deviations.
    b. underestimates the population variance.
    c. fails to take into account the sample size.
    d. creates too little "bias."

3. The shape of the t distribution

    a. changes as the size of the distribution changes.
    b. is typically not normal.
    c. has a steeper curve to reflect the cutoff scores.
    d. is not symmetrical.

4. Having two scores from the same person results in having scores that are

   a. dependent
   b. matched
   c. correlated
   d. all of the above

5. If a study yields a t score of 2.46, and the cutoff t score was 2.36, should you reject the null hypothesis? Why or why not?

   a. Yes, because the computed t score is more extreme than the cutoff score.
   b. No, because the computed t score is more extreme than the cutoff score.
   c. No, because the computed t score is too close to the cutoff t score to be significant.
   d. This can not be determined without knowing the degrees of freedom.

6. A group of students take the SAT, then take an SAT prep class, then take the SAT again. To test the null hypothesis that there is no difference in students' SAT scores from before to after taking the prep class, which population mean would be used?

   a. Zero.
   b. The original (before) SAT score of the test group.
   c. The second (after) SAT score of the test group.
   d. The national mean SAT score.

7. A counselor claims that after attending three sessions with her, clients score higher on a Satisfaction With Life scale than they do before counseling. Her null hypothesis is that there is no difference in clients' scores after counseling. If the cutoff t score is 2.0 and the standard deviation of the comparison distribution is 1.5, by how many points do clients' scores have to change in order to justify rejecting the null hypothesis?

   a. 1.5
   b. 2.0
   c. 2.5
   d. 3.0

8. Which of the following is an assumption you must make before you can use the t test?

   a. The sample is normally distributed.
   b. The sample is skewed.
   c. The population is normally distributed.
   d. The population is skewed.

9. Suppose you are doing research on the general intelligence of people with eidetic memory (that is, people who have exact visual memory), and subjects are so hard to come by that you are limited to 10 subjects. If there is a medium effect size in the population, and you are testing your hypothesis with a t test for dependent means, two-tailed, at the .05 level, what is the power of this study? Refer to Table 8.7 in the text for your answer.

   a. .09
   b. .15
   c. .32
   d. .46

10. A research article reports results of a study using a t test for dependent means as "$t(16) = 2.67, p < .05$." This means

   a. the result is not significant.
   b. there were 16 subjects.
   c. the t score was 16.
   d. the t score was 2.67.

Fill-In Questions

1. When estimating the population variance from the sample variance, the amount of information in the sample that is free to vary is called the _____.

2. The reason that a sample's variance tends to be smaller than the population's is that the sample is less likely to include _____.

3. When figuring the variance of the distribution of means in a t test problem, you divide the estimated population variance by _____.

4. In the t test for dependent means, you reduce the two scores per person to one score by creating _____.

5. The t test for dependent means tests to see if the population of difference scores is equal to _____.

6. An important assumption of the hypothesis testing procedure is the distribution is not _____.

7. An unbiased population variance estimate changes the denominator for this formula from _____ to _____.

8. A t distribution differs from a normal distribution in that there the tails contain a _____ proportion of the scores.

9. To find the score at which the null hypothesis will be rejected, you look on a table of t distributions. But first you need to know whether it is a one- or two-tailed test, the degrees of freedom in the sample, and the _____.

10. The larger the sample size, the more a t distribution becomes indistinguishable from a(n) _____.

Problems and Essays

1. An urban planner is interested in whether people who live in noisy parts of a city have worse hearing. To test this, she administers hearing tests to six randomly selected healthy 18-year-olds that have grown up in one of the noisiest parts of the city. Their scores on the hearing test are 16, 14, 18, 18, 20, and 16. This test was designed so that healthy 18-year-olds should score 20. (The variance is not known.) What should she conclude? Explain your computations and the logic of what you have done to a person who has never had a course in statistics.

2. A linguist theorizes that people will be able to form sentences with pleasant words quicker than with unpleasant words. To test her hypothesis, she creates a list of equal numbers of pleasant and unpleasant words, trying to select words of approximately equal difficulty, putting the words in random order in the list. Subjects are then asked to form a sentence using each word, as soon the word is shown to them on a computer screen. A special timing device records how long it takes from the time the word appears on the screen until the subject starts speaking the sentence. Five subjects are used, and the average time it takes each subject to do the pleasant and unpleasant words are shown in the table below. Is the time it takes subjects to come up with a sentence different for the two kinds of words? Explain your procedures and the logic of what you have done to a person who has never had a course in statistics.

	Mean Reaction Time (in Seconds)	
Subject	*Pleasant*	*Unpleasant*
1	.44	.51
2	.33	.51
3	.60	.74
4	.59	.77
5	.68	.55

3. A developmental psychologist has created a special exercise program intended to improve hand-eye coordination of toddlers. As a first test of the effectiveness of this set of exercises, he arranges for a group of 38 toddlers to participate in the program, testing their hand-eye coordination on a standard test before and after several weeks using the program. In the report of the results of this study, he writes: "Mean scores for the 38 toddlers increased from 61.32 to 68.93, $t(37) = 3.21$, $p < .01$, one-tailed." Explain this result, including the underlying computations that went into it, to a person who has never had a course in statistics.

4. An instructor of a speed reading course claimed that students could increase their reading speed without lowering their reading comprehension. A skeptical student decided to test this. She tested a group of 9 volunteers on their comprehension of a story before and after the class. She also noted their reading speeds, which an analysis showed to be significantly greater after the class, $t(8)=3.5$, $p<.01$. Their scores on the comprehension tests are listed below. Do the data support the claim of the instructor, that reading comprehension does not decrease?

	Subjects' Reading Comprehension Scores	
SUBJECT	*BEFORE*	*AFTER*
1	87	85
2	84	82
3	75	71
4	80	78
5	97	91
6	92	91
7	88	89
8	67	71
9	70	70

Explain to a person who has never had a course in statistics: (a) the meaning of the reading speed result and (b) how you computed (including its logic) and what you found, in the analysis of the comprehension scores.

Using SPSS 10.0 with this Chapter

If you are using SPSS for the first time, before proceeding with the material in this section, read the Appendix on Getting Started and the Basics of Using SPSS.

You can use SPSS to carry out a *t* test for dependent means. It is also possible to carry out a *t* test for a single sample using SPSS, but as noted in the chapter, this procedure is rarely used in practice and was covered mainly as a step towards introducing you to the more widely used *t* tests. You should work through the example, following the procedures step by step. Then look over the description of the general principles involved and try the procedures on your own for some of the problems listed in the Suggestions for Additional Practice. Finally, you may want to try the suggestions for using the computer to deepen your understanding.

I. Example

A. Data: Hand-eye coordination scores for nine surgeons, each measured under both quiet and noisy conditions (fictional data), from the example in the text. The scores for the surgeons, under quiet conditions first, are 18, 12; 21, 21; 19, 16; 21, 16; 17, 19; 20, 19; 18, 16; 16, 17; and 20, 16.

B. Follow the instructions in the SPSS Appendix for starting up SPSS.

C. Enter the data as follows:
  1. Type 18 and press enter. Then click on the next box on the same line and type 12 and enter. This will put the subjects two scores on the same line next to each other.
  2. Click on the first box on the next line and type 21 and enter. Then click on the second box on the second line and type 21 and enter (the quiet score and the noisy score for the second surgeon).
  3. Type the scores for the remaining subjects, on each line one subject's quiet and noisy score, in that order.
  4. As we have done in previous chapters, to name the two variables, click on the variable view tab. In the first row of the first column type in QUIET under the column titled "Name". Repeat this process in the second row for the second variable using the variable name NOISY.
  5. The screen should now appear as shown in Figure SG8-1.

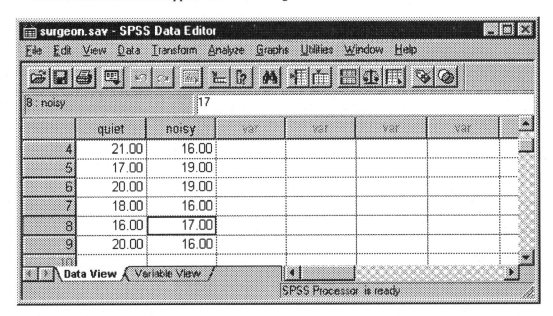

Figure SG8-1

D. Carry out a *t* test for dependent means as follows:

Analyze

Compare Means >

Paired Samples T-test

[Highlight QUIET so that it appears in the Current Selections box. Highlight NOISY so that it appears in the current selections box. Click on the arrow so that both variables appear in the Paired Variables box.]

OK

The results should appear as Figure SG8-2 below.

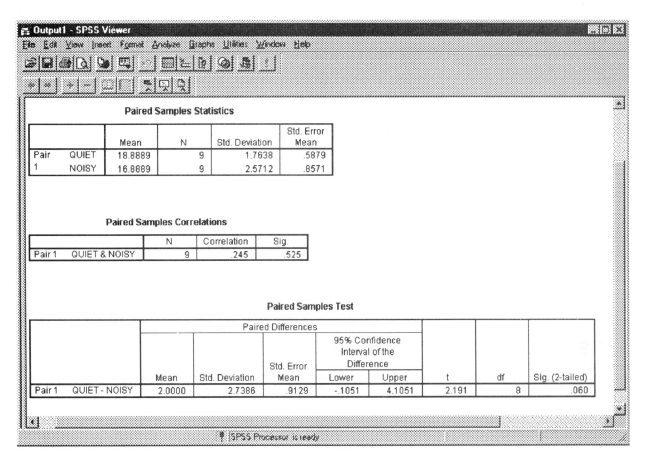

Paired Samples Statistics

		Mean	N	Std. Deviation	Std. Error Mean
Pair 1	QUIET	18.8889	9	1.7638	.5879
	NOISY	16.8889	9	2.5712	.8571

Paired Samples Correlations

		N	Correlation	Sig.
Pair 1	QUIET & NOISY	9	.245	.525

Paired Samples Test

		Paired Differences							
					95% Confidence Interval of the Difference				
		Mean	Std. Deviation	Std. Error Mean	Lower	Upper	t	df	Sig. (2-tailed)
Pair 1	QUIET - NOISY	2.0000	2.7386	.9129	-.1051	4.1051	2.191	8	.060

Figure SG8-2

E. Inspect the result.

1. The first table provides descriptive statistics about the two variables.
2. The second table provides the correlation between the two variables.
3. The third table provides the statistical test.
   a. The first column gives the variable names.
   b. The second column gives the **mean difference** for each pair of scores.
   c. The third column gives the standard deviation of the differences among the pairs of scores.
   d. The fourth column gives the **SE of Mean**, which is the standard deviation of the distribution of means, S_M, corresponding to each variable (based on an estimated population variance).
   e. The fifth column provides the 95% confidence interval surrounding the difference. Describe the correlation between the two variables, which you ignore since your interest is in the difference between these two variables not the extent to which highs go with highs and lows with lows.
   f. The sixth column gives the computed *t* score, which it lists as **2.191**.
   g. The seventh column gives the degrees of freedom, **8**.
   h. Finally, the last column, **2-tail Sig**, gives the probability, the exact chance, of getting a *t* score this extreme on this particular *t* distribution. In this example, the computer reports **.060**. Since the significance level was set in advance at .05, this result does not reach significance. (Note that the figure given is for a two-tailed test, which is appropriate in the example. But if you were using a one-tailed test, you would consider the result significant at the .05 level if this number were .10 or less. To put this another way, the particular result of .060 means that there is .030 higher than 2.191 and .030 lower than -2.191.)

95

F. Print out the result.

G. Save your lines of data as follows:

    File

      Save Data

        [Name your data file followed by the extension ".sav" and designate the drive you would like your data saved in]

          OK

II. Systematic Instructions for Computing the *t* Test for Dependent Means

A. Start up SPSS.

B. Enter the data as follows:

    1. Type 18 and press enter. Then click on the next box on the same line and type 12 and enter. This will put the subjects two scores on the same line next to each other.

    2. Click on the first box on the next line and type 21 and enter. Then click on the second box on the second line and type 21 and enter (the quiet score and the noisy score for the second surgeon).

    3. Type the scores for the remaining subjects, on each line one subject's quiet and noisy score, in that order.

    4. As we have done in previous chapters, to name the two variables, click on the variable view tab. In the first row of the first column type in QUIET under the column titled "Name". Repeat this process in the second row for the second variable using the variable name NOISY.

C. Carry out the *t*-test for dependent means as follows:

    Analyze

      Compare Means >

        Paired Samples T-test

          [Highlight QUIET so that it appears in the Current Selections box. Highlight NOISY so that it appears in the current selections box. Click on the arrow so that both variables appear in the Paired Variables box.]

            OK

D. Save your lines of data as follows:

    File

      Save Data

        [Name your data file followed by the extension ".sav" and designate the drive you would like your data saved in]

          OK

III. Additional Practice

(Compute a *t* test for dependent means for each of these data sets and compare your results to those in the text.)

A. Text examples.

    1. Data in Table 8.4 for husbands' communication quality scores before and after marriage (from Olthoff & Aron, 1993).

    2. Data in Table 8.5 for people's attitude toward their government during war.

B. Practice problems in the text.

    1. Questions 4 and 5 from Chapter 8.

IV. Using the Computer to Deepen Your Knowledge

A. The effect of increasing the mean of the difference scores.

    1. Use SPSS to compute the *t* test for dependent means using the surgeon example, but adding 2 to each Noisy score. Doing the following can do this:

      Transform

        Compute

          [Type NOIPLUS2 in the target variable box to name the new variable. Type NOISY +2 in the Numeric Expression box.]

OK

2. Conduct another *t* test for dependent means using the original data, but this time adding 6 to the first three Noisy scores and nothing to the others. (To do this, you will actually have to change the scores as entered.)

3. Compare the two outcomes: Both have a larger mean difference, but the increase in the *t* score is much greater in the first case. Why is this? (Hint: Consider the variance of the difference scores.)

B. Correlation and the *t* test for dependent means.

1. Examine the correlation reported in the output for the original data and for each of the adjusted data sets in A above (that is, first with adding 2 to each Noisy score and then with adding 6 to a third of them).

2. Compare the correlations and their relation to the effects of these changes in data to the *t* test results.

a. Notice that the size of the correlation is not directly related to the size of the *t* test result (the two procedures are measuring different things).

b. Notice that the adding of 6 to a third of the scores creates a lower correlation than adding 2 to all of them. Why is this? Consider its relation to the results of the *t* tests and to variance in the difference scores.

C. The importance of matching.

1. Rearrange the Noisy scores so that all the same numbers are in the Noisy column, but they are not paired with the same subject's Quiet scores. Then compute a *t* test for dependent means.

2. Try another rearrangement and compute a *t* test for dependent means.

3. Compare these two results to the original.

Chapter 9
The *t* Test for Independent Means

Learning Objectives

By the end of this chapter you should be able to:

- Explain the difference between a *t* test for dependent means and a *t* test for independent means.
- Explain the characteristics of the distribution of differences between means.
- List and perform the steps in conducting a *t* test for independent means.
- Discuss the assumptions for the *t* test for independent means (and the conditions under which it is safe to violate them).
- Figure the effect size and power of a study using the *t* test for independent means.
- Interpret the results of studies using *t* tests for independent means reported in research articles.

Chapter Outline

I. The *t* Test for Independent Means
   A. Used in studies with two samples.
   B. Follows the usual steps of hypothesis testing.
   C. Only differences from a *t* test for dependent means is that the comparison distribution is a distribution of differences between means and the *t* score is based on this distribution.

II. The Distribution of Differences Between Means
   A. It is the comparison distribution in a *t*-test for independent means.
   B. It can be understood as being constructed in four steps.
      1. Construct a distribution of means for each of the two populations.
      2. Randomly select one mean from each distribution of means.
      3. Subtract one from the other.
      4. Repeat a large number of times to create a distribution of these differences.
   C. If the null hypothesis is true, its mean is zero–since the two populations, and hence the two distributions of means, have the same mean, differences between means randomly drawn from these should average out to zero.
   D. Estimating the population variance.
      1. A single overall estimate is made of the variance of the populations, since it is assumed the population variances are equal.
      2. If sample sizes are equal, this pooled population variance estimate is the average of the estimates for the two populations–$S_{\text{POOLED}}^2 = (S_1^2 + S_2^2)/2$.
      3. If samples sizes are different, pooled population variance estimate is based on an average which first weights each estimate by the degrees of freedom on that it is based: $S_{\text{POOLED}}^2 = [df_1/df_{\text{TOTAL}}][S_1^2] + [df_2/df_{\text{TOTAL}}][S_2^2]$.
   E. Variance and standard deviation of the distribution of differences between means.
      1. The variance of each distribution of means is the pooled estimate divided by the corresponding sample size: $S_{M1}^2 = S_{\text{POOLED}}^2/N_1$ and $S_{M2}^2 = S_{\text{POOLED}}^2/N_2$.
      2. Variance of the distribution of differences between means is the sum of the variances of the two distributions of means (because the variance of each contributes to its variance): $S_{\text{DIFFERENCE}}^2 = S_{M1}^2 + S_{M2}^2$.
      3. The standard deviation of the distribution of the difference between means is the square root of its variance: $S_{\text{DIFFERENCE}} = \sqrt{S_{\text{DIFFERENCE}}^2}$.

F. The shape of the distribution of differences between means.
   1. A t distribution (because we are using estimated population variances).
   2. Its degrees of freedom are the sum of the degrees of freedom for the two samples (because each contributes to the pooled estimate of the variance): $df_{TOTAL} = df_1 + df_2$.
G. The t score on this distribution is the difference between the two sample means divided by the standard deviation of this distribution: $t = (M_1 - M_2)/S_{DIFFERENCE}$.

III. **Assumptions of the t Test for Independent Means**
   A. Normal population distributions.
      1. Violation of this assumption is a problem mainly if the two populations are thought to have dramatically skewed distributions, and in opposite directions.
      2. The test is especially robust to violations if a two-tailed test is used and if the sample sizes are not extremely small.
   B. Equal population variances.
      1. The test is fairly robust to even fairly substantial differences in the population variances if there are equal numbers in the two groups.
      2. If the two estimated population variances are quite different, *and* if the samples have different numbers of cases, a modification of the usual t test procedure (not covered in this text) is sometimes used.
   C. It is difficult in practice to determine whether the assumptions hold.
   D. Some procedures that can be applied when the assumptions are clearly violated are described in Chapter 11.

IV. **Effect Size and Power for the t Test for Independent Means**
   A. Effect size.
      1. Effect size = (Population 1M - Population 2 M) / Population SD.
      2. For a completed study, estimate effect size as Effect Size = $(M_1 - M_2) / S_{Pooled}$.
      3. Cohen's convention: Small $d = .20$; medium $d = .50$; large $d = .80$. (Same as for t test for dependent means.)
   B. Power.
      1. Table 9-4 in the text gives approximate power for the .05 significance level for small, medium, or large effect sizes and one- or two-tailed tests.
      2. Power when sample sizes are not equal.
         a. For any given number of subjects, power is greatest when subjects are divided into two equal groups.
         b. The power is equivalent to a study with equal sample sizes in which each of those equal sizes is the harmonic mean of the actual unequal sample sizes: Harmonic Mean = $[(2)(N_1)(N_2)]/[N_1 + N_2]$.
   C. Planning sample size: Table 9-5 in the text gives the approximate number of subjects needed to achieve 80% power for estimated small, medium, and large effect sizes using one- and two-tailed tests, all using the .05 significance level.

V. **How t Tests for Independent Means are Described in Research Articles**
   A. They are usually reported in the article text by giving the two sample means (and sometimes the SDs), followed by the standard format for any t test–for example: $t(38) = 4.72, p < .01$.
   B. Sometimes they are reported in tables that give the means (and sometimes SDs), using stars to indicate significance levels.

Formulas

I. Pooled estimate of population variance (S_{POOLED}^2)

Formula in words: Weighted average of estimates for each population; that is, each estimate contributes the proportion to the overall estimate that its degrees of freedom are to the total degrees of freedom.

Formula in symbols: $S_{\text{POOLED}}^2 = [df_1/(df_1+df_2)][S_1^2] + [df_2/(df_1+df_2)][S_2^2]$ (9-1)

S_1^2 is the unbiased estimate of the variance of Population 1.

S_2^2 is the unbiased estimate of the variance of Population 2.

Note: Each $S^2 = \Sigma(X-M)^2/df = SS/df$ (see Chapter 8).

df_1 is the degrees of freedom for the sample from Population 1.

df_2 is the degrees of freedom for the sample from Population 2.

Note: Each $df = N-1$.

II. Variance of each population's distribution of means (S_{M1}^2 and S_{M2}^2)

Formula in words: The pooled population variance estimate divided by the corresponding sample size.

Formulas in symbols: $S_{M1}^2 = S_{\text{POOLED}}^2 / N_1$ and $S_{M2}^2 = S_{\text{POOLED}}^2 / N_2$ (9-2)

N_1 is the number of subjects in the sample representing Population 1.

N_2 is the number of subjects in the sample representing Population 2.

III. Variance of the distribution of differences between means ($S_{\text{DIFFERENCE}}^2$)

Formula in words: Sum of the variances of the two distributions of means.

Formula in symbols: $S_{\text{DIFFERENCE}}^2 = S_{M1}^2 + S_{M2}^2$ (9-3)

IV. Standard deviation of the distribution of the differences between means ($S_{\text{DIFFERENCE}}$)

Formula in words: The square root of the variance of the distribution of differences between means.

Formula in symbols: $S_{\text{DIFFERENCE}} = \sqrt{S_{\text{DIFFERENCE}}^2}$ (9-4)

V. Degrees of freedom for a *t* test for independent means (df_{TOTAL})

Formula in words: Sum of the degrees of freedom in the two samples.

Formula in symbols: $df_{\text{TOTAL}} = df_1 + df_2$ (9-5)

VI. *t* score for a *t* test for independent means

Formula in words: The difference between the two sample means divided by the standard deviation of the distribution of differences between means.

Formula in symbols: $t = (M_1 - M_2)/S_{\text{DIFFERENCE}}$ (9-6)

M_1 is the mean of the sample representing Population 1.

M_2 is the mean of the sample representing Population 2.

VII. Effect size for a *t* test for independent means (*d*)

Formula in words: The hypothesized difference between the population means divided by the population standard deviation.

Formula in symbols: Effect size = (Population 1 M - Population 2 M)/Population SD   (9-7)

Population 1 M is the mean of Population 1.

Population 2 M is the mean of Population 2.

Population SD is the standard deviation of each of the populations.

VIII. Estimated effect size for a *t* test for independent means (d) for a completed study

Formula in words: The observed difference between the sample means divided by the pooled estimate of the population standard deviation.

Formula in symbols: Estimated effect size = $(M_1 - M_2) / S_{\text{POOLED}}$ (9-8)

S_{POOLED} is the pooled estimate of the population standard deviation ($S_{\text{POOLED}} = \sqrt{S_{\text{POOLED}}^2}$).

IX. Harmonic mean sample size

Formula in words: Twice the product of the two sample sizes divided by the sum of the sample sizes.

Formula in symbols: Harmonic Mean $= [(2)(N_1)(N_2)] / [N_1+N_2]$ (9-9)

How to Conduct a *t* Test for Independent Means

(Based on Table 9-3 in the Text)

I. Reframe the question into a null and a research hypothesis about populations.

II. Determine the characteristics of the comparison distribution.

A. Its mean will be 0.

B. Its standard deviation is computed as follows.

    1. Compute estimated population variances based on each sample (that is, compute two estimates).

    2. Compute pooled estimate of population variance: $S_{POOLED}^2 = [df_1/(df_1+df_2)][S_1^2] + [df_2/(df_1+df_2)][S_2^2]$.
Note: $df_1=N_1-1$ and $df_2=N_2-1$.

    3. Compute variance of each distribution of means: $S_{M1}^2 = S_{POOLED}^2/N_1$ and $S_{M2}^2 = S_{POOLED}^2/N_2$.

    4. Compute variance of distribution of differences between means: $S_{DIFFERENCE}^2 = S_{M1}^2 + S_{M2}^2$.

    5. Compute standard deviation of distribution of differences between means: $S_{DIFFERENCE} = \sqrt{S_{DIFFERENCE}^2}$.

C. Determine its shape: It will be a *t* distribution with df_T degrees of freedom ($df_{TOTAL} = df_1+df_2$).

III. Determine the cut-off sample score on the comparison distribution at which the null hypothesis should be rejected.

A. Determine the degrees of freedom (df_{TOTAL}), desired significance level, and whether to use a one- or two-tailed test.

B. Look up the appropriate cut-off on a *t* table; if exact *df* is not given, use *df* below.

IV. Determine the score of your sample on the comparison distribution: $t = (M_1 - M_2)/S_{DIFFERENCE}$.

V. Compare the scores in 3 and 4 to decide whether or not to reject the null hypothesis.

Outline for Writing Essays for Hypothesis-Testing Problems
Involving the Means of Two Independent Samples
(*t* test for Independent Means)

The reason for your writing essay questions in the practice problems and tests is that this task develops and then demonstrates what matters so very much–your comprehension of the logic behind the computations. (It is also a place for those of you who are better at words than numbers to shine. And for those better at numbers to develop their skills at explaining in words.)

Thus, to do well you need to be sure to do the following in each essay: (a) give the reasoning behind each step; (b) relate each step to the specifics of the content of the particular study you are analyzing; (c) state the various formulas in nontechnical language, because as you define each term you show you understand it (although once you have defined it in nontechnical language, you can use it from then on in the essay); (d) look back and be absolutely certain that you made it clear just why that formula or procedure was applied and why it is the way it is.

The outlines below are *examples* of ways to structure your essays. There are other completely correct ways to go about it. And this is an *outline* for an answer–you must write the answer out in paragraph form.

These essays are necessarily very long for you to write (and for others to grade). But this is the very best way to be sure you understand everything thoroughly. One short cut you may see on a test is to write your answer for someone who understands statistics up to the point of the new material you are studying. You can choose to take the same short cut in these practice problems (maybe writing for someone who understands right up to whatever point you yourself start being just a little unclear). But every time you write for a person who has never had statistics at all, you review the logic behind the entire whole course. You engrain it in your mind. Over and over. The time is never wasted. It is an excellent way to study.

I. **Reframe the question into a research hypothesis and a null hypothesis about populations. (Step 1 of hypothesis testing.)**
   A. State in ordinary language the hypothesis testing issue: Do the two groups of persons studied represent larger groups or "populations" of people whose averages are different?
   B. Explain language (to make rest of essay easier to write by not having to repeat long explanations each time), focusing on the meaning of each term in the concrete example of the study at hand.
      1. Populations.
      2. Sample.
      3. Mean.
      4. Research hypothesis.
      5. Null hypothesis.
      6. Rejecting the null hypothesis to provide support for the research hypothesis.

II. **Determine the characteristics of the comparison distribution. (Step 2 of hypothesis testing.)**
   A. Explain principle that the comparison distribution is the distribution (pattern of spread of differences between means of scores of two groups) that represents what we would expect if the null hypothesis were true and our particular two groups each consist of randomly selected scores from populations that have the same mean.
   B. Thus, the comparison distribution is the distribution of differences between means of two groups where the two groups really are not from two different populations, but the two populations are one and the same.

C. Note that because we are working with a difference between means of two groups, we have to compare our actual difference between the means of two groups to a distribution not of individual cases, but of differences between means of two groups.

D. Give an intuitive understanding of how one might construct a distribution of differences between means of two groups.
  1. Create a distribution of means based on the population the first group represents.
    a. Select a random sample of the size (number of subjects) of your first group from the population it represents and compute its mean.
    b. Select another random sample of this size from this population and compute its mean.
    c. Repeat this process a very large number of times.
    d. Make a distribution of these means.
  2. Create a distribution of means based on the population the second group represents.
  3. Select one mean from each distribution of means and find the difference (subtract the one from the other).
  4. Repeat this process many times.
  5. Make a distribution of these differences.
  6. Note that this procedure is only to explain the idea, and would be too much work and unnecessary in practice.

E. There is an exact mathematical relation of a distribution of differences between means to the population the means are drawn from, so that in practice the characteristics of the distribution of means can be determined directly from knowledge of the characteristics of the population and the size of the samples involved.

F. Since we are still assuming the null hypothesis is true, the mean of a distribution of differences between means is zero because the distributions of means from each will have the same mean, and differences between means taken from them should average out to zero.

G. The standard deviation of a distribution of differences between means is a measure of the amount of spread or variation in the differences. (Define variance and standard deviation in lay language.) This standard deviation is computed in steps.
  1. Estimate the variation in each of the populations which each group represents.
    a. Whatever the distribution a particular group's scores come from, it is reasonable to assume that the variation among the scores in your particular group is representative of the variation in that larger distribution of scores.
    b. A sample's variation is on the average slightly less than the population it comes from because it is less likely to include scores that are far from its mean.
    c. Thus, a special adjustment is made that exactly corrects for this: Instead of taking the average of the squared deviations–the sum of squared deviations divided by the number of subjects–one instead divides the sum of squared deviations by one less than the number of subjects in the sample.
    d. Describe the computations (and state results) for your two groups.
  2. Average the estimates to get a more accurate pooled estimate.
    a. Normally we assume the two populations have the same amount of variation.
    b. The averaging is done so as to give weight to each estimate in proportion to the information it contributes (which is the number of cases minus one).
    c. Describe the computations and state the results.

3. Compute the variance of each distribution of means.
   a. The spread of each distribution of means will be less spread out than the population of individual cases from which the samples are taken because of the following reasoning.
     i. Any one score, even an extreme score, has some chance of being selected in a random sample.
     ii. However, the chance is less of very many extreme scores being selected in the same random sample (what is required to create an extreme sample mean), particularly since scores would have to be extreme in the same direction.
     iii.Thus, there is a moderating effect of numbers: In any one sample the deviants tend to be balanced out by middle cases or by deviants in the opposite direction, making each sample tend towards the middle and away from extreme values.
     iv. With fewer extreme values for the means, the variation among the means is less.
   b. The more cases in each sample, the less spread out is the distribution of means of that sample size: With a larger number of cases in each sample, it is even harder for extreme cases in that sample not to be balanced out by middle cases or extremes in the other direction in the same sample.
   c. The variance of each distribution of means is found by a formula that divides the estimated population variance by the number of subjects in the group representing it (thus making it smaller in proportion to the number of subjects in the group).
   d. Describe the computations and state the results.
4. Find the standard deviation of the distribution of differences between means.
   a. The variance in each distribution of means contributes to the variance in the differences between the means.
   b. The variance of the distribution of means, in fact, comes out to the sum of the variances of the two distributions of means. Its standard deviation is the square root of this result.
   c. Describe the computations and state the results.

H. The shape of the distribution of differences between means.
1. The distribution tends to be bell-shaped, with most cases falling near the middle and fewer at the extremes, due to the same basic process of extremes balancing each other out that we noted in the discussion of the standard deviation–middle values are more likely and extreme values less likely.
2. Specifically, it can be shown that it will follow a precise shape called a *t* distribution.
3. Actually there are different *t* distributions according to the amount of information that goes into estimating the variation in the distribution from the sample, which is the sum of the numbers you divide by in making the estimates (one less than the number of subjects in the first group plus one less than the number of subjects in the second group).
4. But the shape of the comparison distribution is only a precise *t* distribution if both populations of individual scores follow a precise shape called a normal curve (also bell-shaped) that is widely found in nature. Note that in the problem you are told that the distributions of the populations are normal curves so that this condition is met in your case.

III. Determine the cutoff sample score on the comparison distribution at which the null hypothesis should be rejected. (Step 3 of hypothesis testing.)
   A. Before you figure out how extreme the particular difference between the means of your two groups is on this distribution of differences between means, you want to know how extreme your difference would have to be to decide it was too unlikely that it could have been a randomly drawn mean from this comparison distribution.
   B. Since the shape of the comparison distribution follows a mathematically defined formula, you can use a table to tell you how many standard deviations from the mean your score would have to be in order to be in the top so many percent.
   C. Note that the number of standard deviations from the mean on this *t* distribution is called a *t* score. (Explaining this term makes writing simpler as you go along.)
   D. To use these tables you have to decide the kind of situation you have, and there are two considerations.

1. Are you interested in the chances of getting this extreme of a difference between means that is extreme in only one direction (such as only higher for one group than the other) or in either? (Explain which is appropriate for your study.)
2. Just how unlikely would the extremeness of a particular mean have to be? The standard figure used in psychology is less likely than 5% (though 1% is sometimes used to be especially safe). (Say which you are using in your study–if no figure is stated in the problem and no special reason given for using one or the other, the general rule is to use 5%.)

   E. State the cutoff for your particular problem.

IV. Determine the score of your sample on the comparison distribution. (Step 4 of hypothesis testing.)

   A. Find where the actual difference your two groups' means would fall on the comparison distribution, in terms of a t score.

   B. State this t score.

V. Compare the scores obtained in Steps 3 and 4 to decide whether to reject the null hypothesis. (Step 5 of hypothesis testing.)

   A. State whether your difference between means (from Step 4) does or does not exceed the cutoff (from Step 3).

   B. If your difference between means exceeds the cutoff, you write out the following.
1. You can reject the null hypothesis.
2. By elimination, the research hypothesis is thus supported.
3. Say what it means that the research hypothesis is supported. (That is, the study shows that the particular experimental manipulation *appears* to make a difference in the particular thing being measured, or that people in general of the kind represented by one of your groups are probably really different or have been changed on the thing being measured from people in general of the kind represented by your other group.)

   C. If your score does not exceed the cutoff, write out these points.
1. You can not reject the null hypothesis.
2. The experiment is inconclusive.
3. Say what it means that the study is inconclusive. (That is, the study did not yield results that give a clear indication of whether or not the particular experimental manipulation appears to make a difference in the particular thing being measured; or that it is not clear based on this study whether people in general of the kind represented by one of your groups are really different or have been changed on the thing being measured from people in general of the kind represented by your other group.)
4. Explicitly note that even though the research hypothesis was not supported in this study, this is not evidence that it is false–it is quite possibly true but the thing studied has only a small effect, not sufficient to produce a mean extreme enough to yield a significant result in this study.

Chapter Self-Tests

Multiple-Choice Questions

1. A distinguishing feature of the t test for independent means is

   a. dependent populations are treated as if they are unrelated.

   b. the difference between the means of two independent samples is evaluated.

   c. variance is not used in this procedure.

   d. the variance of the parent populations is unrelated to the variance of the samples.

2. When conducting a *t* test for independent means using a two-tailed test, the null hypothesis typically states that

a. the mean of Population 1 is the same as the mean of Population 2.
b. the mean of Population 1 is different from the mean of Population 2.
c. the variance of Population 1 is less than or the same as the variance of Population 2.
d. the variance of Population 1 is different from the variance of Population 2.

3. In a *t* test for independent means, because there are two samples we end up with two estimates of the population variance. If the sample sizes are different, the two estimates are combined by

a. directly averaging the two estimates into one number.
b. finding a weighted average.
c. pooling the raw data of each sample, then finding the variance of the new super sample.
d. finding the difference of the two estimates (that is, the estimate for Population 1 minus the estimate for Population 2), and using a special table to look up the new estimate based on that difference.

4. The distribution of differences between means has a mean of

a. the population variance divided by N.
b. the pooled mean of the sample means.
c. 0.
d. 1.

5. In estimating the population variance, a weighted average is used when

a. there are extreme scores in the sample.
b. the samples are skewed.
c. one sample is considered more representative of the population than the other.
d. the samples are not the same size.

6. The distibution of the difference between means is a _____.

a. raw score distribution
b. *z* distribution
c. *f* distribution
d. *t* distribution

7. With respect to sizes of samples, power is greatest when

a. sample size does not affect power.
b. the sample size of the experimental group is larger than the sample size of the control group.
c. the sample size of the control group is larger than the sample size of the experimental group.
d. the sample sizes are equal.

8. When conducting a *t* test for independent means, if the assumption of normality is seriously violated, you should

a. not be concerned because the *t* test for independent means is highly robust even under extreme violations of the assumptions.
b. use a procedure other than the *t* test for independent means.
c. proceed, but interpret your results with caution.
d. proceed ONLY if the population variances are not skewed.

9. In a study with 30 subjects total (divided into a control group and an experimental group), which of the following cases would be the most powerful?

a. The experimental group has 20 subjects and the control group has 10.
b. Both groups have 15 subjects.
c. The control group has 20 subjects and the experimental group has 10.
d. The control group has 29 subjects and the experimental group has 1 subject.

10. Which of the following is part of the process of computing a *t* test for independent means?

    a. Each sample's standard deviation is divided by its sample size to find the standard deviation of its population's distribution of means.

    b. The population variance, which is known, is used to find the variance of the two samples.

    c. The population variance is estimated, then that estimate is used to find the variance of each of the distributions of means.

    d. An estimate of the population mean, based on pooled sample means, is translated into a *t* score, and then compared to a *t* distribution.

Fill-In Questions

1. In a study of the effects of a particular drug on creativity, subjects were evaluated while taking part in a creative task. During the task 10 subjects were under the influence of the drug and 10 subjects were not. A *t* test for _____ would be conducted to analyze the data.

2. The *t* test for independent means is used to compare the means of two samples of scores coming from _____ group(s) of people.

3. The comparison distribution for a study that employs an independent *t* test is _____.

4. When the variances of the distribution of means for both samples are added together, the result is the variance of _____.

5. In the formula "$t = (M_1 - M_2)/S_{DIFFERENCE}$," $S_{DIFFERENCE}$ is the _____ of the distribution of differences between means.

6. & 7. The assumptions for a *t* test for independent means require that the populations are both _____ and have the same _____.

8. When the sample sizes are not equal, the best estimate of the population variance is a _____ estimate.

9. The _____ mean is used to figure power when your sample sizes are unequal.

10. A study with 15 subjects in one condition and 10 in the other, using a *t* test for independent means, yielded a *t* of 3.21, which was significant at the .01 significance level, one-tailed. Write these results in the standard format (using appropriate symbols, etc.) as they would be reported in the text of a research article. _____.

Problems and Essays

1. As a senior thesis a woman's study major examines the effects of self-defense training on self-confidence. (This is a new program and it is not clear whether it will increase self-confidence, decrease it, or make no difference.) Five of ten volunteers are randomly selected to receive self-defense training. The other five receive no special training. At the end of the training period, all subjects complete a self-confidence questionnaire.

    (a) Is there a difference in self-confidence between the two groups, according to the data below (use the .01 significance level)?

    (b) Explain your analysis to a person who has never had a course in statistics.

Self-Confidence Scores For Subjects Who Do and Do Not Receive Self-Defense Training

TRAINING	NO TRAINING
15	14
18	16
14	19
17	18
15	13

2. A social psychologist conducted a study of whether she could produce a placebo effect on intelligence. (A "placebo" is an inactive drug or a fake treatment. A "placebo effect" occurs when a subject reacts to a placebo as if it were a real drug or treatment.) She randomly divided seven subjects into two groups. All seven were given pills (known to have no true effect) to take at the start of the experiment in which they were told that they would first be given some questionnaires, including an intelligence test, for background information, and then would undergo some physiological testing to measure effects of the "vitamin" on levels of red blood cells. Three of the subjects were randomly assigned to be told that these pills would take an hour to have any effect, and if they noticed anything at all from them even then, it would be some tingling in the feet. The other four were told that this vitamin has been found to enhance alertness and mental agility during the first hour and then to have no special effect except possibly some tingling in the feet. The table below shows the scores on the intelligence test.

(a) Based on these data, is intelligence test performance increased by a placebo pill? (Use the .05 significance level.)

(b) Explain your conclusion and procedure to a person who has never had a course in statistics.

Intelligence Scores of Placebo Group and Control Group

PLACEBO	CONTROL
85	89
97	76
105	99
74	

3. Do people who are health-conscious get better grades? To address this question, a researcher first assessed the degree of health consciousness (using a questionnaire) of a group of college students. Of those, the top 15 and the bottom 15 were selected, forming the High Health-Conscious (HHC) group and the Low Health-Conscious (LHC) group, respectively. The researcher reported: "The HHC group was not found to have a significantly higher GPA than the LHC group (HHC $M=3.2$, $SD=.33$; LHC $M=3.0$, $SD=.68$; $t(28) = 1.06$)." Explain and interpret these results to a person who is not familiar with statistics.

4. An ophthalmologist psychologist is interested in whether males and females differ in their sensitivity to light. Forty males and forty females are each measured in a series of visual tasks and the results are shown in the table below. (Each is a measure of sensitivity, with higher numbers indicating greater sensitivity.) Explain and interpret these results to a person not familiar with statistics.

Means of Males and Females on Perceptual Sensitivity Measures

	Males	Females	t
Light Intensity-A	4.16	13.21	0.78
Light Intensity-B	1422.12	1238.63	4.21**
Color Contrast	107.16	94.16	1.91*
Adaptation-A	.0024	.0013	2.68**
Adaptation-B	1.81	1.93	-1.07

*$p < .05$ **$p < .01$

Using SPSS 10.0 with this Chapter

If you are using SPSS for the first time, before proceeding with the material in this section read the Appendix on Getting Started and the Basics of Using SPSS.

You can use SPSS to carry out a *t* test for independent means. You should work through the example, following the procedures step by step. Then look over the description of the general principles involved and try the procedures on your own for some of the problems listed in the Suggestions for Additional Practice. Finally, you may want to try the suggestions for using the computer to deepen your understanding.

I. Example

A. Data: Employee performance after several months on the job of seven subjects randomly assigned to a special job skills program and seven subjects randomly assigned to the standard job skills program (fictional data), from the example in the text. The scores for those receiving the special program are 6, 4, 9, 7, 7, 3 and 6. The scores for those receiving the standard program are 6, 1, 5, 3, 1, 1, and 4.

B. Follow the instructions in the SPSS Appendix for starting up SPSS.

C. Enter the data as follows.

1. Type **1** and enter. Then click on the next box on the same line and type **6** and enter. The 1 stands for the special program, and the 6 stands for the performance score of the first subject in that special program. (This system is used because SPSS assumes that all scores on the same line are for the same subject-thus, you do not lay out the column for each condition.)

2. Type the program and performance scores for the remaining subjects in the special program.

3. Type **2** and enter. Then click on the next box on the same line and type **6** and enter (the **2** is being used to stand for the standard program, the **6** is for the performance score of the first subject in the standard program.

4. Type the scores of the remaining subjects.

5. As we have done in previous chapters, to name the two variables, click on the variable view tab. In the first row of the first column type in PROGRAM under the column titled "Name". Repeat this process in the second row for the second variable using the variable name PERFORM. The screen should now appear as shown in Figure SG9-1.

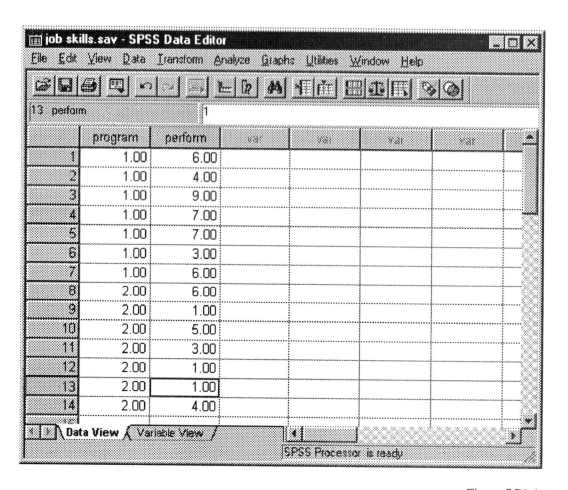

Figure SG9-1

D. Carry out the *t* test for independent means as follows:
    1. Statistics
        Compare Means >
            Independent-Samples T Test
                [Highlight PERFORM and move it into the Test Variable(s) box.
                Highlight PROGRAM and move it into the Grouping Variable box.]
                Define Groups
                    [Type in 1 for Group 1 and 2 for Group 2. Your screen should now look
                    like Figure SG9-2]
                    Continue
                    OK

The result should look like Figure SG9-3.

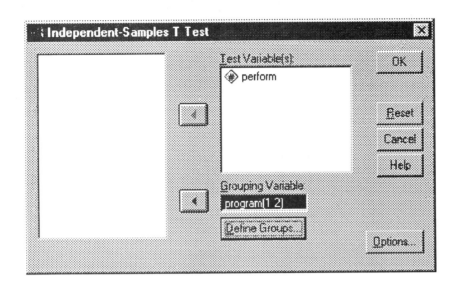

Figure SG9-2

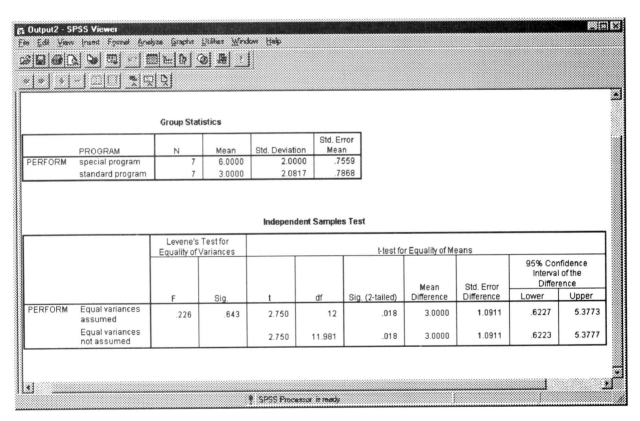

Figure SG9-3

E. Inspect the result.
　　1. The first table provides information about the two variables.
　　　　a. The first column gives the levels and names (if you provided them under the "Values" column using the "Variable View" tab) of the grouping variable (that is, **1** or **2**, corresponding to the numbers used for the special and standard programs, respectively).
　　　　b. The second, third and fourth columns give, respectively, the number of cases, mean, and estimated population standard deviation for each grouping. That is, these numbers correspond to what in the text are called N_1 and N_2; M_1 and M_2; and S_1 and S_2.
　　　　c. The fifth column, **SE of Mean**, is the standard deviation of the distribution of means, S_M for each grouping. Note that these are based on each population variance estimate and not on the pooled estimate—so they are not quite the same for each group as the square root of the S_M^2 computed in the text.
　　2. The second table provides **Levene's Test for Equality of Variances** and the *t* **test for Equality of Means.**
　　　　a. **Levene's Test for Equality of Variances** is a significance test of the null hypothesis that the *variances* of the two populations are the same. This test is important mainly as a check on whether it is reasonable to proceed with the ordinary *t* test for independent means with its assumption that the population variances are equal. If this test is significant (that is, if the **P** is less than .05), this assumption is brought into question. However, in the example, the result is clearly not significant (**.643** is well above .05) so we have no special reason to doubt the assumption of equal population variances.
　　　　b. *t* **test for Equality of Means**
　　　　　　i. The first row (the one labeled **Equal**) gives results of the ordinary *t* test for independent means that assumes equal population variances.
　　　　　　ii. Notice in the first column (of the first row) that the *t* score, degrees of freedom, and standard deviation of the distribution of differences between means (what SPSS labels as **SE of Diff**) are the same as computed in the text for this example, within rounding error.
　　　　　　iii. The column labeled **2-tail Sig** gives the probability, the exact chance, of getting a *t* score this extreme on this particular *t* distribution. In this example, the computer reports **.018**. Since the significance level was set in advance at .05, this result is clearly significant. (Note that the figure given is for a two-tailed test, which is appropriate in the example. But if you were using a one-tailed test, you would consider the result significant at the .05 level if this number were .10 or less. To put this another way, the particular result of .018 means that there is .009 of the curve higher than 2.75 and .009 lower than -2.75.)
　　　　　　iv. The last column, labeled **95% CI for Diff**, refers to what is called the "95% confidence interval." It refers to the raw scores corresponding to the *t* scores at the bottom 2.5% and the top 2.5% of the *t* distribution.
　　　　　　v. The second row of the bottom table, labeled **Unequal**, gives the results of a special *t* test that does not require the assumption of equal population variances.
F. Print out the result.
G. Save your lines of data as follows.
　　File
　　　Save Data
　　　　[Name your data file followed by the extension ".sav" and designate the drive you would like your data saved in.]
　　　　OK

II. Systematic Instructions for Computing the *t* Test for Independent Means
A. Start up SPSS.
B. Enter the data as follows, with one variable consisting of either a 1 or a 2, representing which group a subject is in, and the other variable consisting of the scores on the measured variable.

1. Type **1** and enter. Then click on the next box on the same line and type **6** and enter. The 1 stands for the special program, and the 6 stands for the performance score of the first subject in that special program. (This system is used because SPSS assumes that all scores on the same line are for the same subject-thus, you do not lay out the column for each condition.)
2. Type the program and performance scores for the remaining subjects in the special program.
3. Type **2** and enter. Then click on the next box on the same line and type **6** and enter (the **2** is being used to stand for the standard program, the **6** is for the performance score of the first subject in the standard program).
4. Type the scores of the remaining subjects.
5. As we have done in previous chapters, to name the two variables, click on the variable view tab. In the first row of the first column type in PROGRAM under the column titled "Name". Repeat this process in the second row for the second variable using the variable name PERFORM.

C. Carry out the *t* test for independent means as follows:
   1. Analyze
      Compare Means >
         Independent-Samples T Test
            [Highlight PERFORM and move it into the Test Variable(s) box.
            Highlight PROGRAM and move it into the Grouping Variable box.]
               Define Groups
                  [Type in 1 for Group 1 and 2 for Group 2]
                     Continue
                        OK
   2. Print out a copy of the result.
   3. Inspect the result, attending especially to the first line of the bottom table (the row labeled Equal), which describes the computations for an ordinary *t* test for independent means, with its assumption of equal population variances.

D. Save your lines of data as follows:
   File
      Save Data
         [Name your data file followed by the extension ".sav" and designate the drive you would like your data saved in.]
            OK

III. Additional Practice
(For each data set compute a *t* test for independent means and compare your results to those in the text).
A. Text example: Data in Table 9-1 of perceived academic competence of boys whose mothers' work does or does not involve problem solving (from Moorehouse & Sanders, 1992).
B. Practice problems in the text.
   1. Questions 4-7 from Chapter 9.

IV. Using the Computer to Deepen Your Knowledge
A. The *t* test for independent means versus the *t* test for dependent means.
   1. Use SPSS to compute a *t* test for independent means using the surgeon example from Chapter 8–you will have to retype in the data setting this up as if the Quiet and Noisy scores were from two different groups of people. Notice that the resulting *t* is considerably lower.

2. Now try to set up the *t* test computed in this chapter (the new job program example) as a *t* test for dependent means, by arbitrarily pairing the score of the first subject in the new-program group with the score of the first subject in the standard-program group, and continuing in that fashion over all the scores. (This would not even be possible if there were different numbers of subjects in the group.) Notice that the *t* is not much higher than the *t* test for independent means. (Also note the correlation.)

3. Try another *t* test for dependent means with the same job-program example, but this time pairing the subjects in the two groups differently. (Again, note the correlation.)

4. What is the principle operating here? (Hint: When two sets of scores are from the same people, they tend to be correlated.)

B. Effect of variance on the *t* test for independent means.

1. Compute the *t* test in the example again, but this time use as data for the special-program group three 5s, three 7s, and one 6. This will keep the mean the same, but will much reduce the variance of the scores.

2. Compute another *t* test, but this time use all 6s for the special-program group. This still keeps the mean of this group the same, but reduces the variance to zero.

3. Compare these results (including the original finding). What accounts for the differences?

Chapter 10
Introduction to the Analysis of Variance

Learning Objectives

By the end of this chapter you should be able to:

- Determine when it is appropriate to use an analysis of variance.
- Perform an analysis of variance and determine if it is statistically significant.
- List and perform the steps in conducting a one-way analysis of variance.
- Discuss the assumptions for the analysis of variance (and the conditions under which it is safe to violate them).
- Figure the effect size and power of a one-way analysis of variance.
- Interpret how results of studies using analysis of variance are reported in research articles.

Chapter Outline

I. **Basic Logic of the Analysis of Variance**
   A. Used in studies with three or more samples.
   B. Follows the usual steps of hypothesis testing.
   C. The null hypothesis is that the three or more populations being compared all have the same mean.
   D. Population variance can be estimated by averaging variance estimates from all samples. This is called the *within-group* estimate of the population variance.
      1. The within-group variance does not determine if the null hypothesis is true.
      2. The within-group variance focuses only on the variation inside a population therefore it does not matter how far apart the means of the different populations are.
   E. Population variance can also be estimated based on variation among means of samples. This is called a *between-group* estimate of the population variance.
      1. When the null hypothesis is true.
         a. All populations have same mean.
         b. Any variation among means of your particular samples thus can only represent variation among individual scores in the populations.
         c. Thus, variance of individual scores can be estimated from variation among samples.
      2. When the research hypothesis is true.
         a. The populations have different means.
         b. Any variation among means of your particular samples thus can represent both variation among individual scores in the populations *plus* variation between the population means.
         c. When a between-group estimate is computed in this case, it reflects both sources of variation.
   F. Decisions regarding the null and research hypotheses involve comparing the within-group and between-group estimates of the population variance.
      1. When the null hypothesis is true, the two should be about the same.
      2. When the research hypothesis is true, the between-group estimate should be larger than the within-group estimate.
      3. In terms of proportions (between-group divided by within-group), the proportion should be about 1 when the null hypothesis is true and greater than 1 when it is not.
      4. This proportion is called the *F Ratio*.
   G. The *F* distribution and the *F* table.
      1. Statisticians have developed the mathematics of an *F* distribution–the probabilities of getting *F*s of various sizes under the null hypothesis.

2. Tables are available indicating how extreme the F ratio calculated from your samples has to be in order to reject the null hypothesis at various standard significance levels.

3. You can think of F in terms of an analogy to the signal-to-noise ratio in engineering, in which the signal is like the variation among means and the noise like the variation of individual scores.

II. Analysis of Variance Procedures

A. Within-group population variance estimate.

    1. Compute population variance estimates from the data in each sample–$S^2=SS/df$.

    2. Since all populations are assumed to have equal variances, if sample sizes are equal then a straightforward averaging can combine these estimates.

    3. This is called the *within group variance* and is symbolized as S_{Within}^2.

B. Between-group population variance estimate.

    1. Estimate the variance of the distribution of means, based on the means of your particular samples. Treating each mean as a number, apply the usual formula for estimated population variance.

    2. Extrapolate from the estimated variance of the distribution of means to an estimated variance of the population of individual scores: Multiply by the size of each sample (just the opposite of the dividing you do when going from a population of individual scores to a distribution of means).

    3. This is called the *between-group variance* or *mean-squares between* and is symbolized as $S_{Between}^2$.

C. The F ratio is the between-group variance estimate divided by the within-group variance estimate.

D. The F distribution.

    1. Think of it as constructed by taking one random sample from each of several populations with the same mean, computing an F ratio, repeating this process many times, and constructing a distribution of these F ratios.

    2. In practice, there is an exact mathematical F distribution.

    3. The F distribution is not symmetrical, but is positively skewed because it is a ratio of variances (which must always be positive).

    4. Using the F table requires a numerator degrees of freedom (number of groups minus 1) and a denominator degrees of freedom (sum of degrees of freedom over all the groups–number of subjects in each group minus one).

III. Hypothesis Testing with the Analysis of Variance

A. Follows the same standard five steps we learned in the hypothesis testing process.

IV. Assumptions in the Analysis of Variance

A. Same as in t test: normal populations with equal variance.

B. Also as with the t test, the analysis of variance of the kind considered in this chapter is generally robust to moderate violations.

C. Violation of normality is a problem when there is reason to believe populations are strongly skewed in different directions or your sample size is quite small.

D. Violation of equal variances is a problem when the largest variance estimate of any group is 4 or 5 times that of the smallest.

E. If assumptions are seriously violated, use alternative procedures (covered in chapter 11).

V. Effect Size and Power for the Analysis of Variance

A. Effect size.

    1. For a completed study, estimated effect size = S_M/S_{Within}.

    2. Estimated effect size can also be computed for a published study, which provides only the F and the number of subjects in each group: *Estimated effect size* = $(\sqrt{F})/(\sqrt{n})$.

B. Power.

    1. Main determinants of power are effect size, sample size, significance level, and number of groups.

    2. Table 10.7 in the text gives approximate power for small, medium, and large effect sizes, for 3, 4, or 5 groups, all using the .05 significance level.

C. Planning sample size: Table 10.8 in the text gives the approximate number of subjects needed to achieve 80% power for estimated small, medium, and large effect sizes, for 3, 4, or 5 groups, all using the .05 significance level.

VI. Factorial Analysis of Variance

A. Used when the effect of two or more variables is examined at once.

B. Combinations of all possible groups are created.

C. Major advantage of factorial studies:

1. They allow you to study the effects of the combination of variables, or interactions.

2. An interaction is when the impact of one variable depends on the level of another variable.

3. Interaction effects cannot be determined in studies of one variable so an important result could be missing.

D. Terminology

1. Factorial research designs are analyzed using factorial analysis of variance.

2. One-way analysis of variance indicates there was one independent variable.

3. Two-way analysis of variance indicates there were two independent variables.

4. Each grouping combination is called a cell and the mean for each grouping is called a cell mean.

5. The mean for one variable alone is called a marginal mean.

E. Identifying interactions.

1. Can identify interactions by looking at cell means.

a. Draw a table with levels of one variable as columns and levels of the other variable as rows.

b. Each box represents a cell.

c. Figure the cell means for the table.

d. An interaction is present when the difference in cell means across one row is not the same as the difference in cell means across another row.

2. Can identify interactions graphically.

a. Construct a bar graph with one bar representing each cell mean.

b. Whenever there is an interaction, the patterns of bars on one section of the graph will be different from the pattern on the other section of the graph.

F. Relation of interactions and main effects.

1. Any combination of main effects and interactions can be significant.

2. When there is no interaction, the main effect has a straightforward meaning.

3. When an interaction and main effect are both statistically significant, you need to be careful about drawing conclusions. The main effect could be significant due to one level of one variable.

VII. How Analyses of Variance are Described in Research Articles

A. They are usually reported in the article text by giving the sample means (and sometimes the SDs), followed by a standard format for reporting Fs–for example, $F(3,67) = 5.21$, $p < .01$. The first number in parenthesis is the numerator degrees of freedom, the second number is the denominator degrees of freedom.

Formulas

I.   Within-group estimate of the population variance when sample sizes are equal (S_{Within}^2)

Formula in words: Average of population variance estimates computed from each sample.

Formula in symbols: $S_{\text{Within}}^2 = (S_1^2 + S_2^2 + ... + S_{\text{Last}}^2) / N_{\text{groups}}$ (10-1)

S_1^2 is the unbiased estimate of the variance of Population 1.

S_2^2 is the unbiased estimate of the variance of Population 2.

S_{Last}^2 is the unbiased estimate of the variance of the population corresponding to the last group.

Note: Each $S^2 = \Sigma(X-M)^2/df = SS/df$ refers to where you are supposed to fill in the corresponding figures for the populations between 2 and the last.

N_{Groups} is the number of groups.

II.   Variance of the distribution of means estimated from sample means ($S_M{}^2$)

Formula in words: Sum of squared deviations of each sample's mean minus the overall mean of all subjects, divided by the degrees of freedom for this estimate (the number of groups minus one).

Formula in symbols: $S_M{}^2 = \Sigma(M-GM)/df_{\text{Between}}$ (10-2)

M is the mean of each sample.

GM is the grand mean–the overall mean of all scores (also, when sample sizes are equal, the mean of the means–$GM = \Sigma M/N_G$).

df_{Between} is the degrees of freedom in the between-group estimate–the number of groups minus 1 (that is, $df_B = N_G - 1$).

III.   Between-group estimate of the population variance when sample sizes are equal ($S_{\text{Between}}{}^2$)

Formula in words: Variance of the distribution of means times the sample size.

Formulas in symbols: $S_{\text{Between}}{}^2 = (S_M{}^2)(n)$ (10-3)

n is the number of scores in each sample.

IV.   The F ratio

Formula in words: The between-group estimate of the population variance divided by the within-group estimate of the population variance.

Formulas in symbols: $F = S_{\text{Between}}{}^2/S_{\text{Within}}{}^2$ (10-4)

V.   Numerator degrees of freedom or between-groups degrees of freedom (df_{Between})

Formula in words: The number of groups minus 1.

Formula in symbols: $df_{\text{Between}} = N_{\text{Groups}} - 1$ (10-5)

VI.   Denominator degrees of freedom or within-groups degrees of freedom (df_{Within})

Formula in words: The sum of the degrees of freedom for all of the groups.

Formula in symbols: $df_{\text{Within}} = df_1 + df_2 + \ldots + df_{\text{Last}}$ (10-6)

df_1 is the degrees of freedom for the first sample.

df_2 is the degrees of freedom for the second sample.

df_{Last} is the degrees of freedom for the last sample.

Note: Each $df = N - 1$

VII.   Estimated effect size for analysis of variance (f) for a completed study when calculations are available

Formula in words: the computed estimate of the standard deviation of the distribution of means divided by the computed within-group estimate of the standard deviation of the population of individual scores.

Formula in symbols: *Estimated effect size* $= S_M / S_{within}$ (10-7)

S_M is the estimated standard deviation of the distribution of means.

S_{Within} is the within-group estimate of the standard deviation of each of the populations of individual scores.

VIII. Estimated effect size for analysis of variance for a completed study when only the *F* ratio and size of groups are available

Formula in words: The *F* ratio divided by the square root of the number of subjects in each group.

Formula in symbols: *Estimated effect size = ($\sqrt{F}$)/($\sqrt{n}$)*   (10-8)

How to Conduct a One-Way Analysis of Variance

(with Equal Sample Sizes)

(Based on Table 10-5 in the Text)

I.   Reframe the question into a research hypothesis and a null hypothesis about populations.

II.   Determine the characteristics of the comparison distribution.
   A. The comparison distribution will be an *F* distribution.
   B. The numerator degrees of freedom is the number of groups minus 1: $df_{Between} = N_{Groups} -1$.
   C. The denominator degrees of freedom is the sum of the degrees of freedom in each group (the number of scores in the group minus 1): $df_{Within} = df_1 + df_2 + \ldots + df_{Last}$.

III.   Determine the cutoff sample score on the comparison distribution at which the null hypothesis should be rejected.
   A. Determine the desired significance level.
   B. Look up the appropriate cutoff on an *F* table, using the degrees of freedom calculated above.

IV.   Determine the score of your sample on the comparison distribution. (This will be an *F* ratio.)
   A. Compute the between-groups population variance estimate ($S_{Between}^2$).
      1. Compute the means of each group.
      2. Compute a variance estimate based on the means of the groups: $S_M^2 = \Sigma(M-GM)/df_{Between}$.
      3. Convert this estimate of the variance of a distribution of means to an estimate of the variance of a population of individual scores by multiplying by the number of scores in each group: $S_{Between}^2 = (S_M^2)(n)$.
   B. Compute the within-groups population variance estimate (S_{Within}^2).
      1. Compute population variance estimates based on each group's scores: For each group, $S^2=SS/df$.
      2. Average these variance estimates: $S_{Within}^2 = (S_1^2+S_2^2+\ldots+S_{Last}^2) / N_{Groups}$.
   C. Compute the *F* ratio: $F = S_{Between}^2/S_{Within}^2$

V.   Compare the scores in III and IV to decide whether or not to reject the null hypothesis.

119

Outline for Writing Essays on the Logic and Computations for Conducting a One-Way Analysis of Variance (with Equal Sample Sizes)

The reason for your writing essay questions in the practice problems and tests is that this task develops and then demonstrates what matters so very much–your comprehension of the logic behind the computations. (It is also a place where those better at words than numbers can shine, and for those better at numbers to develop their skills at explaining in words.)

Thus, to do well, be sure to do the following in each essay: (a) give the reasoning behind each step; (b) relate each step to the specifics of the content of the particular study you are analyzing; (c) state the various formulas in nontechnical language, because as you define each term you show you understand it (although once you have defined it in nontechnical language, you can use it from then on in the essay); (d) look back and be absolutely certain that you made it clear just *why* that formula or procedure was applied and *why* it is the way it is.

The outlines below are *examples* of ways to structure your essays. There are other completely correct ways to go about it. And this is an *outline* for an answer–you are to write the answer out in paragraph form.

These essays are necessarily very long for you to write (and for others to grade). But this is the very best way to be sure you understand everything thoroughly. One short cut you may see on a test is that you may be asked to write your answer for someone who understands statistics up to the point of the new material you are studying. You can choose to take the same short cut in these practice problems (maybe writing for someone who understands right up to whatever point you yourself start being just a little unclear). But every time you write for a person who has never had statistics at all, you review the logic behind the entire course. You engrain it in your mind. Over and over. The time is never wasted. It is an excellent way to study.

I. Reframe the question into a null and a research hypothesis about populations. (Step 1 of hypothesis testing.)
A. State in ordinary language the hypothesis testing issue.
B. The interest in these groups is as representatives, or "samples," of larger groups, or "populations," of particular types of individuals (such as those exposed to various experimental manipulations).
C. Thus you construct a scenario in which the populations do not differ, then do computations based on that scenario to see how likely it is such populations would produce samples of scores whose averages are as different from each other as are the averages of the particular samples in this study.

II. Determine the characteristics of the comparison distribution. (Step 2 of hypothesis testing.)
A. Explain logic of overall approach.
1. We make and compare two estimates of the variation within these populations (which are assumed to be the same).
2. If the scenario of no difference is true, then an estimate based on the variation among the averages of the samples should give the same result as an estimate based on the average variation within each sample.
3. But if the scenario is false (and the population averages differ), then this will increase the estimate based on the differences among the averages of the samples but will not affect the estimate based on the variation within them.

4. Thus, if the scenario of no difference is true, the ratio of the two estimates (one based on differences divided by one based on variation within) should be about 1. If the scenario is false, the ratio should be greater than one.

B. Explain F distribution.

1. Statisticians have determined the probability of getting samples that produce ratios of different sizes under the conditions in which the scenario of no difference is true.
2. The probabilities depend on how many groups there are, and how many subjects within each group.

III. Determine the cutoff sample score on the comparison distribution at which the null hypothesis should be rejected. (Step 3 of hypothesis testing.)

A. Procedure: Determine significance level and look up cutoff on an F table.

B. Explanation.

1. Begin by figuring out how large this ratio of the two variation estimates would have to be in order to decide that the probability was so low that it is unlikely that the scenario of no difference could be true.
2. There are standard tables that indicate the size of these ratios associated with various low probabilities.
3. To use these tables you have to decide the kind of situation you have. There are two considerations.
   a. How many groups and how many subjects in each group. (State the numbers for your study.)
   b. Just how unlikely would a ratio have to be to decide the whole scenario on which these tables are based (the scenario of no difference) should be rejected? The standard figure used in psychology is less likely than 5% (though 1% is sometimes used to be especially safe). (Say which you are using in your study–if no figure is stated in the problem and no special reason given for using one or the other, the general rule is to use 5%.)
4. State the cutoff F ratio for your situation.

IV. Determine the score of your sample on the comparison distribution. (Step 4 of hypothesis testing.)

A. Estimate the populations' variances based on scores within the samples.

1. Procedure: Compute $S^2 = SS/df$ for each, then $S_{Within}^2 = (S_1^2 + S_2^2 + ... + S_{Last}^2) / N_{Groups}$.
2. Explanation.
   a. The variation in a sample ought to be representative of the population it comes from.
   b. State variance formula in lay terms, noting a reason for squaring–to eliminate signs that would cancel each other out.
   c. State unbiased variance formula in lay terms, noting a reason for dividing by N-1 instead of N–to adjust for the tendency of sample variance to be smaller than population variance.
   d. In doing this kind of problem, we assume that all populations have equal variation (unless we have reason to think otherwise).
   e. Thus, we can average the estimates of the variation of the populations to get a better overall estimate.

B. Estimate the variance of the distribution of means.

1. Procedure: $S_M^2 = \Sigma(M-GM)/df_{Between}$.
2. Explanation.
   a. Purpose: Intermediate step to computing the population's variation based on the variation among averages of samples.
   b. Think of a population of averages of samples taken at random from a population.
   c. The variation among the averages of these samples ought to reflect the variation among the individual scores in the population (the more variation in one, the more variation in the other).
   d. If the scenario of no difference among population averages is true, then taking one sample from each population is the same as taking the samples all from the same population.
   e. Thus, you can make an estimate of the variation in this population based on the variation among the averages of your sample.
   f. Remind the reader of the variance formula and unbiased variance formula already described.

C. Estimate the populations' variances based on variation among the averages of the samples:
   1. Procedure: $S_{Between}^2 = S_M^2 \text{ X } n$.
   2. Explanation.
      a. The variation in a distribution of averages is less than in a distribution of individual scores (note that the exact relation is in proportion to the number of scores in each sample).
      b. Thus, to estimate a population's variation based on the variation in a distribution of averages of samples taken from it, you multiply by the size of each sample.
D. Compute the ratio of the two variance estimates.
   1. Procedure: $F = S_{Between}^2 / S_{Within}^2$.
   2. Explanation and purpose: This is where you compute the crucial ratio of variation estimates for your particular samples by dividing the estimate based on variation between groups by the estimate based on the variation within.

V. **Compare the scores in Steps 3 and 4 to decide whether or not to reject the null hypothesis. (Step 5 of hypothesis testing.)**
   A. Note whether or not your F ratio exceeds the cutoff and draw the appropriate conclusion.
      1. Reject the null hypothesis: The variation among the averages of your particular samples is so great that it seems unlikely that their populations are the same. So they seem to be different and the null hypothesis seems untrue.
      2. Fail to reject the null hypothesis: The result is inconclusive. On the one hand, these results were not extreme enough to persuade you that the variation was due to the populations being different. On the other hand, it is still possible that they really are different, but because of the people who happened to be selected to be in your samples from the populations, this difference did not show up.
   B. Be sure to state your conclusion in terms of your particular measures and situation, so it is clear to a lay person just what the real bottom line of the study is.

Chapter Self-Tests

Multiple-Choice Questions

1. When conducting an analysis of variance,

   a. the null hypothesis is that the populations have the same means.
   b. the sample variances are assumed to be the same.
   c. population variances must differ by no more than 1 *SD*.
   d. preliminary *t* tests are often conducted between the different populations.

2. Which of the following is true about the within-group estimate of the population variance in analysis of variance:

   a. it is unaffected by whether or not the null hypothesis is true.
   b. it reflects the variance caused by experimental conditions.
   c. if the research hypothesis is true, it is larger than the true variance.
   d. its size is a reliable indicator of effect size.

3. When calculating an analysis of variance, if the research hypothesis is in fact true, then

   a. the F ratio will always be significant.
   b. the between-group variance estimate is likely to be bigger than the within-group variance estimate.
   c. the within-group variance estimate is likely to be bigger than the between-group estimate.
   d. small sample sizes are sufficient to detect small differences among the variance of sample means.

4. Suppose IQ was tested with children divided into three groups according to their parents' parenting styles. Within the group of children of each parenting style, the IQ scores would

   a. be equal, because within-group variance is always 0.
   b. be equal, because the IQ's of different children within a parenting style grouping are more alike than they are different.
   c. vary, due to differences among the parenting styles.
   d. vary, reflecting variation normally found within the population of children of each parenting style.

5. In a factorial analysis of variance, a main effect is

   a. the cell mean with the largest mean.
   b. the largest difference between any two cell means.
   c. a significant result for a variable.
   d. the most important variable in the study.

6. Marginal means are

   a. the means of one variable alone in a factorial analysis of variance.
   b. estimated means.
   c. means that are close to statistical significance.
   d. means figured from small sample sizes.

7. An important advantage of factorial designs is

   a. the ability to determine between groups variance estimates.
   b. being able to study interactions.
   c. the increased sample size required.
   d. the ability to determine within groups variance estimates.

8. One characteristic of the F distribution is that

   a. there is an inherent bias toward increased positive findings for an alpha level of .01.
   b. the degrees of freedom of the F ratio's numerator solely determines which F distribution is used as a comparison distribution.
   c. its range is -1 to $+\infty$.
   d. it is positively skewed (the long tail to the right).

9. For the analysis of variance, estimated effect size is determined by

   a. the degrees of freedom of the numerator of the F ratio divided by the degrees of freedom of the denominator.
   b. dividing the population standard deviation by the number of groups.
   c. dividing the difference between the means of the two groups with the most different means by the estimated population standard deviation.
   d. dividing the computed estimate of the standard deviation of the distribution of means by the computed estimate of the standard deviation within populations.

10. After conducting an analysis of variance, if a researcher wanted to present his findings for publication and he had used 8 subjects in each group, what should the "___" be in "$F(3, ___) = 4.93, p < .05$"?

    a. 8
    b. 11
    c. 28
    d. 32

Fill-In Questions

1. When conducting an analysis of variance, the null hypothesis is that population means are _____.

2. When conducting an analysis of variance, the _____-group estimate of the population variance should always be pretty accurate, regardless of whether the null hypothesis is true or not.

3. When conducting an analysis of variance if the null hypothesis is true, then the ratio of the between-group variance estimate to the within-group variance estimate should be about _____.

4. A research design with two independent variables is a _____ research design.

5. Each grouping in a factorial design is a(n) _____.

6. In a one-way analysis of variance the between-group variance is computed by first finding the estimate of the variance of the _____, then multiplying this estimate by the sample size.

7. When conducting an analysis of variance, one assumption that must be met is that the variance is the same in each _____.

8. Numerically, an interaction exists when the difference in cell means across one row _____ the difference in cell means across another row.

9. A research design in which participants are measured on more than two testings is a _____.

10. In general, when subjects are selected so that the averages of the groups come out the same on such variables as intelligence, age, etc., the power of such a design is _____ the power of a study in which the subjects are just randomly assigned to groups regardless of their scores on these variables.

Problems and Essays

1. A social psychologist interested in the effects of media violence arranged to have 15 children watch a popular children's television program that included a lot of violence. Five were randomly assigned to watch the show on a small-screen television set, five on a standard screen set, and five on a large-set. Immediately after, each child was left in a room with various toys, and the number of seconds of play (during a short observation period) with violent toys was systematically recorded.

    (a) Do the data below (which are fictional) suggest that the size of screen on which children watch a violent show makes any difference in the subsequent amount of play with violent toys? (Use the .05 significance level.)
    (b) Explain your analysis to a person who has never had a course in statistics.

    Time Playing with Violent Toys After Watching a Violent
    Program on Televisions of Different-Sized Screens

SMALL	STANDARD	LARGE
65	76	45
68	54	58
59	59	56
54	60	64
57	52	48

2. A researcher was interested in how different groups perceive psychologists. She asked college students, psychologists, lawyers, and people in the general public how important they thought psychologists were to the current United States society (1=Not important, 10=Very important).

    (a) Do the data below (which are fictional) suggest that the different groups have differing opinions? (Use the .01 significance level.)
    (b) Explain your analysis to a person who has never had a course in statistics.

    Importance of Psychologists According to College Students,
    Psychologists, Lawyers, and General Public

COLLEGE	PSYCHOLOGISTS	LAWYERS	PUBLIC
4	6	5	4
3	7	6	4
6	5	7	5

3. A health psychologist wanted to examine the relation of social support provided by people in different categories of relationship to the ability of a person to cope with a serious illness. The researcher identified 80 women, all of about the same age and suffering from the same serious illness, 20 of whom during the illness only had had contact with their husband; 20, only contact with their children; 20, only contact with a close woman friend; and 20, only contact with their parents. The (fictional) mean reported level of coping was 4.21 (S=3.0) for the husband-only group, 3.81 (S=2.0) for the children-only group, 5.29 (S=4.0) for the friend-only group, and 2.16 (S=3.0) for the parent-only group.

    (a) According to these data, is the type of relationship with the person who provides social support associated with different amounts of coping? (Use the .05 level.)
    (b) Explain your analysis to a person who has never had a course in statistics.

4. A personality psychologist hypothesized that working adults in the general population, college students, and high school students would differ in their levels of satisfaction with life. She administered a Satisfaction With Life Index to 20 subjects in each group. She reported her results as follows: "The means were 6.52 (SD = .87) for working adults, 5.47 (SD = 1.13) for college students, and 4.80 (SD = 1.87) for the high school students. The difference was significant, $F(2, 57)$ = 8.04, $p < .01$." Explain and interpret these results to a person who has never had a course in statistics.

Using SPSS 10.0 with this Chapter

If you are using SPSS for the first time, before proceeding with the material in this section read the Appendix on Getting Started and the Basics of Using SPSS.

You can use SPSS to carry out the kind of analysis of variance described in this chapter (as well as more advanced analyses of variance). But SPSS requires the raw data to conduct the analysis of variance–it is not set up to handle a problem in which you already have the means and standard deviations.

You should work through the example, following our procedures step by step. Then look over the description of the general principles involved and try the procedures on your own for some of the problems listed in the Suggestions for Additional Practice. Finally, you may want to try the suggestions for using the computer to deepen your understanding.

I. Example
   A. Data: Ratings of a defendant's guilt by subjects randomly assigned to groups that receive either information that the defendant has a criminal record, information that the defendant has a clean record, or no information about the defendant's criminal record (fictional data), from the example in the text. The ratings for those in the Criminal Record group are 10, 7, 5, 10, and 8; for those in the Clean Record group, 5, 1, 3, 7, and 4; and for those in the No Information group, 4, 6, 9, 3, and 3.
   B. Follow the instructions in the SPSS Appendix for starting up SPSS.
   C. Enter the data as follows.
      1. Type **1** and press enter. Then click on the next box on the same line and type **10** and enter. This will put the subjects two scores on the same line next to each other. The **1** stands for the Criminal Record group (which is arbitrarily labeled **1**, and the **10** is the rating of guilt given by the first subject in the Criminal Record group).
      2. Type the data in the same way for each of the remaining subjects, using **1** for those in the Criminal Record Group, **2** for those in the Clean Record Group, and **3** for those in the No Information group.
      3. As we have done in previous chapters, to name the two variables, click on the variable view tab. In the first row of the first column type in INFOTYPE under the column titled "Name". Repeat this process in the second row for the second variable using the variable name GUILT. Your screen should now look like Figure SG10-1.

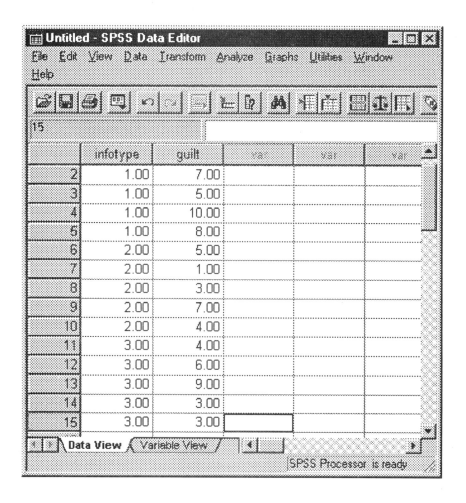

	infotype	guilt	var	var	var
2	1.00	7.00			
3	1.00	5.00			
4	1.00	10.00			
5	1.00	8.00			
6	2.00	5.00			
7	2.00	1.00			
8	2.00	3.00			
9	2.00	7.00			
10	2.00	4.00			
11	3.00	4.00			
12	3.00	6.00			
13	3.00	9.00			
14	3.00	3.00			
15	3.00	3.00			

Figure SG10-1

D. Carry out the analysis of variance.
    1. Analyze
        Compare Means >
           One-Way ANOVA
              [Highlight GUILT and move it into the Dependent List box. Highlight
              INFOTYPE and move it into the Factor box.]
                  Your screen should now look like Figure SG10-2.
                Options
                    [Check Descriptives]
                    Continue
                      OK
    2. Your results should appear as shown in Figure SG10-3. You may have to scroll your output screen
      up to the first line in order to see the section of results that match Figure SG10-3.

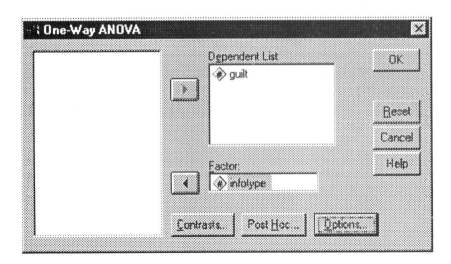

Figure SG10-2

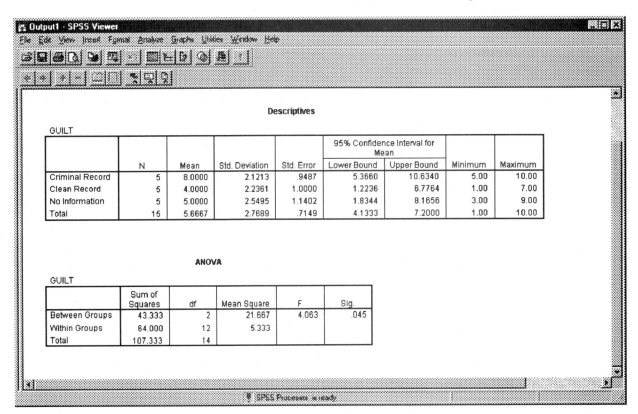

Figure SG10-3

E. Inspect this screen of results.

    1. The first table displays the descriptive statistics for each of the cells of the variables GUILT.

    2. The second table, entitled **ANOVA,** is the analysis of variance.

    3. The first column of this table lists the types of population variance estimates.

    4. The second column displays the population variance estimates calculated for these data.

5. The third column, **df**, gives the degrees of freedom. In the **Between Groups** row, this corresponds to $df_{Between}$; in the **Within Groups** row, this corresponds to df_{Within}. The figures in this example, **2** and **12**, respectively, correspond to those computed in the text.

6. The fourth column, **Mean Squares**, gives the population variance estimates ($S_{Between}$ and S_{Within}), with the between-group estimate (**21.6667**) given first and then the within-group estimate (**5.3333**). (The text, using rounded-off figures, computed 21.7 and 5.33, respectively.)

7. The next column, **F**, gives **4.063**, which corresponds closely to the 4.07 computed using rounded figures in the text.

8. Finally, the last column, **Sig.**, gives the probability–the exact chance of getting an F ratio this extreme on this particular F distribution. In this example, the probability is **.045**. Since the significance level was set in advance at .05, this result is significant.

F. Print out this screen of results by clicking on File and then Print.

G. Save your lines of data as follows.

    1. File

      Save Data

        [Name your data file followed by the extension "CH10XMPL.SAV" and designate the drive you would like your data saved in.]

        OK

II. Systematic Instructions for Computing a One-Way Analysis of Variance

A. Start up SPSS.

B. Enter the data as follows, with one variable consisting of numbers (such as 1, 2, 3, etc.) representing which group a subject is in and the other variable consisting of the scores on the measured variable.

    1. Type **1** and press enter. Then click on the next box on the same line and type **10** and enter. This will put the subjects two scores on the same line next to each other. The **1** stands for the Criminal Record group (which is arbitrarily labeled **1**, and the **10** is the rating of guilt given by the first subject in the Criminal Record group).

    2. Type the data in the same way for each of the remaining subjects, using **1** for those in the Criminal Record Group, **2** for those in the Clean Record Group, and **3** for those in the No Information group.

    3. As we have done in previous chapters, to name the two variables, click on the variable view tab. In the first row of the first column type in INFOTYPE under the column titled "Name". Repeat this process in the second row for the second variable using the variable name GUILT. Your screen should now look like Figure SG10-1.

C. Carry out the analysis of variance as follows.

    1. Analyze

      Compare Means >

        One-Way ANOVA

          [Highlight GUILT and move it into the Dependent List box. Highlight INFOTYPE and move it into the Factor box.]

            Options

              [Check Descriptives]

                Continue

                  OK

D. Save your lines of data as follows.

    1. File

      Save Data

        [Name your data file followed by the extension ".SAV" and designate the drive you would like your data saved in.]

        OK

III. Additional Practice

(For each data set, conduct an analysis of variance and compare your results to those in the text).

A. Questions 2 and 4 from Chapter 10.

IV. Using the Computer to Deepen Your Knowledge

A. Impacts on the two population variance estimates.

  1. Use SPSS to compute an analysis of variance using the criminal-record example but add 3 points to every subject in the Criminal-Record group. (This increases the differences among the means of the groups but does not change the variance within any of the groups.)

  2. Compute the analysis of variance again with the original data, except this time for the two subjects in the Criminal Record group with 10s make one of them a 0 and one a 20. (This keeps the differences among the means the same, but increases the variance dramatically in the Criminal-Record group.)

  3. Compute the analysis of variance yet again with the original data, except this time make all the subjects in the Criminal-Record group have 8s. (This keeps the differences among the means the same, but decreases the variance in the Criminal-Record group to 0.)

  4. Compare the results of these analyses, focusing on how these modifications affect the two population variance estimates.

B. Effect of outliers on analysis of variance: Compute an analysis of variance for the criminal-record example, but change one of the scores in the Criminal-Record group to a very high number, say a 40. Compare this to the original result.

Chapter 11
Chi-Square Tests and Strategies When Population Distributions Are Not Normal

Learning Objectives

By the end of this chapter you should be able to:

- Identify whether a variable is nominal or rank-ordered.
- Describe the chi-square distribution.
- Perform the steps for figuring the chi-square test of goodness of fit and the chi-square test for independence.
- Construct a contingency table.
- Discuss the assumptions for the chi-square tests (and the conditions under which it is safe to violate them).
- Figure the effect size (ϕ and Cramer's ϕ), power and needed sample size for a study using a chi-square test of independence.
- Interpret results of studies using chi-square tests that are reported in research articles.
- Recognize when assumptions for the major parametric statistical tests have been violated and understand their implications.
- Perform data transformations.
- Discuss the difference between parametric and nonparametric tests.
- Perform rank-order tests.

Chapter Outline

I. **Categorical (Nominal) Variables**
II. **Chi-Square Test for Goodness of Fit**
    A. Tests the probability that a distribution of observed frequencies in various categories could have arisen from a population with a hypothesized distribution of frequencies in these categories.
    B. The chi-square statistic reflects the degree of divergence between these observed and expected frequencies.
        1. Discrepancy in a category is observed frequency minus expected (based on the proportion of the total observed sample that would be expected to be in this category given the hypothesized population distribution).
        2. The squared discrepancy in each category is divided by the expected frequency to keep these discrepancies in proportion to the number of scores that would have been expected.
        3. The chi-square statistic is the sum, over the categories, of each squared discrepancy divided by its expected frequency.
    C. If samples are randomly taken from a population and a chi-square statistic computed on each, these chi-squares follow a mathematically defined distribution (the chi-square distribution).
        1. The distribution is skewed with the long tail to the right.
        2. The distribution's exact shape depends on the degrees of freedom.
        3. Table A-4 (in Appendix A of the text) gives the cutoff chi-squares for various significance levels and degrees of freedom.
    D. In a chi-square test for goodness of fit, the degrees of freedom are the number of categories minus 1.
    E. The steps of hypothesis testing are otherwise the same as we have been using all along.

III. Chi-Square Test for Independence
    A. Tests the probability that a sample in which people are measured on two categories could have come from a population in which the distribution of frequencies over categories on one variable is independent of the distribution of frequencies over categories on a second variable.

    B. Data are usually displayed on a contingency table, a two-dimensional breakdown in which the columns represent the categories of one variable, the rows represent the categories of the other variable, and the number in each cell is the frequency for the combination of categories that cell represents.

    C. If the two variables are independent, then the expected frequencies for a given cell is the proportion of its row's observed frequency of the total observed frequency, times the observed frequency for its column. (That is, if the two variables are independent, then the distribution of the frequencies among the cells in any particular column should be in proportion to the distribution of frequencies among the rows overall.)

    D. The chi-square statistic is computed using the observed and expected frequencies in each cell.

    E. The degrees of freedom for a chi-square test for independence are the number of rows minus 1 times the number of columns minus 1. (This is the number of cells whose frequency-data are needed in order to fill in all the other cell's frequency-data, assuming the column and row frequencies are known.)

    F. The steps of hypothesis testing are otherwise the same as we have been using all along.

IV. Assumption for Chi-Square Tests
    A. Chi-square tests are not limited by the kinds of assumptions required for the t test and analysis of variance.

    B. They do require that each observed case be independent of all other cases.

V. Effect Size and Power for Chi-Square Tests for Independence
    A. Estimated effect size for a test of a 2 X 2 contingency table is the phi coefficient, or (ϕ).
        1. $\phi = \sqrt{(X^2/N)}$.
        2. ϕ has the same range, meaning, and conventions for small, medium, and large effect sizes as the correlation coefficient (r), but is always positive.

    B. Estimated effect size for a test of a contingency table larger than 2 X 2 (Cramer's ϕ).
        1. Cramer's $\phi = \sqrt{[X^2/(N)(df_{Smaller})]}$, where $df_{Smaller}$ is the degrees of freedom corresponding to the smaller dimension of the contingency table.
        2. Cramer's ϕ is interpreted approximately as a correlation coefficient, but the corresponding conventions for small, medium, and large effect sizes depend on the value of $df_{Smaller}$ (see Table 11-7 in the text).

    C. Power:
        1. Main determinants of power are effect size, sample size, and degrees of freedom.
        2. Table 11-8 in the text gives approximate power for various sample sizes using the .05 significance level for small, medium, or large effect sizes, over 1 through 4 degrees of freedom.

    D. Planning sample size: Table 11-9 in the text gives the approximate number of subjects needed to achieve 80% power for estimated small, medium, and large effect sizes for 1 through 4 degrees of freedom using the .05 significance level.

VI. Chi-Square Tests as Reported in Research Articles
    A. All observed frequencies are usually reported.
    B. Chi-square test results follow a standard format--for example, "$X^2(2, N=531) = 28.35, p < .001$."

VII. Assumptions in the Standard Hypothesis-Testing Procedures
    A. Most require meeting two assumptions.
        1. Populations have normal distributions.
        2. Populations have equal variances.
    B. Recognizing violations of assumptions.
        1. Difficult to do with only sample data.
        2. Extreme skewness, kurtosis, or outliers of samples suggest population distribution is not normal.

VIII. Data Transformations
    A. Application of some regular mathematical procedure to each score (such as taking the square root of each).
    B. Done to make scores in the sample follow normal distribution in the hope that they will then represent a population that is normally distributed.
    C. Justified when underlying meaning of intervals between scores is arbitrary.
    D. Major types of transformations:
        1. Square root.
        2. Log.
        3. Inverse.
    E. Transformations do not change order of scores.
    F. Carried out by trial and error until a transformation creates a distribution in the sample that appears normal.
    G. After the transformation, the ordinary parametric test is applied.

IX. Rank-Order Methods
    A. Involve converting scores to ranks.
    B. Distribution free and nonparametric.
    C. Rank-order tests are available that correspond to each major parametric method (see Table 11-13 in text).
    D. Rank-order tests operate based on a known distribution of any set of ranks (rectangular) and involve precise computations of probability of getting a pattern of ranks as extreme as that observed in the study.
    E. Recently, some statisticians have recommended applying ordinary parametric tests after making a rank-order transformation.

X. Comparison of Methods
    A. Data transformation.
        1. Advantage is that it permits the use of familiar and sophisticated parametric techniques.
        2. Disadvantages.
           a. No transformation may work to make the data meet assumptions.
           b. May distort meaning of scores.
    B. Rank-order tests.
        1. Advantages.
           a. Can always be applied.
           b. Particularly suitable for rank-order data.
           c. Underlying logic is very simple and direct.
        2. Disadvantages.

a. Less commonly understood than standard parametric methods.

b. In many complex situations no standard rank-order methods have been developed.

c. May distort meaning of scores.

3. In the past, ease of computation by hand was an advantage.

XI. Procedures Used When Populations Appear Nonnormal, as Described in Research Articles

A. Data transformations are typically described at the start of the Results section, with a description of the distribution of the data that were transformed.

B. Rank-order tests are described in the same way as other tests, often giving a Z statistic (for the normal approximation of the distribution of the underlying rank-order statistic).

Formulas

I. Chi-square statistic (X^2)

Formula in words: Sum, over all the categories or cells, of the squared difference between observed and expected frequencies divided by the expected frequency.

Formula in symbols:
$$X^2 = \Sigma \; \frac{(O-E)^2}{E} \tag{11-1}$$

O is the observed frequency for a category or cell.

E is the expected frequency for a category or cell.

II. Expected frequency of a cell in a contingency table (E)

Formula in words: The proportion that a cell's row's observed frequency is of the total observed frequency, times the observed frequency for its column.

Formulas in symbols: $E = (R/N)(C)$ $\tag{11-2}$

R is the number of cases observed in this cell's row.

N is the number of cases total.

C is the number of cases observed in this cell's column.

III. Degrees of freedom (df) for a chi-square test for independence

Formula in words: The number of columns minus one, times the number of rows minus one.

Formulas in symbols: $df = (N_{Columns}-1)(N_{Rows}-1)$ $\tag{11-3}$

$N_{Columns}$ is the number of columns.

N_{Rows} is the number of rows.

IV. Estimated effect size for a test of a 2 X 2 contingency table (ϕ).

Formula in words: Square root of result of dividing the computed chi-square statistic by the number of cases in the sample.

Formula in symbols: $\phi = \sqrt{(X^2/N)}$ $\tag{11-4}$

V. Estimated effect size for a test of a contingency table larger than 2 X 2 (Cramer's ϕ).

Formula in words: Square root of result of dividing the computed chi-square statistic by the product of the number of cases in the sample times the degrees of freedom in the smaller dimension of the contingency table.

Formula in symbols: Cramer's $\phi = \sqrt{[X^2 / (N)(df_{Smaller})]}$ (11-5)

$df_{Smaller}$ is the degrees of freedom corresponding to the smaller dimension of the contingency table.

How to Conduct a Chi-Square Test for Goodness of Fit

I.   Reframe the question into a research hypothesis and a null hypothesis about populations.
   A. Populations.
      1. Population 1 are people like those in the study.
      2. Population 2 are people who have the hypothesized distribution over categories.
   B. Hypotheses.
      1. Research: Two populations have different distributions of cases over categories.
      2. Null: Two populations have the same distributions of cases over categories.

II. Determine the characteristics of the comparison distribution.
   A. The comparison distribution will be a chi-square distribution.
   B. Its degrees of freedom are the number of categories minus 1.

III. Determine the cutoff sample score on the comparison distribution at which the null hypothesis should be rejected.
   A. Determine the desired significance level.
   B. Look up the appropriate cutoff on a chi-square table, using the degrees of freedom calculated above.

IV. Determine the score of your sample on the comparison distribution. (This will be a chi-square statistic.)
   A. Determine the actual, observed frequencies in each category.
   B. Determine the expected frequencies in each category (multiply the proportion this category is expected to have times the total number of cases in the sample).
   C. In each category compute observed minus expected and square this difference.
   D. Divide each squared difference by the expected frequency for its category.
   E. Add up the results of Step D over the different categories.

V.   Compare the scores in III and IV to decide whether or not to reject the null hypothesis.

How to Conduct a Chi-Square Test for Independence

I.   Reframe the question into a research hypothesis and a null hypothesis about populations.
   A. Populations.
      1. Population 1 are people like those in the study.
      2. Population 2 are people whose distribution of cases over categories on the first variable is independent of the distribution of cases over categories for the second variable.

135

B. Hypotheses.
    1. Research: Two populations are different.
    2. Null: Two populations are the same.

II. **Determine the characteristics of the comparison distribution.**
    A. The comparison distribution will be a chi-square distribution.
    B. Its degrees of freedom are the number of rows (the number of categories in one of the variables) minus 1 times the number of columns (the number of categories in the other variable) minus 1.

III. **Determine the cutoff sample score on the comparison distribution at which the null hypothesis should be rejected.**
    A. Determine the desired significance level.
    B. Look up the appropriate cutoff on a chi-square table, using the degrees of freedom calculated above.

IV. **Determine the score of your sample on the comparison distribution. (This will be a chi-square statistic.)**
    A. Set up a two-dimensional contingency table, placing the observed frequencies in each cell.
    B. Determine the expected frequencies in each cell.
        1. Find the marginal totals for each column and row.
        2. Find the overall total.
        3. For each cell multiply the proportion of cases its row represents of the total (the row total divided by the overall total) times the number of cases in its column.
    C. For each cell compute observed minus expected and square this difference.
    D. Divide each squared difference by the expected frequency for its cell.
    E. Add up the results of Step D over all the cells.

V. **Compare the scores in III and IV to decide whether or not to reject the null hypothesis.**

How to Conduct Hypothesis Tests When Populations Appear Nonnormal

I. **Examine data to see if the distributions suggest a nonnormal population distribution, then decide which method to use.**
    A. If data transformation does not distort the underlying meaning of the data and there is a transformation that makes the data meet the assumptions, this method is appropriate.
    B. If the data are rank-order scores or most reasonably considered as ranks, and if a rank-order test is available, this method is particularly appropriate.

II. **Carry out one of the following methods:**
    A. Data transformation.
        1. Examine the sample data to estimate the kind and degree of nonnormal shape of the population distribution.
        2. Apply the transformation that seems to offer the best correction.
          a. Square root for a moderately skewed distribution.
          b. Log for a highly skewed distribution.
          c. Inverse for a very highly skewed distribution.
        3. Examine the transformed sample distribution; if it still clearly suggests a nonnormal population distribution, try a different transformation.

4. Once an appropriate distribution has been created, carry out a standard parametric hypothesis test using the transformed scores.

B. Rank-order test.

1. Transform all scores to ranks, ignoring which group the subject is in (however, if computing a correlation, rank each variable's scores separately), giving average ranks for ties.

2. Carry out the hypothesis test in one of these ways.

a. Use one of the standard nonparametric tests (for which you have not learned the procedures in this text).

b. Carry out a standard parametric hypothesis test using the ranks instead of scores.

Outline for Writing Essays on the Logic and Computations for Conducting Chi-Square Tests

The reason for your writing essay questions in the practice problems and tests is that this task develops and then demonstrates what matters so very much--your comprehension of the logic behind the computations. (It is also a place where those better at words than numbers can shine, and for those better at numbers to develop their skills at explaining in words.)

Thus, to do well, be sure to do the following in each essay: (a) give the reasoning behind each step; (b) relate each step to the specifics of the content of the particular study you are analyzing; (c) state the various formulas in nontechnical language, because as you define each term you show you understand it (although once you have defined it in nontechnical language, you can use it from then on in the essay); (d) look back and be absolutely certain that you made it clear just *why* that formula or procedure was applied and *why* it is the way it is.

The outlines below are *examples* of ways to structure your essays. There are other completely correct ways to go about it. And this is an *outline* for an answer--you are to write the answer out in paragraph form.

These essays are necessarily very long for you to write (and for others to grade). But this is the very best way to be sure you understand everything thoroughly. One short cut you may see on a test is that you may be asked to write your answer for someone who understands statistics up to the point of the new material you are studying. You can choose to take the same short cut in these practice problems (maybe writing for someone who understands right up to whatever point you yourself start being just a little unclear). But every time you write for a person who has never had statistics at all, you review the logic behind the entire course. You engrain it in your mind. Over and over. The time is never wasted. It is an excellent way to study.

Chi-Square

I. Reframe the question into a null and a research hypothesis about populations.

A. Introduce the situation.
   1. State the given (observed) distribution of cases over categories.
   2. State the expected proportional distribution of cases over categories.
   3. Note that there is a discrepancy.

B. State in ordinary language the hypothesis testing issue.
   1. Is this discrepancy so large that we can reject the hypothesis that our observed cases (our sample) represent a world in which the distribution is true generally (that is, in the population).
   2. Thus, you construct a scenario (the null hypothesis) in which the observed distribution is a random sample from a population like that which is expected and see how likely it is under this scenario that just by chance you could have obtained a sample with a discrepancy as large as you actually have.

II. Determine the characteristics of the comparison distribution.

A. This step involves figuring out the probabilities of getting different degrees of discrepancy by chance (assuming the null hypothesis is true).

B. The distribution of chance discrepancies (assuming the null hypothesis is true) for a particular way of measuring discrepancy (called chi-square) is called a chi-square distribution.

C. The chi-square distribution is mathematically defined and depends only on the number of categories involved (technically, on the number of categories minus 1).

III. Determine the cutoff sample score on the comparison distribution at which the null hypothesis should be rejected.

A. In this step one figures out how large an actual discrepancy would have to be in order to decide that the probability of getting such a discrepancy under the null hypothesis is so low that this whole scenario of the null hypothesis being true could be confidently rejected.

B. There are standard tables that indicate the size of these discrepancies associated with various low probabilities.

C. Just how unlikely would a discrepancy have to be to decide the whole scenario on which these tables are based (the scenario of no difference) should be rejected? The standard figure used in psychology is less likely than 5% (though 1% is sometimes used to be especially safe). (Say which you are using in your study--if no figure is stated in the problem and no special reason given for using one or the other, the general rule is to use 5%.)

D. Once this decision is made, the cutoff level of discrepancy can be determined from the table. (State the level for your situation.)

IV. Determine the score of your sample on the comparison distribution.

A. Compute the degree of discrepancy for your actual situation.

B. This requires computing a number called a chi-square, which reflects the degree of divergence between observed and expected frequencies over the categories. It is computed in four steps (which you should describe for your example).
   1. For each category find the discrepancy between observed and expected in terms of actual scores. (That is, for the expected, multiply the proportion expected times the number of cases in your sample.)

2. Square this discrepancy. (This eliminates the problem of some discrepancies being positive and some negative.)
3. Divide the squared discrepancy in each category by the expected frequency. (This keeps these discrepancies in proportion to the number of cases that would have been expected.)
4. The chi-square statistic is the sum, over the categories, of each squared discrepancy divided by its expected frequency.

V. Compare the scores in Steps III and IV to decide whether or not to reject the null hypothesis.

A. Note whether or not your chi-square exceeds the cutoff and draw the appropriate conclusion. Either:

1. Reject the null hypothesis: The distributions of cases over categories is so discrepant from what you would expect if your sample represents a population with a distribution like that hypothesized that you reject this scenario.
2. Fail to reject the null hypothesis: The result is inconclusive. On the one hand, these results were not extreme enough to persuade you that the discrepancy was due to chance. On the other hand, it is still possible that your sample really does represent a population whose proportional distribution over categories is different from what was expected, but because of the people who happened to be selected to be in your samples from the population, this discrepancy did not show up strongly enough.

B. Be sure to state your conclusion in terms of your particular measures and situation, so it is clear to a lay person just what the real bottom line of the study is.

Chi-Square Test for Independence

I. Reframe the question into a research hypothesis and a null hypothesis about populations.

A. Introduce the situation.

1. Make (if it is not given) a contingency table of the observed data and describe it.
2. Explain the notion of independence: That the distribution of cases over categories on one variable is unrelated to the distribution of cases over categories on the other variable.
3. Compute the expected frequencies for the cells in your contingency table under the assumption of independence. (The number in each cell should be the proportion of cases in its column that its row is a proportion of the total.)
4. Note the discrepancy between observed and expected.

B. State in ordinary language the hypothesis-testing issue.

1. The hypothesis-testing question is whether this discrepancy is so large that we can reject the hypothesis that our observed cases (our sample) represents a world in which the expected distribution of independence is generally true (that is, in the population).
2. Thus, you construct a scenario (the null hypothesis) in which the observed distribution is a random sample from a population in which the distributions of cases over categories are independent and see how likely it is that you could have gotten a discrepancy as large as you actually have under this scenario just by chance.

II. Determine the characteristics of the comparison distribution.

A. This step involves figuring out the probabilities of getting different degrees of discrepancy by chance under the null hypothesis.

B. The distribution of chance discrepancies under the null hypothesis for a particular way of measuring discrepancy (called chi-square) is called a chi-square distribution.

C. The chi-square distribution is mathematically defined and depends only on the number of expected cell frequencies that are free to take on any possible value once the overall numbers in each row and column are set. (This is figured out by multiplying the number of rows minus 1 times the number of columns minus 1.)

III. Determine the cutoff sample score on the comparison distribution at which the null hypothesis should be rejected.

A. In this step one figures out how large an actual discrepancy would have to be in order to decide that the probability of getting such a discrepancy under the null hypothesis is so low that this whole scenario of the null hypothesis being true could be confidently rejected.

B. There are standard tables that indicate the size of these discrepancies associated with various low probabilities.

C. Just how unlikely would a discrepancy have to be to decide the whole scenario on which these tables are based (the scenario of no difference) should be rejected? The standard figure used in psychology is less likely than 5% (though 1% is sometimes used to be especially safe). (Say which you are using in your study—if no figure is stated in the problem and no special reason given for using one or the other, the general rule is to use 5%.)

D. Once this decision is made, the cut-off level of discrepancy can be determined from the table. (State the level for your situation.)

IV. Determine the score of your sample on the comparison distribution.

A. Compute the degree of discrepancy for your actual situation.

B. This requires computing a number called a chi-square, which reflects the degree of divergence between observed and expected frequencies over the categories. It is computed in four steps (describe these steps in terms of your example).

1. For each cell find the discrepancy between the number observed and expected.
2. Square this discrepancy (this eliminates the problem of some discrepancies being positive and some negative).
3. Divide the discrepancy in each cell by the expected frequency. (This keeps these discrepancies in proportion to the number of cases that would have been expected.)
4. The chi-square statistic is the sum, over the categories, of each squared discrepancy divided by its expected frequency.

V. Compare the scores in Steps III and IV to decide whether or not to reject the null hypothesis.

A. Note whether or not your chi-square exceeds the cutoff and draw the appropriate conclusion. Either:

1. Reject the null hypothesis: The distributions of cases over categories in the two variables is so discrepant from what you would expect if your sample represents a population in which the distributions over the two variables are unrelated to each other that you reject this scenario.
2. Fail to reject the null hypothesis: The result is inconclusive. On the one hand, these results were not extreme enough to persuade you that the discrepancy from the two variables being unrelated was due to chance. On the other hand, it is still possible that your sample really does represent a population in which the variables are related, but because of the people who happened to be selected to be in your samples from the population, this discrepancy did not show up strongly enough.

B. Be sure to state your conclusion in terms of your particular measures and situation, so it is clear to a lay person just what the real bottom line of the study is.

VI. Compute effect size and evaluate any nonsignificant results in terms of power.

A. The degree of association between the distributions of cases over categories for the two variables can be indexed by a number that ranges from 0 (no association) to 1 (perfect association).

B. This number is the square root of the result of dividing the computed chi-square by the number of cases (or if greater than a 2 X 2 table, the division is by the number of cases times one less than the number of rows or columns in the smaller side of the table).

C. Give the result for your study and compare it to Cohen's conventions for small, medium and large effect sizes, discussing it as an indication of the degree of association in relation to what is typical in psychology research.

D. If you get a nonsignificant result, compute power (using the table).

1. Explain concept of power as probability of deciding that the population distributions are not independent on the basis of a study with this many subjects, given that there is a true association of a given size in the population.

2. Compute power twice, once for a small and once for a large effect size in the population and discuss implications for the likelihood of there actually being an effect of a small and large size in the population.

Outline for Writing Essays on the Logic and Computations for Conducting Hypothesis Tests When Populations Appear Nonnormal

I. **Explain that ordinarily one could use a standard statistical procedure to resolve the issue (test the hypothesis raised by the essay question).**
   A. Name the procedure that would be appropriate (such as a *t* test or analysis of variance).
   B. However, explain that these standard procedures require certain conditions be met to use them.
   C. One of these conditions is that the distribution of scores in the larger groups (populations) that your data are supposed to represent must follow a bell-shaped pattern known as a normal curve.
   D. However, in the data at hand, the scores do not seem to come from populations distributed in the shape of a normal curve. (Explain what leads you to this conclusion.)
   E. Thus, one of several alternatives have to be used.

II. **If data transformation is selected, explain it.**
   A. The purpose is to make data more likely to be representative of a normally distributed population.
   B. Data transformation is acceptable when the underlying meaning of the intervals between scores are arbitrary and the transformation does not change the order of the scores.
   C. Deciding which transformation to use depends on which will make the sample data most closely follow a normal curve; summarize the trial-and-error process you carried out in working the problem.
   D. Once the data are transformed, one can carry out the normal hypothesis test.
   E. Describe the logic and computations in the steps of the appropriate hypothesis-testing procedure you apply.

III. **If a rank-order method is selected, explain it.**
   A. This method is used in three situations.
      1. The data suggest a nonnormal population and transforming to ranks creates a situation with a known distribution. This is acceptable when the underlying meaning of the values of the variable are arbitrary.
      2. The meaning of the intervals between values of the variables is inconsistent; converting to ranks, while reducing the amount of information, leaves only that information that one can be confident is accurate.
      3. The data are in the form of ranks to begin with and standard methods assume equal interval measurement.
   B. Describe transformation into ranks, noting how any ties are handled.
   C. Explain that you will then carry out a normal hypothesis test using the ranked data.
   D. Describe the logic and computations in the steps of the appropriate hypothesis- testing procedure you apply.
   E. Note that statisticians have found that although ranks do not have a normal distribution, using the standard statistical procedures (parametric tests) with ranked data gives approximately accurate results.

Chapter Self-Tests

Multiple-Choice Questions

1. A variable such as a person's nationality is usually considered to be
   a. rank-order.
   b. quantitative.
   c. nominal.
   d. fractional.

2. The chi-square statistic is the sum, over all categories or cells, of the following calculation made within each category or cell:
   a. the difference between the squared expected frequency and the squared observed frequency.
   b. the product of the expected frequency times the total number of cases observed in all categories or cells.
   c. the squared difference between the observed and expected frequency, divided by the expected frequency.
   d. the difference between observed and expected frequencies, divided by the expected frequency.

3. In a chi-square test for goodness of fit, the research hypothesis is that
   a. the population distribution of means fits the expected distribution of means.
   b. the population distribution of means is different between the two populations.
   c. the distribution of cases over categories differs between Population 1 and Population 2.
   d. the distribution of cases over categories is the same for Population 1 and Population 2.

4. "Independence" in the chi-square test for independence refers to a situation in which
   a. knowing a score's category on one variable gives no information about its category on the other variable.
   b. observed frequencies equal twice the expected frequencies.
   c. the independent variable is truly causal and not merely predictive.
   d. if any relation exists between the two variables, either could be the cause of the other, but there are no third variables that might explain this relation.

5. The shape of the chi-square distribution is
   a. normal.
   b. rectangular.
   c. skewed to the left.
   d. skewed to the right.

6. The situation of no relation between variables in a contingency table is called
   a. covariation.
   b. correlation.
   c. independence.
   d. dependence.

7. ϕ is identical to a
   a. percentile rank.
   b. proportion.
   c. z-score.
   d. correlation coefficient.

8. A square-root transformation is often used when the data are

   a. bimodally skewed.
   b. positively skewed.
   c. negatively skewed.
   d. normally distributed.

9. Data transformations are justified by all of the following arguments, EXCEPT

   a. the transformed data might better represent a population that is normally distributed.
   b. if there is not an inherent meaning in a score's number (as in the case of most psychological scales), transformations give a reflection of reality that is at least as accurate as the original picture.
   c. transformation makes the hypothesis-testing procedure more stringent by increasing sample sizes.
   d. after transformations, scores that were higher are still higher (that is the order of the scores is unchanged).

10. "Non-parametric tests" use data that

   a. are transformed using antilogs.
   b. do not require estimating population parameters.
   c. are transformed using logs.
   d. are normally distributed.

Fill-In Questions

1. _____ invented the chi-square test.

2. You have taken a random sample of people at your college and asked each which of three fast-food chains he or she prefers. There is a tendency for one chain to be picked more often. To examine whether this preference would be likely to hold in the general population that this sample represents, you would conduct _____.

3. The formula for computing chi-square is $\Sigma[(O\text{-}E)^2/$ _____].

4. In the chi-square test for goodness of fit, the degrees of freedom are _____.

5. If there is no relationship between the variables in a contingency table, they are said to be _____ of each other.

6. In a chi-square test for independence, the expected frequency of a particular cell equals the percent of total observed cases in the cell's _____ times the number of observed cases in the cell's column.

7. Because the chi-square test does not require that the parent populations be _____, it is called a "nonparametric" or "distribution-free" test.

8. Data transformations are used when the distribution of the population is thought to be _____.

9. A single score that has a big effect on the mean of a group and therefore likely to distort significance tests comparing that group to other groups is called a(n) _____.

10. Because there is no need to estimate population values, rank-order tests are called _____.

Problems and Essays

1. An industrial psychologist working for a particular manufacturing company was concerned that one of their four plants might have consistently more worker grievances than the others. Records are kept for a month, during which Plant A had 15 grievances; Plant B, 34; Plant C, 17; and Plant D, 18.

   (a) Do these data (which are fictional) suggest that the four plants are different in how many grievances arise? (Use the .05 significance level.)
   (b) Explain your analysis to a person who has never had a course in statistics.

2. A survey is conducted of the weight of newborns (recorded as below average, average, and above average) and depression of mothers during pregnancy (rated as severe, mild, or not depressed).

   (a) Do the data (which are fictional) in the following table suggest birthweight is related to mother's depression during pregnancy? (Use the .05 significance level.)
   (b) Compute the effect size and indicate whether it is large, medium, or small.
   (c) Explain your analyses to a person who has never had a course in statistics.

   Level of Mother's Depression During Pregnancy

Birthweight	Severe	Mild	Not Depressed
below average	8	5	1
average	3	8	12
above average	9	7	7

3. In a study of the effect on attraction of expecting to be liked, ten subjects were randomly assigned to meet a stranger under conditions in which they did or did not expect the stranger to like them. This was followed by a short interaction after which the subjects indicated how attracted they were to the person as a friend. Here are the scores:

   Did not expect to be liked: 77, 83, 88, 91, 98
   Did expect to be liked: 46, 57, 58, 66, 99
   (a) Conduct a t test for independent means using the raw scores (use the .05 level, two-tailed).
   (b) Conduct another t test using square-root transformed scores.
   (c) Discuss the reasons for using the transformation and the implications of the difference in results of these two methods.

4. Do adults who changed elementary schools over five times in their childhood have a different number of "good friends" than those who only attended one school? A small sample was drawn, and the frequent movers had 3, 1, 9, 13, and 6 good friends, while those who had not moved had 1, 4, 5, 2, and 1 good friend.

   (a) Conduct the appropriate standard parametric hypothesis-testing procedure, but using ranks. (Use the .05 significance level.)
   (b) Explain your analysis to a person who has never had a course in statistics.

Using SPSS 10.0 with this Chapter

If you are using SPSS for the first time, before proceeding with the material in this section read the Appendix on Getting Started and the Basics of Using SPSS.

You can use SPSS to carry out a chi-square test for independence. You should work through the example, following the procedures step by step.

I. **Example**

A. Data: A survey was conducted in which 25 people were asked about their religious and political party affiliations. The results for 25 subjects are as follows (with Religion being the first score listed and Political Party being the second score listed):

1, 1
0, 0
0, 1
0, 1
1, 1
1, 1
1, 0
0, 0
1, 1
1, 0
1, 0
1, 0
1, 0
1, 0
1, 0
1, 1
0, 0
0, 0
1, 0
0, 0
0, 1
0, 1
0, 1
1, 0
1, 0

B. Follow the instructions in the SPSS Appendix for starting up SPSS.

C. Enter the data as follows.

1. Type 1, the score for Religion for the first subject, and press Enter.
2. Type 0, the score for Religion for the second subject, and press Enter.
3. Type the remaining scores for this variable, one per line.
4. In the first space in the second column, type 1, the score for Political Party for the first subject.
5. Type 0, the score for Political Party for the second subject.
6. Type the remaining scores for this variable, one per line.
7. As we have done in previous chapters, to name the two variables, click on the variable view tab. In the first row of the first column type in RELIGION under the column titled "Name". Repeat this process in the second row for the second variable using the variable name POLPAR. Your screen should now appear like Figure SG11-1.

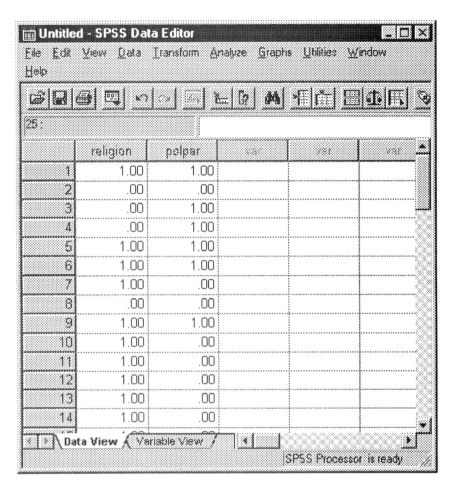

Figure SG11-1

D. Compute the chi-square test as follows:

    Analyze

        Descriptive Statistics >

            Crosstabs

                [Highlight RELIGION and bring it into the Row(s) box. Highlight POLPAR and bring it into the Column(s) box.]

                [Expected Range: check Get from Data]

                    Statistics

                    [Check Chi-Square]

                    Continue

                    OK

The results should appear as shown in Figure SG11-2 below.

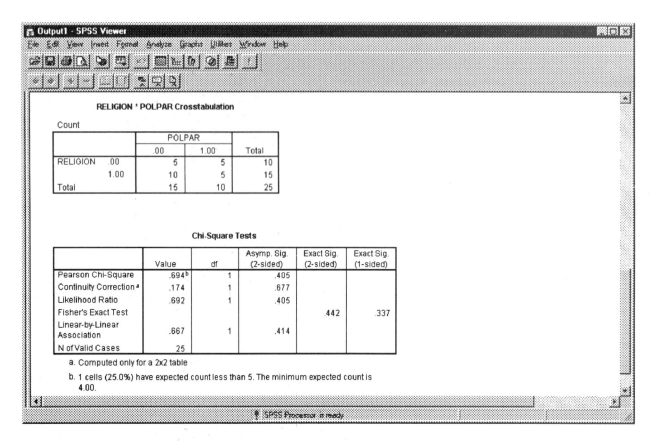

RELIGION * POLPAR Crosstabulation

Count

		POLPAR		
		.00	1.00	Total
RELIGION	.00	5	5	10
	1.00	10	5	15
Total		15	10	25

Chi-Square Tests

	Value	df	Asymp. Sig. (2-sided)	Exact Sig. (2-sided)	Exact Sig. (1-sided)
Pearson Chi-Square	.694[b]	1	.405		
Continuity Correction[a]	.174	1	.677		
Likelihood Ratio	.692	1	.405		
Fisher's Exact Test				.442	.337
Linear-by-Linear Association	.667	1	.414		
N of Valid Cases	25				

a. Computed only for a 2x2 table

b. 1 cells (25.0%) have expected count less than 5. The minimum expected count is 4.00.

Figure SG11-2

1. Print out this screen of results by going to File and then Print.
    a. The second table labeled **Chi-Square Tests**, provides several statistics. The only one you need attend to is labeled **Pearson Chi-Square** (this is the ordinary chi-square test). The **Value** of the chi square statistic is **.694** and the **df** (degrees of freedom) is **1**. The **Asymp. Sig.** refers to the probability of getting a chi-square this extreme. A probability of **.405** is clearly not sufficient enough to reject the null hypothesis of independence at the .05 level.
2. Print out this screen of results by going to File and then Print.

E. Save your lines of data follows.
    File
    Save Data
        [Name your data file followed by the extension ".sav" and designate the drive you would like your data saved in.]
        OK

II. Systematic Instructions for Computing a Chi-Square Test of Independence

A. Start up SPSS.

B. Enter the data as follows.
    1. Type 0, the score for Religion for the first subject, and press Enter.
    2. Type 1, the score for Religion for the second subject, and press Enter.
    3. Type the remaining scores for this variable, one per line.
    4. In the first space in the second column, type 1, the score for Political Party for the first subject.
    5. Type 1, the score for Political Party for the second subject.
    6. Type the remaining scores for this variable, one per line.

7. As we have done in previous chapters, to name the two variables, click on the variable view tab. In the first row of the first column type in RELIGION under the column titled "Name". Repeat this process in the second row for the second variable using the variable name POLPAR.

C. Compute the chi-square test as follows:

Analyze
    Descriptive Statistics >
        Crosstabs
            [Highlight RELIGION and bring it into the Row(s) box. Highlight POLPAR and bring it into the Column(s) box.]
               [Expected Range: check Get from Data]
                Statistics
                 [Check Chi-Square]
                 Continue
                   OK

D. Interpret the results.
1. The contingency table (check it for accuracy).
2. The chi-square statistic, its degrees of freedom, and its probability (all listed in the row for **Pearson**).

E. Save your lines of data as follows.

File
    Save Data
        [Name your data file followed by the extension ".sav" and designate the drive you would like your data saved in.]
           OK

Using SPSS to Carry Out Data Transformations

I. Example

A. Data: Number of books read in the past year by four children who are not, and four children who are, highly sensitive. These are fictional data from a text example. For the children who are not highly sensitive, the numbers of books read are 0,3,10, and 22; for the highly sensitive children, 17, 36, 45, and 75.

B. Follow the instructions in the SPSS Appendix for starting up SPSS and be sure the cursor is in the Scratch Pad window.

C. Enter the data as follows.
1. Type one line per subject, using a 1 for not highly sensitive and a 2 for highly sensitive.
2. Name your variables HIGHSENS and BOOKS. Your screen should now look like Figure SG11-3.

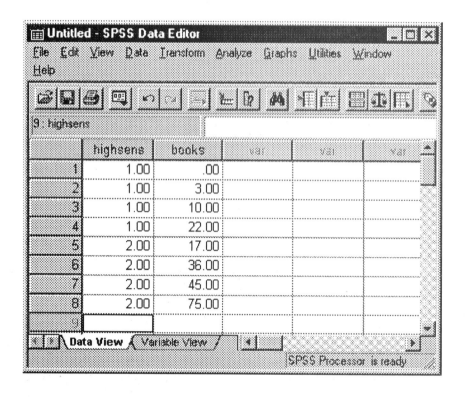

Figure SG11-3

D. Carry out a square root transformation:

    Transform

      Compute

        [Name your new variable by typing SQRBOOKS in the Target Variable box.]

          [Type SQRT(BOOKS) in the Numeric Expression box. Your screen should now look

           Figure SG11-4.]

             OK

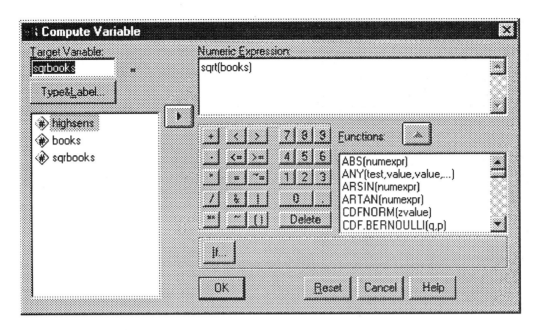

Figure SG11-4

E. Carry out a t test for independent means, using the square-root transformed variable:
> Analyze
>> Compare Means >
>>> Independent Samples t test
>>>> [Move SQRBOOKS into Test Variable(s) box and HIGHSENS into
>>>> Grouping Variable box.]
>>>>> Define Groups
>>>>>> [Type 1 for Group 1 and 2 for Group 2]
>>>>>>> Continue
>>>>>>> OK

F. The results should look like Figure SG11-5.

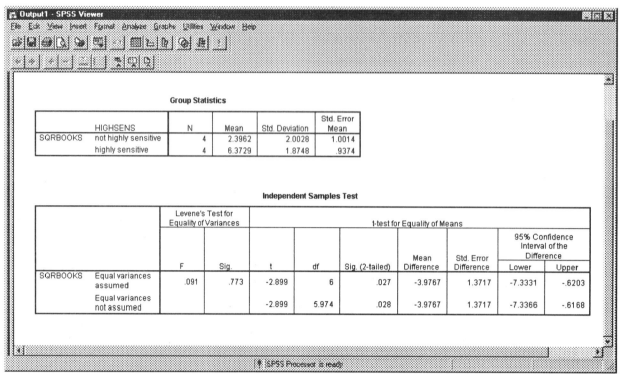

Group Statistics

	HIGHSENS	N	Mean	Std. Deviation	Std. Error Mean
SQRBOOKS	not highly sensitive	4	2.3962	2.0028	1.0014
	highly sensitive	4	6.3729	1.8748	.9374

Independent Samples Test

		Levene's Test for Equality of Variances		t-test for Equality of Means					95% Confidence Interval of the Difference	
		F	Sig.	t	df	Sig. (2-tailed)	Mean Difference	Std. Error Difference	Lower	Upper
SQRBOOKS	Equal variances assumed	.091	.773	-2.899	6	.027	-3.9767	1.3717	-7.3331	-.6203
	Equal variances not assumed			-2.899	5.974	.028	-3.9767	1.3717	-7.3366	-.6168

Figure SG11-5

G. Save your lines of data as follows:

> File
> > Save Data
> > > [Name your data file using the '.sav' extension and designate the drive you
> > > would like your data saved in.]
> > > > OK

II. Additional Practice

A. For each data set carry out the appropriate data transformation followed by the appropriate statistical procedure and compare your results to those in the text.

B. Use any of the data sets from Chapters 3 and 8 through 10.

III. Using the Computer to Deepen Your Knowledge

A. Effects of data transformation.

1. Use SPSS to compute a *t* test for independent means using the books-read example, comparing a square root, log, and inverse transformation; and make a histogram for the untransformed scores and for each transformation. Record the *t* score obtained under the various conditions.

2. Do the same with the *t* test example from Chapter 9 (the new-job-program experiment). Record the *t* score obtained under the various conditions.

3. Do the same with the example of a *t* test for dependent means in Chapter 8 (the surgeons'-reaction-time study), being sure to modify both Quiet and Noisy scores in the same way. Record the *t* scores obtained under the various conditions.

4. Do the same with the correlation example from Chapter 3 (the manager's-stress example). Change each variable separately, keeping the other in its original form. Then try some combinations. Record the correlations obtained under the various conditions.

5. Compare the results. What trends are there and what do they mean? (Evaluate these trends in terms of how well the transformations do and do not approximate a normal curve.)

B. Evaluate the effect of transformations in creating normal sample distributions: Using one of the larger data sets from Chapter 1 or 2 of the text, try several data transformations.

For each, produce a histogram. (You may also want to compute skew and kurtosis, as described in the advanced procedures section of the SPSS discussion in Chapter 2 of this *Study Guide and Computer Workbook*.)

Chapter 12
Making Sense of Advanced Statistical Procedures in Research Articles

Learning Objectives

To understand each of the following statistical techniques in a general way, so that you can recognize it in a research article, understand why it was done and what the results reported in an article mean, and make sense of the key terminology:

■ Hierarchical and stepwise multiple regression.
■ Partial correlation.
■ Reliability.
■ Factor analysis.
■ Causal modeling, including path analysis and latent variable modeling.
■ Analysis of covariance.
■ Multivariate analysis of variance and covariance.

Chapter Outline

I. The Two Main Categories of Advanced Statistical Techniques
   A. Those that focus on associations among variables (these are variations and extensions of correlation and regression).
      1. Hierarchical and stepwise multiple regression.
      2. Partial correlation.
      3. Reliability.
      4. Factor analysis.
      5. Causal modeling.
   B. Those that focus on differences among groups (these are variations and extensions of analysis of variance).
      1. Analysis of covariance.
      2. Multivariate analysis of variance and covariance.

II. Brief Review of Multiple Regression
   A. Multiple regression is about predicting a criterion or dependent variable based on two or more predictor variables.
      1. A multiple-regression prediction rule includes a set of regression coefficients, one to be multiplied by each predictor variable.
      2. The sum of these multiplications is the predicted value on the dependent variable.
      3. When working with Z scores, the regression coefficients are standardized regression coefficients, called beta weights (βs).
   B. Hypothesis testing: Significance can be computed both for each regression coefficient and the overall prediction rule.

III. Hierarchical and Stepwise Multiple Regression
   A. Both methods examine the influence of several predictor variables in a sequential fashion.

B. Hierarchical multiple regression follows a hypothesized order.
   1. Procedure: It computes the correlation of the first predictor variable with the dependent variable, then how much is added to the overall multiple correlation by including the second-most-important predictor variable, and then perhaps how much more is added by including a third predictor variable, and so on.
   2. It requires a specific theoretical basis for the order in which the regression is carried out.
C. Stepwise multiple regression is used in exploratory studies–it determines which, of the several, predictor variables usefully contribute to the prediction.
   1. Procedure.
      a. It computes the correlation of each predictor variable with the dependent variable and identifies the one with the highest correlation. (If none of these correlations are significant, the procedure stops.)
      b. It next computes the multiple correlation of each of the other variables in combination with the one just identified as having the highest correlation by itself to see which combination produces the highest multiple correlation. (If none of these multiple correlations add significantly to the predictability over just using the first variable, the procedure stops.)
      c. It next computes the multiple correlation of each of the remaining variables in combination with the highest two to see which combination produces the highest multiple correlation. (If none of these multiple correlations add significantly to the predictability over just the first two, the procedure stops.)
      d. The process continues in this way until all variables are included in the prediction rule or adding the next best variable does not add significantly to the predictability.
   2. Caution: The prediction formula that results is the optimal small set of variables for predicting the dependent variable, *as determined from the sample studied*–when tried with a new sample, somewhat different combinations often result.

IV. Partial Correlation
A. This is the degree of association between two variables, over and above the influence of one or more other variables.
B. A variable over and above the influence of which the partial correlation is computed is said to be *held constant*, *partialled out*, or *controlled for*. (These terms are interchangeable.)
C. The partial correlation coefficient is interpreted like an ordinary bivariate correlation except one should remember that some third variable is being controlled for.
D. You can think of a partial correlation as the average of the correlations between two variables, each correlation computed among just those subjects at each level of the variable being controlled for.
E. Partial correlation is often used to help sort out alternative explanations in a correlational study.
   1. If the correlation between two variables dramatically drops or is eliminated when a third variable is partialled out, it suggests that the third variable was behind the correlation.
   2. If the correlation between two variables is largely unaffected when a third variable is partialled out, it suggests that the third variable is not behind the correlation.

V. Reliability Coefficients
A. Reliability, the accuracy and consistency of a measure, is the extent to which if you were to give the same measure again to the same person under the same circumstances, you would obtain the same result.
B. Reports of computations of reliability of a measurement are very common in research articles.
C. Test-retest reliability.
   1. This is the correlation between the scores of the same people who take a measure twice.

2. It is often an impractical or inappropriate approach to reliability, since having taken the test once could influence the second taking.
D. Reliability as internal consistency.
1. Split half reliability is the correlation between two halves of the same test.
2. Cronbach's alpha can be thought of as the correlation between scores on two halves of a test, averaging such computations for all possible divisions of the test into halves.
E. In general a test should have a reliability of at least .7, and preferably closer to .9, to be considered useful.
F. If a measure has low reliability, it tends to reduce the correlation between it and any other variable. This can be adjusted for in bivariate correlation using a correction for attenuation.

VI. Factor Analysis
A. This is a widely used procedure applied when a researcher has measured people on a large number of variables.
B. It identifies groupings of variables (called *factors*) such that those within each group correlate with each other but not with variables in other groupings.
C. The correlation between a variable and a factor is called the variable's *factor loading* on that factor.
D. A widely used convention is to consider a variable part of a factor on which it has a loading of .3 or greater.
E. Researchers usually give each factor a name based on the variables that load highly on it. (These names can be misleading.)
F. Tables of the results of factor analyses usually give the factor loadings for each factor and also often give the percentage of variance that the factor as a whole accounts for in the entire set of original variables.

VII. Causal Modeling
A. Path analysis.
1. This procedure focuses on a diagram with arrows connecting the variables, indicating the hypothesized pattern of causal relations among them.
2. It is based on the correlations among the variables; for each arrow the researcher can compute a path coefficient.
   a. A path coefficient indicates the extent to which the variable at the start of the arrow is associated with the variable at the end of the arrow, after controlling for all variables that also point to this variable.
   b. A path coefficient is the same as a beta in multiple correlation/regression, with the variable at the start of the arrow as a predictor variable, the variable at the end of the arrow the dependent variable, and all the other variables in the path diagram, which also point to the variable at the end of the arrow as other predictor variables in the regression equation.
3. A path analysis is considered to provide support for the hypothesized causal pattern if the path coefficients for the major arrows are all significant and in the predicted directions.
B. Latent variable models.
1. This procedure is also widely known as structural equation modeling or LISREL.
2. It is an extension of path analysis with several advantages.
   a. It produces an overall measure of how good the model fits the data.
   b. It includes a significance test–but the null hypothesis is that the model fits.
   c. It permits modeling of latent variables (as assessed by a set of manifest variables).
3. The path diagram.
   a. Manifest variables are shown in squares.

b. Latent variables are shown in circles.

c. The measurement model, the relation of the manifest to the latent variables they assess, usually involves arrows from each latent variable to its associated manifest variables.

d. The causal model usually involves arrows showing the relations among the latent variables.

4. Limitations.

a. A well-fitting model that is not a significantly bad fit is still only one of the possible models that could fit the data.

VIII. Analysis of Covariance (ANCOVA)

A. This procedure is the same as an ordinary ANOVA, except that one or more variables are partialled out.

B. A variable partialled out is called a covariate.

C. The rest of the results are interpreted like any other analysis of variance.

D. The analysis of covariance is generally used in one of two situations.

1. One situation is the analysis of a random-assignment experiment in which some nuisance variable is partialled out.

2. The other situation is in a study in which it is not possible to employ random assignment, and variables on which groups may differ are partialled out. (This use is more controversial.)

E. ANCOVA assumes that the correlation between the covariate and the dependent variable is the same in all the cells.

IX. Multivariate Analysis of Variance (MANOVA) and Multivariate Analysis of Covariance (MANCOVA)

A. Multivariate statistical techniques involve more than one dependent variable.

B. The most widely used multivariate techniques are MANOVA and MANCOVA.

C. MANOVA is simply an analysis of variance in which there is more than one dependent variable.

D. MANOVA tests each main and interaction effect of the independent variables on the combination of dependent variables.

E. A significant effect in MANOVA, which could be due to any one of the dependent variables, is usually followed up by a series of ordinary "univariate" analyses of variance on each dependent variable separately.

F. MANCOVA is a MANOVA in which one or more variables are partialled out of the analysis.

X. Overview of Statistical Techniques Considered

A. Most of the techniques covered in this course can be understood as representing the various combinations of the following possibilities.

1. Association versus difference test.

2. One versus many independent variables.

3. One versus many dependent variables.

4. Whether or not any variables are controlled.

XI. How to Read Results Involving Unfamiliar Statistical Techniques

A. Even well-seasoned researchers periodically encounter unfamiliar statistical methods in research articles.

B. In these cases, you can usually figure out the basic idea.

1. Usually there will be a p level given and just what pattern of results is being considered significant can be discerned from the context.

2. Usually there will be some indication of effect size (degree of association or the size of the difference).

Chapter Self-Tests

Multiple-Choice Questions

1. Suppose a researcher wants to know what the correlation between one predictor variable and the dependent variable will be, and then how much is added by adding another predictor variable, and then perhaps even a third predictor variable. The sequence is planned in advance based on theory. What is this called?
   a. Multivariate analysis of variance
   b. Time-series analysis
   c. Hierarchical multiple regression
   d. Canonical correlation analysis

2. A _____ variable is a variable that is not actually measured but stands for a true variable that you would like to measure but can only approximate with real-life measures.
   a. dependent
   b. latent
   c. independent
   d. partial

3. The measure of overall fit is called
   a. factor loadings
   b. path coefficient
   c. fit index
   d. R^2

4. Which of the following is the best example of test-retest reliability?
   a. The responses of half the items on a test are correlated with the responses on the other half of the test.
   b. A group of people are given a test, but half are given one test and half are given a different but similar test and their scores on the two tests are correlated.
   c. A group of people are given a test on one occasion and then later the same people are given another very similar test and the two sets of scores are correlated.
   d. A group of people are given the same test on two separate occasions and the scores are correlated.

5. Computing reliability by correlating scores on two halves of a test raises the problem of which way to split the items in half. With Cronbach's alpha, in effect
   a. the halves are split by comparing odd and even numbered items.
   b. the test is simply split in half by top half and bottom half.
   c. it is split randomly.
   d. all possible splits are done and then the results are averaged.

6. Suppose that a researcher wants to look at the relations among a large number of variables measured in a study. She wants to know how the variables clump together and which variables don't seem to correlate. What procedure would be best for her to use?
   a. Factor analysis
   b. Hierarchical multiple regression
   c. Stepwise multiple regression
   d. Partial correlation

7. A correlation coefficient between 2 variables with a 3rd variable held constant is called a

   a. standardized regression coefficient.
   b. partial correlation coefficient.
   c. factor loading.
   d. multiple correlation coefficient.

8. Which of the following is NOT an advantage of latent variable modeling over ordinary path analysis?

   a. The computer calculates an overall measure of how good the model fits the data.
   b. It includes latent variables in the analysis.
   c. It rules out the possibility that any other pattern might create a better path diagram.
   d. A kind of significance test can be computed.

9. How is an analysis of covariance (ANCOVA) different from an analysis of variance (ANOVA)?

   a. ANCOVA allows you to control for the effect of an unwanted variable, whereas an ANOVA does not.
   b. ANOVA allows you to control for the effects of an unwanted variable, whereas an ANCOVA does not.
   c. ANCOVA allows you to use a factorial design, whereas an ANOVA does not.
   d. ANOVA allows you to use a factorial design, whereas an ANCOVA does not.

10. How are MANOVAs and MANCOVAs different from ANOVAs and ANCOVAs?

   a. They allow you to use two or more predictor variables, whereas ANOVAs and ANCOVAs do not.
   b. They allow you to partial out variables, whereas ANOVAs and ANCOVAs do not.
   c. They are more accurate than ANOVAs and ANCOVAs, but you can only use one predictor variable.
   d. They allow you to use more than one dependent variable, whereas ANOVAs and ANCOVAs do not.

Fill-In Questions

1. _____ is an exploratory technique in which the researcher is trying to find the best small set of predictor variables for some dependent variable based on results of a study that measured a large number of predictor variables.

2. A _____ is a correlation coefficient between two variables with a 3rd variable held constant.

3. _____ gives you a measure of the overall consistency of a test.

4. A value of at least _____ is needed to be considered a useful measure of internal consistency.

5. In one type of causal modeling, some of the variables included in the model are not actually measured, but can be included because they are considered to be the cause of variables that are measured in the study. These variables that are not measured are called _____ variables.

6. LISREL is a computer program that is widely used for a type of causal modeling known as _____.

7. The variable held constant in a partial correlation is analogous to an _____ in an analysis of covariance.

8. A researcher is planning a study comparing the effects of three kinds of psychotherapy on depression. Depression will be measured in each subject by both a behavioral and a questionnaire measure. In addition, the

researcher wants to control for initial differences in expectations of benefits prior to therapy. The appropriate statistical technique for the entire analysis is a(n) _____.

9. Multiple-regression techniques and causal modeling techniques are examples of methods that focus on association, while analysis of variance and multivariate analysis of variance are examples of techniques that focus on _____.

10. A _____ variable is a variable not actually measured but stands for a true variable you would like to measure but can only approximate in real life.

Problems/Essays

1. A study is conducted that examines the influence of various factors on success in graduate school. Explain the (fictional) results, as shown in the following table, to a person who has never had a course in statistics.

Hierarchical Multiple Regression (Dependent Variable = Reported Success in Graduate School)

Predictor Variable	R^2 for All Variables Entered	Increment in R^2
Social Class	.04	.04
Undergraduate Record	.15*	.11*
Social Skills	.18**	.03
Desire to Succeed	.25**	.07*

*$p < .05$ **$p < .01$

2. A study was conducted in which women rated themselves on their practice of seven health behaviors. Explain the (fictional) results, as shown in the following table, to a person who has never had a course in statistics.

Factor Analysis

	Factor Loadings	
Variable	Factor 1	Factor 2
Eats Adequate Fiber	.73	.13
Controls Fat Intake	.68	.21
Controls Sugar Intake	.71	.14
Tooth Flossing	-.03	.53
Daily Exercise	.23	.49
Wears Seat Belts	.06	.38
Breast Self-Exams	.25	.38

3. A (fictional) study is conducted comparing achievement-test scores of high school students of five different ethnic groups. The researchers report their results as follows:

Although previous studies have shown differences among these ethnic groups on this achievement test, the present study, which used parental income and language skills as covariates, did not find any reliable difference; the analysis of covariance was not significant, $F(4,248) = 1.63$. This nonsignificant finding is especially impressive in light of the large sample size employed in our study.

Explain this result (including discussing issues of power regarding a null hypothesis result) to a person who has never had a course in statistics.

4. A study was conducted that examined marital happiness among four groups of married adults–women with no children, mothers of a newborn infant, men with no children, and fathers of a newborn infant. This created a 2

160

X 2 design (parental status X gender). Marital happiness was measured using three variables: a standard marital happiness questionnaire, number of positive words included in a story written in an experimental setting about the spouse, and ratings of the subject's marital happiness by the subject's closest friend. The (fictional) results of the study were reported as follows:

A multivariate analysis of variance (MANOVA) yielded a main effect for gender, Wilks' Lambda $F(1,418)$ = 14.31, $p < .01$, and an interaction effect, Wilks' Lambda $F(1,418) = 9.38$, $p < .01$. The main effect for parental status was not significant, Wilks' Lambda $F(1,418) = 2.13$. Follow-up univariate analyses were significant only for the questionnaire measure. For the gender main effect, women were less satisfied with their marriage than men, $F(1, 361) = 16.33$, $p < .01$. The interaction effect was also significant, $F(1, 361) = 8.14$, $p < .01$. Based on a post-hoc analysis (Neuman-Keuls), the pattern of means associated with this interaction suggest that, for women, being a parent of a newborn is associated with less marital happiness, whereas for men there is little difference in marital happiness between those who are and are not fathers of newborn infants. Explain this result to a person who has never had a course in statistics.

Answers to Self-Test Problems

Note. Answers to problems and essays include numerical results only.

Chapter 1

Multiple-Choice: 1-b, 2-d, 3-a, 4-c, 5-b, 6-c, 7-a, 8-b, 9-a, 10-c

Fill-Ins:

1. values, intervals
2. grouped frequency table
3. interval, interval size
4. histogram
5. bimodal
6. rectangular
7. positively, skewed to the right
8. ceiling effect
9. normal curve
10. Kurtosis

Problems/Essays

A grouped frequency table is preferred over an ordinary frequency table when the scores range over a great many different values. Using an ordinary frequency table in such a situation would fail to give a simple description because there would be so many different values to look at, while the grouped frequency table in this situation gives a more readily grasped summary of the pattern of scores.

2a.

Interval	f
70-79	5
60-69	2
50-59	1
40-49	2
30-39	0
20-29	2
10-19	8
0-9	4

2b. Bimodal. (Kurtotic is also correct and one could argue that it is slightly positively skewed-- that is, skewed to the right.)

3a.
Interval	f
40-44	1
35-39	1
30-34	0
25-29	2
20-24	6
15-19	9
10-14	12
5-9	8
0-4	4

3b. Shape: Unimodal, skewed to the right.

4. A floor effect is when most of the scores are near the bottom of the scale because it is not possible to get a lower score on this measure. For example, if you were to measure number of words spelled wrong on a second grade spelling test completed by fifth graders, most of the fifth graders would spell none of the words wrong so the scores would pile up at zero.

Chapter 2

Multiple Choice: 1-b, 2-d, 3-a, 4-b, 5-b, 6-d, 7-a, 8-c, 9-b, 10-d

Fill-Ins:

1. mean
2. sum of squares
3. 5
4. mode
5. median
6. outlier
7. median
8. mode
9. standard deviation
10. normal

Problems/Essays

1. $M = \sum X/N = 40/8 = 5$
   $SS = (3.1-5)^2 + (3.8-5)^2 + (4-5)^2 + (4.5-5)^2 + (5.4-5)^2 + (6-5)^2 + (8.7-5)^2 = 21.4$
   $SD^2 = SS/N = 21.4/8 = 2.68$; $SD = \sqrt{SD^2} = \sqrt{2.68} = 1.64$

2. Z for sales aptitude: $Z = (X-M)/SD = (50-40)/4 = 10/4 = 2.5$
   Z for education aptitude: $Z = (95-80)/20 = 15/20 = .75$
   Greater aptitude in relation to others: Sales.

3. Raw score for Mary: $X = (Z)(SD) + M = (1.23)(6.5) + 42 = 50$
   Raw score for Susan: $(-.62)(6.5) + 42 = 38$

Chapter 3

Multiple Choice: 1-a, 2-d, 3-c, 4-d, 5-b, 6-d, 7-d, 8-c, 9-a, 10-d

Fill-Ins:

1. multiple correlation
2. multiple regression
3. a curvilinear correlation
4. a negative correlation
5. multiple correlation coefficient
6. closer
7. significant
8. β
9. -.77
10. 39

Problems/Essays
1a.

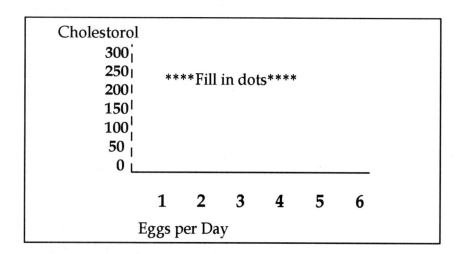

1b. General pattern: positive linear correlation

166

1c.   Eggs/Day   Cholesterol
        Raw   Z   Raw   Z $Z_X Z_Y$
         2   0   210   .33   0
         0   -1.07   100   -1.47   1.57
         1   -.53   180   -.16   .09
         5   1.6   270   1.31   2.09

              M=2   M=190   ∑=3.75
              SD=1.87   SD=61.24

$r = Z_X Z_Y / N = 3.75/4 = .94$

1d.   Proportion of variance accounted for $= r^2 = .94^2 = .88$

1e.   Example answer: Eating eggs could cause higher cholesterol; people who have high
        cholesterol may choose to eat more eggs; some third factor, such as upbringing or genetic
        influences, may have the effects of making people have high cholesterol and also a liking
        for eggs.

2a.

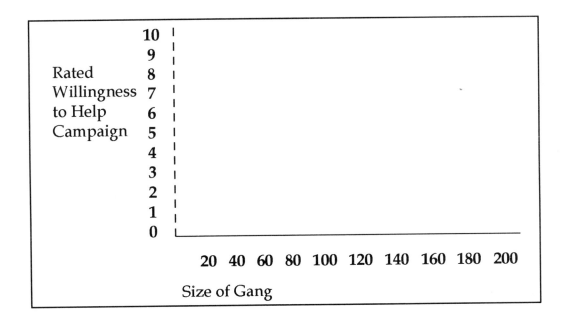

2b. Negative linear correlation.

2c. Size of Gang   Related Willingness to Help Campaign

Raw	Z	Raw	Z	$Z_X Z_Y$
24	-1.2	10	1.6	-1.92
106	.4	4	-.5	-.20
42	-.9	7	.5	-.45
70	-.3	6	.2	-.06
90	.1	5	-.2	-.02
178	1.9	1	-1.6	-3.04

$\Sigma = -5.69$

$r = -5.69/6 = -.95$

2d. $r^2 = -.95^2 = .90$

2e. Example answer: Being in a bigger gang causes leaders to be less willing to help; leaders who are willing to help attract more members; the kind of gang that attracts leaders who are willing to help also attracts large numbers of members.

3. There may be a restriction in range.

4. Predicted Z for performance = .87 X Z for hours of exercise per week.

5.

Person Tested	Hours Prediction Per Week		Performance in Training Program		
	X	Z_X	Y	Z_Y	$Z_Y X_Y$
1	3	-.59	45	-.54	.32
2	11	1.76	90	1.47	2.6
3	6	.29	53	-.18	-.05
4	1	-1.17	25	-1.43	1.67
5	4	-.29	72	.67	-.19
	M=5		M=57		Σ=4.35
	SD=3.41		SD=22.35		

$r=4.35/5=.87$

8 hours: $Z=(X-M)/SD=(8-5)/3.41=3/3.41=.88$

Predicted $Z_Y = (r)(Z_X)=(.87)(.88)=.77$

Chapter 4

Multiple Choice: 1-b, 2-c, 3-a, 4-d, 5-b, 6-c, 7-c, 8-a, 9-b, 10-c

Fill-Ins:

1. 34
2. unimodal; normal
3. standard
4. proportion
5. standard deviation units
6. haphazard
7. parameter
8. statistic
9. probability
10. Population parameter

Problems/Essays

1a. $Z = (X-M)/SD = (55-50)/5 = 5/5 = 1$. Approximation is that 34% are between mean and Z=1. 50% are above the mean, thus 16% (50% - 34%) are above 55.

1b. $z = (40-50)/5 = -2$. 34% + 14% = 48% are between mean and 2 SD from mean. Thus, 2% (50% - 48%) are below 40.

1c. $z = (45-50)/5 = -1$. 34% are between mean and 1 SD below mean. 50% are above mean. Thus total above 40 is 84% (50% + 34%).

Note: It is easier to solve such problems if you draw pictures of the normal curve and the areas involved.

2a. From normal curve table, top 5% (45% between mean and Z) begins at 1.64 (or you can use 1.65). Thus, corresponding raw score is $X = (Z)(SD) + M = (1.64)(2.8) + 15.3 = 4.59 + 15.3 = 19.89$.

2b. From normal curve table, bottom 10% (40% between mean and Z) begins at -1.28. Thus, corresponding raw score = $(-1.28)(2.8) + 15.3 = 11.72$.

3a. $p = (8+7)/30 = 15/30 = 1/2$ or .5
3b. $p = (8+4)/30 = 2/5$ or .4

Chapter 5

Multiple Choice: 1-b, 2-d, 3-c, 4-b, 5-a, 6-c, 7-b, 8-a, 9-c, 10-d

Fill-Ins

1. Hypothesis testing
2. people in general
3. Population 1 is taller than Population 2
4. Population 1 is not taller than Population 2
5. Population 2, people in general
6. supported
7. .01 and .05, 1% and 5%
8. reject the null hypothesis, the research hypothesis is supported
9. 7.5%
10. statistically significant

Problems/Essays

1. Cutoff (.05 level, one-tailed) = -1.65
   Z score on comparison distribution of time to fall asleep is -1.86
   Reject the null hypothesis that time to fall asleep is unaffected by a glass of warm milk.

2. Cutoff (.05 level, one-tailed) = -1.65
   Z score on comparison distribution of bus times is 2.17
   Reject the null hypothesis that the planes from this company arrive no later than planes of airlines in general.

3. Cutoff (.05 level, two-tailed) = ± 1.96
   Z score on comparison distribution of number of items recalled is -1.5
   Do not reject the null hypothesis, the study is inconclusive.

Chapter 6

Multiple Choice: 1-c, 2-c, 3-b, 4-d, 5-b, 6-b, 7-a, 8-c, 9-b, 10-a

Fill-Ins

1. distribution of means, distribution of means of all possible samples of a given size from the population, sampling distribution of the mean
2. sample mean
3. point estimate
4. central limit theorem
5. -2
6. standard error of the distribution of means
7. the standard deviation of the distribution of means, SD_M
8. interval estimate
9. reject
10. Z test

Problems/Essays

1. Cutoff (.01 level, one-tailed) = 2.33
   Distribution of means: Population M = 48; SD^2_M=Population SD^2/N=144/5=28.8, SD_M=5.37; shape=normal.
   M=63; Z score for test group: Z=(63-48)/5.37 = 15/5.37 = 2.79
   Conclusion: Reject the null hypothesis.

2. Cutoff (.05 level, one-tailed) = -1.64.
   Distribution of means: Population M = 38; SD^2_M=Population SD^2/N=36/10=3.6, SD_M=1.90; shape=normal.
   Z score for test group: Z = (36-38)/1.90 = -2/1.90 = -1.05
   Conclusion: Do NOT reject the null hypothesis.

Chapter 7

Multiple Choice: 1-c, 2-d, 3-d, 4-a, 5-b, 6-b, 7-b, 8-b, 9-d, 10-c

Fill-Ins

1. Type I
2. Decision
3. Type I
4. .80
5. power
6. effect size
7. sample size
8. standard deviation of the population of individual cases, variance of the distribution of individual cases
9. standard deviation of the distribution of means, variance of the distribution of means
10. Large

Problems/ Essays

1a. A type I error would be to conclude from the hypothesis-testing process that the data support the contention that the new learning technique works when in fact it does not. A type II error would be if the hypothesis-testing process led to an inconclusive result (failure to reject the null hypothesis) about whether the learning technique works, when in fact it does work.

1b. A Type I error would be to conclude from the hypothesis-testing process that the data support the contention that the new drug speeds learning of symbolic communication for chips, when in fact the new drug does not speed such learning. A Type II error would be if the hypothesis-testing process led to an inconclusive result (failure to reject the null hypothesis) about whether the new drug speeds learning, when in fact the new drug does speed the learning.

2a. Effect size = (3.55-3.80)/1.50= -.17; small effect size.

2b. Example answers:
   1. Give a stronger lecture-thus provide a basis for increasing the expected difference between known and hypothesized means.
   2. Use only children of a particular age-and thus hopefully reduce the population variation.
   3. Use more accurate measurement of consumption of candy (perhaps use records over a two-week period)-and thus hopefully further reduce the population variance.
   4. Use more subjects-and thus reduce the variance of the distributions of means.

3. Conclusion is that the research hypothesis (that ball players like to chew gum more than general public) is probably false and the null hypothesis (that ball players liking of gum is no different from that of the general public) is probably true.
Explanation: With high power, it is easy to reject the null hypothesis if it is false. Thus, had it been false, it probably would have been rejected. Since it was not rejected, it probably is not false.

4. Conclusion: Result could be due to a very small effect size so that it may not be of practical importance.
Explanation: With very high power, it would have been easy to reject the null hypothesis even if the true effect were very small.

Chapter 8

Multiple Choice: 1-c, 2-b, 3-a, 4-d, 5-a, 6-a, 7-d, 8-c, 9-c, 10-d

Fill Ins:

1. degrees of freedom
2. extreme scores
3. N, sample size, number of cases in the sample
4. difference scores
5. zero
6. skewed
7. N; N-1
8. greater, larger
9. level of significance, alpha level
10. normal distribution, normal curve

Problems/Essays

1. t test for a single sample
   t needed (df=5), $p<.05$, 1-tailed = -2.015
   $M = 17$; S^2=4.4; S_M= .85; t= -3.53
   Reject null hypothesis.

2. t test for dependent means
   t needed ($df = 4$), $p<.05$, 1-tailed = 2.132
   Difference scores = .07, .18, .14, .18, -.13
   M=.088; S^2= .017; S_M = .055; t= 1.600
   Do NOT reject null hypothesis.

3. t needed (df=8), $p < .05$, 1-tailed = -1.86
   Difference scores = -2, -2, -4, -2, -6, -1, +1, +4, 0
   $M = -1.33$; $S^2 = 8.25$; $S_M = .96$; $t = -1.39$
   Do NOT reject null hypothesis.

Chapter 9

Multiple Choice: 1-b, 2-a, 3-b, 4-c, 5-d, 6-d, 7-d, 8-b, 9-b, 10-c

Fill Ins:

1. independent means
2. two
3. distribution of difference between means
4. the distribution of differences between means
5. standard deviation
6. normally distributed
7. variance
8. pooled
9. harmonic
10. $t(23) = 3.21$, $p < .01$, one-tailed

Problems/Essays

1. *t*-test for independent means; *t* needed (df, $p < .01$, 2-tailed) $= \pm 3.3356$.
   TRAINING: $N=5$, $df=4$, $M=15.8$, $S^2=2.7$; NO TRAINING: $N=5$, $df=4$, $M=16$, $S^2=6.5$.
   $S_{POOLED} = [(4/8)(2.7)]+[(4/8)(6.5)] = 4.6$; $S_{M1}^2 = 4.6/5 = .92$; $S_M^2 = .92$;
   $S_{DIFFERENCE} = .92 + .92 = 1.84$; $S_{DIFFERENCE} = 1.36$.
   $t = (15.8-16)/1.36 = -.15$.
   Do NOT reject the null hypothesis. The results of the study are inconclusive as to whether self-defense training enhances self-confidence.

2. t-test for independent means; *t* needed ($df=5$, $p<.05$, 1-tailed) $= 2.015$.
   PLACEBO: $N=4$, $df=3$, $M=90.3$, $S^2=184.9$; CONTROL: $N=3$, $df=2$, $M=88$, $S^2=133$.
   $S_{POOLED}^2 = [(3/5)(184.9)]+[(2/5)(133)] = 164.15$; $S_{M1}^2 = 164.15/4 = 41$;
   $S_{M2}^2 = 164.15/3 = 54.7$; $S_{DIFFERENCE}^2 = 41 + 54.7 = 95.7$; $S_{DIFFERENCE} = 9.78$.
   $t = (90.3-88)/9.78 = .24$.
   Do NOT reject the null hypothesis. The results of the study are inconclusive as to whether this placebo procedure can produce an increase in intelligence.

Chapter 10

Multiple Choice: 1-a, 2-a, 3-b, 4-d, 5-c, 6-a, 7-b, 8-d, 9-d, 10-c

Fill Ins

1. equal (the same)
2. within
3. one
4. two-way factorial
5. cell
6. distribution of means
7. population
8. is different from
9. repeated measures analysis of variance
10. less than

Problems/Essays

1. F needed (df=2,12; $p<.05$) = 3.89
   Small: M=60.6, S^2=33.3; Standard: M=60.2 S^2=89.2; Large: M=54.2, S^2=59.2
   GM= 58.3; S_M^2=12.9; $S_{BETWEEN}^2$=64.5; S_{WITHIN}^2= 60.6; F=1.06.
   Do NOT reject the null hypothesis.

2. F needed (df=3,8; $p< .01$) = 7.59
   COLLEGE: M=4.33, S^2=2.33; PSYCHOLOGISTS: M=6, S^2=1; LAWYERS: M=6,
   S^2=1; PUBLIC: M=4.33, S^2=.33.
   GM=5.17; S_M^2=.93; $S_{BETWEEN}^2$=2.8; S_{WITHIN}^2=1.17; F=2.39.
   Do not reject null hypothesis.

3. F needed (df=3, 76; $p<.01$)=4.06 (using figure for df=3,75).
   GM=3.87; S_M^2=1.70; $S_{BETWEEN}^2$=34; S_{WITHIN}^2=3; F=11.33
   Reject the null hypothesis; the research hypothesis is supported.

Chapter 11

Multiple Choice: 1-c, 2-c, 3-b, 4-a, 5-d, 6-c, 7-d, 8-d, 9-c, 10-b

Fill Ins

1. Karl Pearson
2. chi-square test for goodness of fit
3. E
4. the number of categories minus 1
5. independent
6. row
7. normal; normal distributions; normally distributed
8. nonnormal; skewed; kurtotic
9. outlier
10. nonparametric tests; distribution free tests

Problems/Essays

1. X^2 needed (df=3, p<.05) = 7.815

	O	E	O-E	$(O-E)^2$	$(O-E)^2/E$
Plant A	15	21	-6	36	1.71
Plant B	34	21	13	169	8.05
Plant C	17	21	-4	16	.76
Plant D	18	21	-3	9	.43
	84	60	0		X^2=10.95

Decision: Reject null hypothesis.

2. X^2 needed (df=4, p< .05) = 9.488

	Level of Mother's Depression During Pregnancy				
Birthweight	Severe	Mild	Not Depressed	Total	Percent
below average	(4.7) 8	(4.7) 5	(4.7) 1	14	23.3
average	(7.7) 3	(7.7) 8	(7.7) 12	23	38.3
above average	(7.7) 9	(7.7) 7	(7.7) 7	23	38.3
TOTAL	20	20	20	60	99.9

X^2= 10.87

Decision: Reject null hypothesis.

Cramer's ϕ = $\sqrt{[10.76/(60)(2)]}$ = .30, medium effect size

3. a. t needed (df=8, 1-tailed, p < .05) = 2.306

	Did Not Expect	Did Expect
M	87.4	65.2
S^2	63.3	407.7
S_M^2	47.1	47.1

S_{POOLED}^2 = 235.5, $S_{DIFFERENCE}^2$=94.2, $S_{DIFFERENCE}$=9.71,
t= (87.4-65.2)/9.71=2.29

Did not expect to be liked: 77, 83, 88, 91, 98
Did expect to be liked: 46, 57, 58, 66, 99

Do not reject the null hypothesis.

b. SQUARE ROOT TRANSFORMED DATA

	Did Not Expect	Did Expect
	8.77	6.78
	9.11	7.55
	9.38	7.62
	9.54	8.12
	9.90	9.95
M	9.34	8.00
S^2	.18	1.41
S_M^2	.16	.16

$S_{POOLED}^2 = .80$
$S_{DIFFERENCE}^2 = .32$; $S_{DIFFERENCE} = .57$
$t = (9.34-8.00)/.57 = 2.35$
Reject the null hypothesis.

4. t needed ($df=8$, two-tailed, $p<.05$) = 2.306

Movers		Non-Movers	
Raw	Rank	Raw	Rank
3	5	1	2
1	2	4	6
9	9	5	7
13	10	2	4
6	8	1	2

M	6.80	4.20
S^2	10.70	5.20
S_M^2	1.59	1.59

$S_{POOLED}^2 = 7.95$
$S_{DIFFERENCE}^2 = 3.18$; $S_{DIFFERENCE} = 1.78$
$t = (6.8-4.2)/1.78 = 1.46$
Do not reject the null hypothesis.

Chapter 12

Multiple Choice: 1-c, 2-b, 3-c, 4-d, 5-d, 6-a, 7-b, 8-c, 9-a, 10-d

Fill-Ins

1. Stepwise multiple regression, stepwise regression
2. partial correlation coefficient
3. Cronbach's alpha
4. .6 or .7
5. latent
6. latent variable causal modeling, structural equation modeling
7. covariate
8. analysis of covariance, ANCOVA
9. differences
10. latent

Appendix I

How to Get Started and the Basics of Using SPSS

When working through your first SPSS example in the chapters in this *Study Guide and Computer Workbook*, you will need to have either first learned the basics of using SPSS by studying this appendix or you will need to be turning back and forth to this appendix as you work through that first example. Either way, allow an extra hour or so for your first attempt at SPSS.

SPSS is very easy to use once you have learned a few basics of how the program operates. It is also easy to master these basics—or at least it will seem that way after you are started. But facing starting up on your own, particularly if you are not a computer whiz, can seem daunting. Thus, the easiest way to begin is to have someone who is familiar with the program lead you through it.

If you need to learn on your own, the manual that comes with your SPSS disks provides everything you need. Indeed, if it has any faults it is that it provides more than you need. That is, it teaches you every bell and whistle of the program, when all you really need for your purposes is a very small subset of all these details. Thus, this Appendix is designed to help you get started by covering the very minimum of what you need to start up and use SPSS. Once you are comfortable with these basics, if you choose to you can go back to the manual and start getting fancy. But all you will ever need for purposes of this course are the basics we cover here, plus what is covered in the SPSS section of each chapter in this *Study Guide and Computer Workbook*.

In this Appendix we do assume that you are familiar with basic computer terminology such as "file," "saving a file," and "cursor." We also assume you are familiar with the fundamental operations of the computer system you will be using—how to turn it on, type in instructions, move between directories, and how to quit a session at the computer. Finally, we assume you are a little used to working with computers and how finicky they are about your giving instructions exactly.

Before You Start

To use SPSS, the program must be saved onto the hard disk of the computer you will be using (the program is too long to fit on a single soft disk). This is called installing the program. If the program has not been already installed for you onto the computer you will be using, you will have to do so yourself, following the instructions in the manual that came with the disks. Actually, once you get started, instructions on the screen lead you through the process fairly effortlessly. However, the best recommendation is to work through the installation with the help of someone knowledgeable. (But, once again, try to deter that person from doing anything beyond the standard, straight-forward setup.)

Throughout the various chapter sections on using SPSS in *this Study Guide and Computer Workbook*, we will assume that you have set up SPSS on your computer in such a way that you know how to move to the appropriate directory to begin an SPSS session and that once in that directory you can save and recall files.

Beginning an SPSS Session

1. Go to the Start menu at the bottom of your screen. Choose Programs. A list of programs on your computer should appear. Choose SPSS 10.0 for Windows Student Version. Wait a few seconds and then a screen should appear as shown in Figure S-1. Choose "Type in Data" and then click on OK. This should then create the screen shown in Figure S-2.

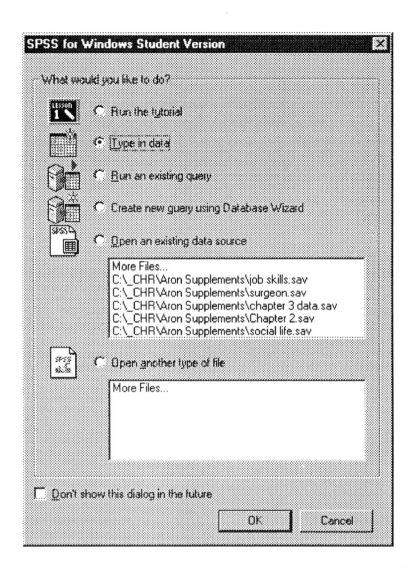

Figure S-1

183

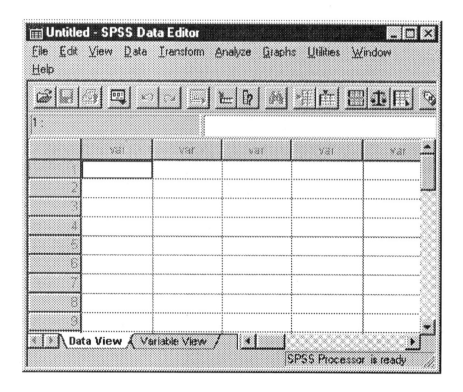

Ending an SPSS Session

1. If you wish to keep the data you have already entered into the data window, and have not already saved it as a file, do so now. (See section below on Saving your Files.)
2. Click on File on the toolbar.
3. Click on Exit.

The Data Lines

The data you use in statistics are usually set up so that each subject studied has a score on one or more variables. For example, in a particular study, each of 10 subjects might have a score on an anxiety test and also a score on an intelligence test. Thus, the data set-up would consist of two variables ("anxiety" and "intelligence"), with scores for each of 10 subjects.

When carrying out a statistical analysis using SPSS, you first name the variable, then type in the lines of data, and finally you tell SPSS what statistical analysis you would like to run by choosing options from the toolbar.

Naming a Variable

Click on the Variable View tab at the bottom of the screen. This will bring a spreadsheet (as seen in Figure S-3) that allows you to define certain characteristics about your variables. Under the name column you can type in an 8 character (no spaces allowed) abbreviated name of your variable. Each row represents each variable that you have in your dataset thus, the first variable name will appear in the cell for the first column of the first row. The name for a second variable will occur in the cell for the first column of the second row, and so on.

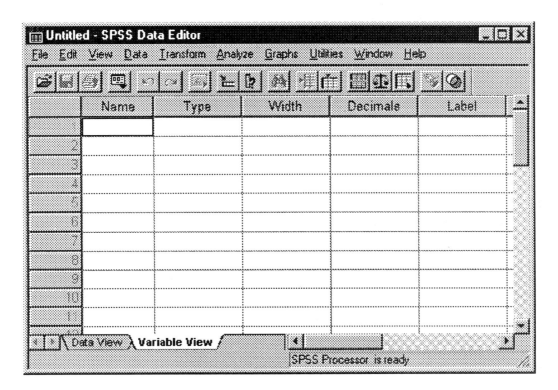

Typing in Lines of Data
     The cursor should appear in the window above the data grid, and the first box in the grid should be highlighted. Type a number and press enter. The number should now appear in the highlighted box and the second box in that column will be highlighted. The columns represent all the data for a single variable, while the rows represent all the data for a single person. SPSS will prompt you to enter each person's data for a particular variable at the same time before moving on to another variable. However, in some instances it may be easier to enter all the data for a person at one time before moving on to the next person's data. In this case, you can use the mouse to click on the box that you would like the data entered into.

Using the Toolbar
    In order to run a statistical analysis in SPSS, you must choose options from the toolbar located at the top of the screen. In this *Study Guide and Computer Workbook*, commands on the toolbar will be denoted as such:

Analyze
> Descriptive Statistics >
>> Frequencies
>>> [Highlight VAR00001 and click on the arrow to enter it into the
>>> Variable(s) box.]
>>>> OK

In this example, you would click on Analyze on the toolbar. A menu will drop down and you will highlight Descriptive Statistics from this menu. A second menu will drop down, and you will highlight Frequencies. Your screen should now look like Figure S-4 below. Click the mouse button on frequencies. This will bring up a Frequencies screen. In order to tell SPSS which variables you are interested in analyzing, you need to highlight the variable and click on the arrow. This will move the variable over into the Variable(s) box. Now click on OK. The results will appear in the Output Window. You may have to scroll the window up and down in order to see all of the output. If you would like to print out the output, click on File and then Print.

To get back to the data window, click on the Output icon in the upper left corner, then click on Next.

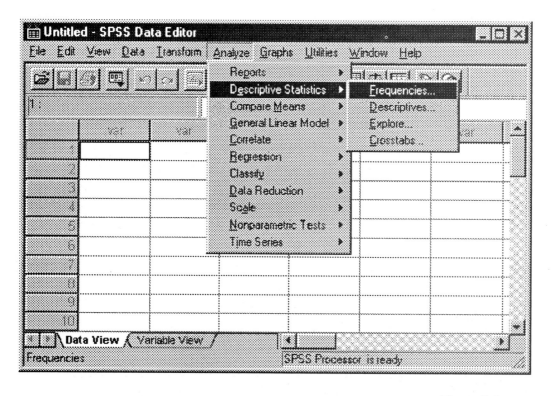

Figure S-4

Creating a New Variable

Sometimes you may want to create a new variable based on existing variables. For example, you may want to create a new variable that is the sum of two existing variables. Or perhaps you want to create a variable that is the square root of an existing variable.
1. First enter your data and name your variables (see preceding section).
2. Transform

Compute

    [Name your new variable in the Target Variable box]

        [Type the computations—using the name of any existing variables along with arithmetic symbols. You can use parentheses to group computations.]

        OK

3. Your new variable will now appear in the Data Window.

4. Example:

    a. To create a variable called SUMXY that is the sum of X and Y, type SUMXY in the Target Variable box. In the Numeric Expression box, type X+Y. You can also highlight the existing variables and use the arrow to move them over into the Numeric Expression box. Your screen should now look like Figure S-5.

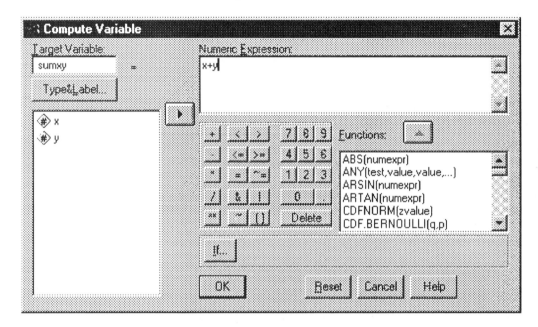

Figure S-5

Saving the Data in a File

Save your lines of data as follows:

 File

  Save Data

    [Name your data file followed by the extension ".sav" (for example Ch1.sav) and designate the drive you would like your data saved in.]

      OK

Recalling a Set of Data

In order to call up an existing data file you would go through the same steps as you did to begin an SPSS session. However this time, instead of choosing to Type in Data, you would choose "Open and existing data source" and then choose one of the SPSS datasets listed for you as seen in Figure S-6.

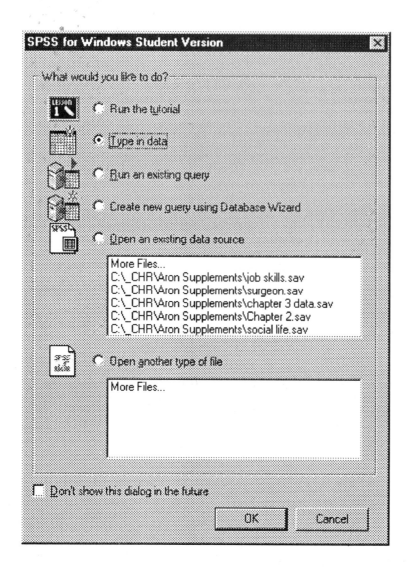

Figure S-6

188

Glossary

Flash Cards

(to Cut Out)

Descriptive statistics

Value

Inferential statistics

Score

Frequency table

Grouped frequency table

Variable

Interval

A possible number or category that a score can have.

1

Procedures for summarizing or otherwise making more comprehensible a set of scores.

1

A particular subject's value on a variable.

1

Procedures for drawing conclusions based on, but going beyond, the scores actually collected in a research study.

1

A frequency table in which the number of subjects is indicated for each interval of values.

1

A listing of the number of subjects receiving each of the possible values that the scores on the variable being measured can take.

1

In a grouped frequency table, each of a specified-sized grouping of values for which frequencies are reported.

1

A characteristic that can take on different values.

1

Rectangular distribution

Frequency distribution

1

1

Histogram

Unimodal distribution

1

1

Frequency polygon

Bimodal distribution

1

1

Symmetrical distribution

Multimodal distribution

1

1

The pattern of frequencies over the various values; what a frequency table, histogram, or frequency polygon describes.

1

A frequency distribution in which all values have approximately the same frequency.

1

A frequency distribution with one value clearly having a larger frequency than any other.

1

A bar-like graph of a distribution in which the are along the horizontal axis and the height of each bar corresponds to the frequency of that value.

1

A frequency distribution with two approximately equal frequencies, each clearly larger than any of the others.

1

A type of line graph of a distribution in which the values are along the horizontal axis and the height of each point which connects the lines corresponds to the frequency of that value.

1

A frequency distribution with two or more approximately equal frequencies, each clearly larger than any of the others.

1

A distribution in which the pattern of frequencies on the left and right side are mirror images of each other.

1

Skewness

Normal curve

1

1,4

Floor effect

Kurtosis

1

1

Ceiling effect

Mean

1

2

Mode

Standard deviation

2

2

A specific, mathematically defined, bell-shaped frequency distribution that is symmetrical and unimodal.

1,4

The extent to which a frequency distribution has the preponderance of cases on one side of the middle.

1

The extent to which a frequency distribution is too peaked and pinched together or too flat and spread out, in comparison to the normal curve.

1

The situation in which many scores pile up at the low end because it is not possible to have any lower score.

1

The arithmetic average of a group of scores; the sum of the scores divided by the number of scores.

2

The situation in which many scores pile up at the high end because it is not possible to have a higher score.

1

The square root of the average of the squared deviations from the mean; roughly the average amount scores in a distribution vary from the mean.

2

The value with the greatest frequency in a distribution.

2

Median

Z-score

2

2

Outlier

Positive linear correlation

2

3

Variance

Negative linear correlation

2

3

Independent variable

Linear correlation

3

3

The number of standard
deviations a score is above
(or below, if it is negative) the
mean in its distribution.

If you line up all the scores from highest
to lowest, the middle score.

2

2

A relation between two variables in
which high scores on one go with
high scores on the other, mediums
with mediums, and lows with lows.

A score with an extremely (very high
or very low) value in relation to the
rest of the scores in the distribution.

3

2

A relation between two variables
in which high scores on one go with
low scores on the other, mediums
with mediums, and lows with lows.

The average of the squared
deviations from the mean.

3

2

A relation between two variables
that shows up on a scatter diagram
as the dots roughly following a
straight line.

A variable that is considered to be
a cause (or, in regression, any
predictor variable.)

3

3

Dependent variable   Curvilinear correlation

3   **3**

Predictor variable   Perfect correlation

3   **3**

Scatter diagram   Correlation coefficient

3   **3**

Statistical significance   Correlation matrix

3   **3**

A relation between two variables that shows up on a scatter diagram as the dots roughly following a systematic pattern that is not a straight line.

3

A variable that is considered to be a cause (or, in regression, any predictor variable).

3

A relation between two variables that shows up on a scatter diagram as the dots exactly following a straight line; a correlation of r equals 1 or -1.

3

A variable that is used as a basis for estimating scores of individuals on another variable.

3

The average of the cross-products of Z scores of two variables.

3

A graphic display of the pattern of relationship between two variables.

3

A table in which the variables are named on the top and along the side, and the correlations among them are all shown.

3

The extent to which the results of a study would be unlikely if in fact there were no association or difference in the populations the measured scores represent.

3

Regression coefficient

Multiple regression

4

4

Subjective interpretation of
probability

Haphazard selection

4

4

Population

Parameter

4

4

Sample

Probability

4

4

201

The number multiplied by a person's score on the independent variable as part of a formula for predicting scores on the dependent variable.

The prediction of scores on one variable based on scores of two or more other variables.

4

4

A procedure of selecting a sample of individuals to study by taking whoever is available or happens to be first on a list.

Understanding probability as the degree of one's certainty that a particular outcome will occur.

4

4

A descriptive statistic for a population.

The scores of the entire group of subjects to which a researcher intends the results of a study to apply.

4

4

The expected relative frequency of a particular outcome.

The scores of the particular set of subjects studied that are intended to represent the scores in some larger population.

4

4

Hypothesis testing

Cutoff sample score

5

5

Research hypothesis

Statistical significance

5

5

Null hypothesis

Level of significance (α)

5

5

Comparison distribution

Conventional levels of significance

5

5

The point on the comparison distribution which, if the sample score reaches or exceeds it, the null hypothesis will be rejected.

5

A systematic procedure for determining whether results of an experiment provide support for a particular theory or practical innovation thought to be applicable to a population.

5

An outcome of hypothesis testing in which the null hypothesis is rejected.

5

A statement about the predicted relation between populations.

5

The probability of obtaining statistical significance if the null hypothesis is actually true.

5

A statement that there is no difference between the populations.

5

The levels of significance widely used in psychology ($p < .05$ and $p < .01$).

5

The distribution representing the situation if the null hypothesis is true and to which you compare your sample.

5

Directional hypothesis

Distribution of means

5

6

One-tailed test

Variance of a distribution of means

5

6

Nondirectional hypothesis

Z-test

5

6

Two-tailed test

Type I error

5

7

A distribution of all the possible means of samples of a given size from a particular population.

A research hypothesis predicting a particular direction of difference between populations.

6

5

The variance of the population divided by the number of cases in each sample.

The hypothesis-testing procedure for a directional hypothesis.

6

5

A hypothesis-testing procedure in which there is a single sample and the population variance is known.

A research hypothesis that does not predict a particular direction of difference between populations.

6

5

Rejecting the null hypothesis when in fact it is true.

The hypothesis-testing procedure for a nondirectional hypothesis.

7

5

Type II error

Meta-analysis

7

7

Statistical power

Effect size

7

7

t test

Effect-size conventions

8

7

Repeated-measures design

Unbiased estimate of the population variance

8

8

A statistical method for combining the results of independent studies, usually focusing on effect sizes.

7

Failing to reject the null hypothesis when in fact it is true.

7

The separation (lack of overlap) between or among populations due to the independent variable.

7

The probability that the study will yield a significant result if the research hypothesis is true.

7

Conventions about what to consider a small, medium, and large effect size.

7

A hypothesis-testing procedure in which the population variance is unknown.

8

An estimate of the population variance, based on sample scores, which is equally likely to over or underestimate the true population variance.

8

A research strategy in which each subject is tested more than once; same as within-subject design.

8

Degrees of freedom

t-test for dependent means

8

8

t distribution

Difference scores

8

8

Weighted average

Pooled estimate of the population variance

9

9

t test for independent means

Variance of a distribution of differences between means

9

9

A hypothesis-testing procedure in which there are two scores for each subject and the population variance is not known.

8

The number of scores free to vary when estimating a population parameter.

8

The difference between a subject's score on one testing and the same subject's score on another testing.

8

A mathematically defined curve describing the comparison distribution used in a *t* test.

8

An average of the estimates of the population variance from two samples, each estimate weighted by the proportion of its degrees of freedom of the total degrees of freedom.

9

An average in which the scores being averaged do not have equal influence on the total.

9

It equals the sum of the variances of the distributions of means corresponding to each of two samples.

9

Hypothesis-testing procedure in which there are two separate groups of subjects whose scores are independent of each other and in which the population variance is not known.

9

Distribution of differences
between means

Harmonic mean

9

9

Analysis of variance

F distribution

10

10

Between group population variance
estimate

Within-group population variance
estimate

10

10

F ratio

Factorial design

10

10

A special kind of average that is more influenced by smaller scores.

9

A mathematically defined curve describing the comparison distribution used in an analysis of variance; the distribution of F ratios when the null hypothesis is true.

10

In analysis of variance, the estimate of the variance of the distribution of the population of individual cases based on the variation among the scores within each of the groups studied.

10

A way of organizing a study in which the influence of two or more variables is studied at once by constructing groupings that include every combination of the levels of the variables.

10

The number of scores free to vary when estimating a population parameter.

9

A mathematically defined curve describing the comparison distribution used in a t test.

10

An average in which the scores being averaged do not have equal influence on the total.

10

Hypothesis-testing procedure in which there are two separate groups of subjects whose scores are independent of each other and in which the population variance is not known.

10

Cell mean   Interaction effect

                        10   10

Main effect   One-way analysis of variance

                        10   10

Marginal mean   Two-way analysis of variance

                        10   10

Rank order test   Phi coefficient

                        11   11

Situations in factorial analysis of variance in which the combination of variables has a special effect that you could not predict from knowing about the effects of each of the two variables separately.

10

The mean of a particular combination of levels of the independent variables in a factorial design.

10

Analysis of variance in which there is only one independent variable.

10

Difference between groups on one dimension of a factorial design (sometimes used only for significant differences).

10

Analysis of variance for a two-way factorial design.

10

In a factorial design, the mean score for all the subjects at a particular level of one of the independent variables; row mean or column mean.

10

A hypothesis-testing procedure that makes use of rank-ordered data.

11

In a factorial design, the mean score for all the subjects at a particular level of one of the independent variables; row mean or column mean.

11

Nominal variable   Chi-square statistic (X^2)

11   11

Chi-square test for goodness of fit   Contingency table

11   11

Expected frequency   Independence

11   11

Observed frequency   Chi-square test for independence

11   11

215

A statistic that reflects the overall lack of fit between the expected and observed frequencies; the sum, over all categories or cells, of the squared difference between observed and expected frequencies divided by the expected frequency.

11

A variable with values that are categories, with no numeric relation; same as a categorical variable.

11

A two-dimensional chart showing frequencies in each combination of categories of two categorical variables.

11

A hypothesis-testing procedure that examines how well an observed frequency distribution of a categorical variable fits some expected pattern of frequencies.

11

The situation of no systematic relationship between two variables.

11

In a chi-square test, the number of cases in a category or cell expected if the null hypothesis were true.

11

A hypothesis-testing procedure that examines whether the distribution of frequencies over the categories of one categorical variable are unrelated to the distribution of frequencies over the categories of another categorical variable.

11

In a chi-square test, the number of cases in a category or cell actually obtained in the study.

11

Cramer's phi

Data transformation

11

11

Stepwise multiple regression

Reliability

12

12

Partial correlation coefficient

Test-retest reliability

12

12

Partialing out

Split-half reliability

12

12

The application of one of several mathematical procedures (e.g., taking the square root, log, inverse) to each score in a sample in order to make the sample distribution closer to normal.

11

A measure of association between two categorical variables that is applicable regardless of the number of levels of the two variables.

11

The degree of consistency of a measure.

12

An exploratory procedure that identifies the best subset of potential predictor variables.

12

The correlation between scores obtained on a measure at two different testings of the same people.

12

The correlation between two variables, over and above the influence of one or more other variables.

12

Correlation of the scores from items representing two halves of a test.

12

Removing the influence of a variable from the association among the other variables; same as controlling for.

12

Cronbach's alpha

Path coefficient

12

12

Factor analysis

Hierarchical multiple regression

12

12

Factor loading

Controlling for

12

12

Path analysis

Multivariate analysis of covariance

12

12

The degree of relation associated with an arrow in a path analysis (including latent variable models).

12

A widely used index of a measure's reliability in terms of the correlations among the items.

12

A procedure in which predictor variables are added in a planned sequential fashion to examine the contribution of each over and above those already included.

12

An exploratory statistical procedure that identifies groupings of variables (factors) correlating maximally with each other and minimally with other variables.

12

Removing the influence of a variable from the association among the other variables; same as partialing out.

12

The correlation of a variable with a factor.

12

An analysis of covariance in which there is more than one dependent variable.

12

A method of analyzing the correlations among a group of variables in terms of a predicted pattern of causal relations.

12

Multivariate analysis of variance

Analysis of covariance

12

12

Structural equation modeling

Covariate

12

12

An analysis of variance in which there is more than one dependent variable.

12

A sophisticated type of path analysis involving latent (unmeasured) variables, permits a kind of significance test, and provides measures of the overall fit of the data to the hypothesized causal pattern.

12

A variable controlled for in an analysis of covariance.

12

Same as latent variable modeling.

12